How to do Shakespeare

'How can I bring the text alive, make it vivid, make people hear it for the first time? How can I enter into that world and not feel a stranger? How can I feel less clumsy and inept? How can I speak it without sounding artificial or "actory"? In other words, how can I make it real . . .?'

Adrian Noble has worked on Shakespeare with everyone from Oscar-nominated actors to groups of schoolchildren. Here he draws on several decades of top-level directing experience to shed new light on how to bring some of theatre's seminal texts to life.

He shows you how to approach the perennial issues of performing Shakespeare, including:

- Word play – using colour vs. playing plain, wit vs. comedy, making language muscular
- Building a character – different strategies, using the text, Stanislavski vs. Shakespeare
- Shape and structure – headlining a speech, playing soliloquies, determining the purpose of a speech, letting the verse empower you
- Dialogue – building tension, sharing responsibility, passing the ball

This guided tour of Shakespeare's complex but unfailingly rewarding work stunningly combines instruction and inspiration. Whether you are an actor or a student, you will miss it at your peril.

Adrian Noble was the Artistic Director and Chief Executive of the Royal Shakespeare Company between 1990 and 2003, having previously served as Associate Director for nine years. He has also held key positions at the Bristol Old Vic and the Manchester Royal Exchange. He regularly works in theatre and opera in Canada, France and the USA, as well as the UK. He has received over 20 Olivier Award nominations during his career.

Adrian
Noble

How to do Shakespeare

Routledge
Taylor & Francis Group

LONDON AND NEW YORK

First published 2010
by Routledge
2 Park Square, Milton Park, Abingdon, Oxon OX14 4RN

Simultaneously published in the USA and Canada
by Routledge
270 Madison Avenue, New York, NY 10016

Routledge is an imprint of the Taylor & Francis Group, an informa business

Typeset in Joanna by
Swales & Willis Ltd, Exeter, Devon
Printed and bound in Great Britain by
TJ International Ltd, Padstow, Cornwall

British Library Cataloguing in Publication Data
A catalogue record for this book is available from the British Library

Library of Congress Cataloging in Publication Data
Noble, Adrian.
   How to do Shakespeare / Adrian Noble.
      p. cm.
   1. Shakespeare, William, 1564–1616—Dramatic production.   2. Acting.
   I. Title.
   PR3091.N63 2009
   792.9'5—dc22   2009019517

ISBN10: 0–415–54926–4 (hbk)
ISBN10: 0–415–54927–2 (pbk)
ISBN10: 0–203–86605–3 (ebk)

ISBN13: 978–0–415–54926–4 (hbk)
ISBN13: 978–0–415–54927–1 (pbk)
ISBN13: 978–0–203–86605–4 (ebk)

For Joanne

CONTENTS

FOREWORD

The first time I heard Shakespeare spoken was listening to recordings of Laurence Olivier on my parent's stately mono record-player. I remember being mesmerized by the intensity of language, the thrill of trying to understand words and meanings coiled in the extraordinary range of Olivier's voice. Probably the reason I wanted to be an actor was hearing that voice – and then, growing older, sensing the infinite possibilities of Shakespeare's world. I mean the infinite possibilities of interpretation. Shakespeare continues to challenge us.

In 1988 Adrian Noble invited me to play King Henry VI in his production of "The Plantagenets" for the RSC. During the three month rehearsal period Adrian carved out time to investigate with the actors the mechanics, or as he calls it "the plumbing" of Shakespeare's language. By making us, the actors, alert to essential points of form in metre, apposition, antithesis, line endings and metaphor, Adrian encouraged us to look for where Shakespeare might be suggesting the imaginative pulse of his characters. He asked us to sense where Shakespeare is directing the actor into the mind and soul of the character. How they think. How they speak.

This book simply and directly offers up a path into experiencing the speaking of Shakespeare's words. Adrian Noble vigorously highlights the extraordinary rhythmic, linguistic patterns Shakespeare gives the speaker. Any actor will find this book invaluable. For any student of Shakespeare it should be essential. For anyone who doubts that Shakespeare's language still has purchase on our lives, it will provide a passionate and uplifting challenge.

Ralph Fiennes

INTRODUCTION

This book will not turn you into a good actor. It won't turn you into a good director. It certainly won't write your essays for you. What it will do is show you how to do Shakespeare. Whether 'doing Shakespeare' for you is reading him, playing him or hearing him, this book will improve your understanding and appreciation of his plays.

When did you last go and see a play? This week, last week, a year ago? Hamlet tells the actors newly arrived in Elsinore 'We'll hear a play tomorrow.' We won't *see* a play; we'll *hear* a play. Hear a play.

Sometime, somewhere in the last 400-odd years, there has been a shift; a shift either in meaning or perception, from the ear to the eye. One could argue that by the time we get to the twenty-first century, sight has achieved primacy among the senses. Nowadays, more often than not, we go to see a play at the Royal Court or the National Theatre. The other day I even heard someone say they were going to see the London Symphony Orchestra at the Barbican. Cinema has replaced theatre as the dominant, commercial dramatic form. Cinema and its siblings – television and photography – are the great shapers of our culture, the source of our inspiration and the spark of our imagination.

Let's take what Hamlet says at face value. When he asks Polonius 'Will the king hear this piece of work?', referring to the play he has commissioned, let us assume that this is not a figure of speech, but that he expects Claudius to engage with the play principally through what he hears. We can also probably deduce then that Shakespeare, like Hamlet, wrote his plays first and foremost to be heard. Let's imagine for a moment that we are in the audience at the Globe Theatre for the first performance of Hamlet in 1601. Let's imagine Shakespeare's first company of actors going out onto the stage with the objective of astonishing, electrifying, enrapturing and thrilling the audience. How would they do this? Principally through the power of language. They would make the audience listen; they would make the audience hear, for the very first time, this magnificent work. I think we can get our imaginations round this idea quite easily. What would it be like? On the one hand, it would be intellectually quite exhilarating, because of the subject matter and the philosophical content. On the other hand, it would have a sensuous, almost visceral feeling to it because of the sound of the poetry and the intensity of the passions held; it is a ghost story, a tale of revenge and a thrilling existential journey. So at one and the same time it would be sophisticated and have a child-like storytelling quality to it. Of course what we're trying to define here, what we are groping backwards towards is the Elizabethan experience; a moment of creative paradox, of sensuous thought, of emotional touch. Shakespeare would almost certainly have described himself as a poet, and it is, of course, in the verse that all these contradictions co-exist.

Herein lies the most exciting challenge for the young actor or student of Shakespeare. How can I bring the text alive, make it vivid, make people hear it for the first time? How can I enter into that world and not feel a stranger, not feel a foreigner in an alien land? How can I not feel clumsy and inept? You may also think how can I speak it without sounding artificial or 'actory'? In other words, how can I make it real and contemporary?

Well, I think the first step lies in your imagination. Just try and imagine language, speech, words as a powerful, intoxicating medium. Try and think what it must have been like for those actors, that audience in Shakespeare's day. Or look around you now. You may have heard a leader, maybe a politician, speaking in a way that mesmerised you. It may be the message they were delivering or the way they spoke, maybe the cadence of their voice. Think of Nelson Mandela or John Kennedy. Or possibly a singer. Think of Bob Marley, Bob Dylan. Maybe Eminem. Like Shakespeare, they all use language in an exciting, purposeful way. You don't need to be able to talk like them or sing like them, just have a smell, the slightest sniff of what words can do.

The next step is to appreciate that Shakespeare, as well being a great visionary, was also a very practical man of the theatre. He wrote plays to be performed after a relatively short rehearsal period to an audience that consisted of a broad cross-section of society: from the highly educated and well-read to the illiterate, from the sophisticated aristocrat to the lowest apprentice. The protean audience that crammed inside the walls of the Globe Theatre in Southwark was almost certainly hard to please and pretty volatile. Shakespeare had to grab their attention and keep it. To do this, he had to make them listen. How did he do this? He chose stories and characters that would capture the imagination and he wrote texts that gave the actors all the ammunition they would need to engage the audience for the two to three hours of the show. So one of the main things we will be examining is what means he used to achieve this. We will examine the techniques, the tricks, if you like, the mechanics of his craft.

By discovering the 'how', we will begin to understand the 'why' and the 'what'. What is he trying to communicate with this speech? Why has he written this passage in such a way? So we will seek meaning starting from the detail of the text.

I've always believed Shakespeare is a 'do it yourself' playwright. It's best if you speak or hear his words, rather than read them. I've worked with some of the greatest actors in the land: brilliant Shakespearean actors like Derek Jacobi, Kenneth Branagh and Ralph Fiennes; I've worked with young actors still at drama school; I've worked with students in high school and children as young as twelve. The same processes and methods apply to them all. You learn about Shakespeare by saying him out loud. You learn to identify the patterns, rhythms, sounds and surprises he used; you appreciate the choices he made and the shape of the speeches. We will work empirically and discover how he wrote his plays; we will try things out and proceed by trial and error.

Before we get under way, I want to deal with the issue of reality. A lot of actors (quite rightly) have a reaction against a style of verse speaking that they feel is phoney and old fashioned; a manner of speaking that seems to be more concerned with the sound of the language than with the meaning, where the main aim is to make the verse sound beautiful rather than reflect the character or the situation. This is a style of acting that was much more prevalent in the 1940s and 1950s than it is today and it perhaps suited the more middle-class theatre of the time. The arrival on the scene of a number of brilliant, working-class actors like Albert Finney and Tom Courteney, as well as the pioneering work on verse done at Stratford by the newly formed Royal Shakespeare Company, did much to banish the dreary old ways.

But there are important underlying issues here that still pertain and must be addressed. Shakespeare wrote principally in verse and whichever way you look at it the language is heightened. There is a density of expression that you only get in poetry and poetry is not a naturalistic form of expression. This doesn't mean it's not real and it doesn't mean it's not truthful. But it does mean that to arrive at a truthful expression of a speech you have to be able to deal with the 'hows' we were talking about above. It's not enough to just overlay Shakespeare with the rhythms of modern speech – it probably won't make much sense and will certainly be very boring to listen to. You'll need to use all the craft, all the techniques you can to make it sound real! The greater the actor, the greater the dancer, the greater the singer, the easier they make it look.

Let's look at the differences between how we approach Shakespeare and how his actors might have looked at their texts. Let's look at the context we are working in. The great thinkers of the mid- to late nineteenth century – Darwin, Freud and Marx – profoundly altered the way we see ourselves and our relationships with the world around us. Freud created a methodology whereby we could look inside ourselves and understand our actions, our desires and our subconscious. Konstantin Stanislavski, working as a writer, director and actor in Russia at the beginning of the twentieth century, revolutionised the way an actor approaches a role. Like Freud, he began with the inner life of the character and worked outwards towards his social behaviour. It is a process of empathy with the emotions, thoughts and, indeed, the subconscious of the character. For an actor living in the West in the twenty-first century, the work of Stanislavski is the very air they breathe, whether or not they have undertaken a specific training in the 'method', as the system has come to be known. This means that, instinctively, a modern actor will approach a character from the inside out.

As we have already observed, Shakespeare's actors would have started with the text and built a character from there. In other words, they would work from the outside in. It's worth remembering the scene in *A Midsummer Night's Dream* when Bottom and his friends rehearse their play. Each actor is only given his part and the end of the previous speech (his cues). There's plenty of evidence to suggest that this was the normal way of working in the Elizabethan theatre. It's also worth noting that the word 'character' would have had a totally different meaning for Shakespeare's actors. They would have understood the word to mean a letter in the alphabet or a written sign or symbol. The current meaning of 'character', a person or personality, comes from the eighteenth century in reference to the early novel. (Incidentally, in the English language, nouns rarely carry a gender with 'his' or 'her'. In the frequent uses of the word 'character' in this book, I have chosen to attribute the male gender for consistency and convenience. I mean no offence and hope that none is taken.)

As a director of Shakespeare's plays, it is the collision of these two traditions, 'inside–out' and 'outside–in', that I find really exciting. When I get an actor to come at a piece of text simultaneously from the Stanislavskian method and the Shakespearean route, then I can expect something highly original, truthful and, yes, realistic. I'll give some examples of how this may work later in the book, but first we have to learn how to read the text.

In any passage of Shakespearean text there are seven basic elements you should learn to look out for. These, in summary, are:

1   apposition (the juxtaposition of words, phrases and ideas inside a speech);
2   metaphor (similes, comparisons and flights of fancy);

3   metre and pulse;
4   line endings;
5   word play (rhyme, alliteration and assonance);
6   vocabulary;
7   shape and structure.

I shall call these the 'plumbing'.

Plumbing is a useful analogy because pipes carry an essential commodity, water, all around the house and, by and large, are invisible. These seven elements in Shakespeare's writing are also essential because they carry the meaning, the character, the atmosphere and the cosmology of the play. It's a hugely valuable lesson to learn the basics of the plumbing, to learn the rules and the dos and the don'ts of the craft, because they will give you the power and the authority to appreciate the magnificence of the building, the play.

We will examine these one by one, looking at lots of examples from the plays. Our aim is to become so familiar with these techniques that we can virtually sight-read a passage. As we go along, we will consider what the impact of each of these is on an audience and what significance they have for the interpretation of the plays. We will consider what choices they throw up for you as a reader or an actor.

After that, we will look at how these elements come together in practice and start to consider the bigger picture. We will look at soliloquies, dialogue, comedy, prose and character building. We will look at some of the differences between Shakespeare's early plays, his middle plays and his last plays.

I will start with a brief overview of Shakespeare's work so that you can appreciate the context of any play or speech you are looking at.

1

JOURNEYS

Early, middle and late Shakespeare

Shakespeare died on 23 April 1616, the day traditionally believed to be his birthday. This ultimate act of tidiness was not, unfortunately, reflected in other aspects of his life, especially in the publication of his plays. Although eighteen plays were published in Quarto editions during his lifetime, it was not until 1623 that John Heminges and Henry Condell, two actors in his company, published what is now known as the First Folio. It is the first collected works of his 'Comedies, Histories and Tragedies', comprising thirty-six of the plays, but excluding *Pericles, Prince of Tyre* and *The Two Noble Kinsmen*, presumably because Shakespeare was not the sole author.

For my twelfth birthday, my grandma gave me a copy of the complete works, printed on cheap paper, which she bought from Woolworth's. I think this once-cherished but now lost-in-a-dozen-moves copy must have been based upon the First Folio because it contained the thirty-six plays as well as the Preface. I'll never know why this loving but poorly educated woman who left school at thirteen chose to give me this book, but it was this copy that started me on a journey in life that took me to university, to drama school, into the theatre and eventually to the RSC. At first, the book was rarely glanced at, but after I watched Laurence Olivier's films of *Henry V* and *Hamlet*, I caught the bug and began to speak some of the speeches aloud in the privacy of my bedroom. I became intoxicated by the sound of the language – it gave me a voice and a private reality. Gradually the plays grew more familiar until they became my constant companions. With familiarity came understanding, not just of the texts, but also of myself. So, over a period of time, I grew up with the plays.

Back to the Folio and in particular to the Preface to the Folio. In the Preface you will read these words:

The Names of the Principall Actors in all these Playes.

William Shakespeare.
Richard Burbadge.
Iohn Hemmings.
Augustine Phillips.
William Kempe.
Thomas Poope.
George Bryan.
Henry Condell.
William Slye.
Richard Cowly.
Iohn Lowine.
Samuell Crosse.
Alexander Cooke.
Samuel Gilburne.
Robert Armin.
William Ostler.
Nathan Field.
Iohn Vnderwood.
Nicholas Tooley.
William Ecclestone.
Ioseph Taylor.
Robert Benfield.
Robert Goughe.
Richard Robinson.
Iohn Shancke.
Iohn Rice.

I find that list of twenty-six names deeply moving. I imagine their lives as actors and try to imagine their thoughts and feelings as they received the pages containing their parts and read the words of these plays for the very first time.

Look at the way he introduces them: 'The Names of the Principall Actors in all these Playes.' The meaning is quite clear: between them, these twenty-six men created practically all the parts in the canon. We know that some actors, such as Will Kempe the Clown, left the company and others, like Robert Armin, joined. The artistic evolution of Shakespeare's work imposed changing demands on casting. Nevertheless, what Heminges and Condell are referring to in this list is the first Shakespearean company; the first ensemble, if you like.

This means that many of the actors would have taken parts in the raw, early plays that fizz with energy and invention; the same actors would have played the mature, more complex middle work; finally, they would have originated roles in the last great, mysterious plays that Shakespeare wrote before he retired to Stratford and completed his own mortal journey.

If you think about the careers of those actors, you will realize that, inevitably, their skills and craft would have developed and matured alongside the rapidly evolving talent of their principal playwright. And, of equal significance, Shakespeare's art matured with the involvement and support of a semi-permanent acting company. He would certainly have benefited from the regular exposure of his work to a discerning, protean, passionate audience, but common sense tells us that he would also have positive, practical input from his actors – or at least the senior ones. So Shakespeare's company of actors, both individually and as a group, undertook a remarkable artistic journey from early to middle to late, developing their skills with language as each play set new demands.

An actor approaching a Shakespeare play in the twenty-first century does not have the opportunity to develop his craft in the sequential way that our twenty-six had. The bus is already travelling and you have to jump on while it is in motion. However, it is very useful to practice with the early works; you should always know where an individual text sits in the canon so you can get an idea of the challenges you are facing. As you mature as an actor you will possibly get to try out different roles, written at a later stage in Shakespeare's career. Let's quickly look at three passages, one from each period, so we can get an idea of the way his work matured and the nature of the artistic journey that his actors underwent. A younger member of the company would most likely have spoken each of these texts, though almost certainly not the same one, and each contains vivid description.

EARLY

The first is from *Henry VI Part III*, written in the early 1590s, when Shakespeare was in his mid- to late twenties. Richard of Gloucester, later to become Richard III, describes his father, the Duke of York, on the battlefield. The speech has a powerful irony, because the audience has just watched York be butchered by the Lancastrians.

RICHARD

I cannot joy, until I be resolved
Where our right valiant father is become.
I saw him in the battle range about;
And watch'd him how he singled Clifford forth.

Methought he bore him in the thickest troop
As doth a lion in a herd of neat;
Or as a bear, encompass'd round with dogs,
Who having pinch'd a few and made them cry,
The rest stand all aloof, and bark at him.
So fared our father with his enemies;
So fled his enemies my warlike father:
Methinks, 'tis prize enough to be his son.

Henry V, II. i. 9–20

Read the passage through a couple of times to get the sense, but, more importantly, to get a flavour of the language. I will go into the detail of exactly how such a passage is written and how to tackle it in later chapters. First off, I want you to get a broad picture. So speak it out loud and try to get a feel for the pulse of the verse, the directness of the language and the vivacity of the pictures that are conjured. As you speak it, you will get a strong idea of this boy's feelings for his father; he is a 'lion', a 'bear'. He closes the description with these simple lines:

So fared our father with his enemies;
So fled his enemies my warlike father:
Methinks, 'tis prize enough to be his son.

Notice the repetition of the rhythm and the uncomplicated expression of his emotion in the last line. It's fascinating that this character was to become one of Shakespeare's most notorious killers when he came to power.

MIDDLE

Now let us look at a speech written ten years later, at the beginning of the new century. This is Ophelia describing an encounter with Hamlet to her father.

OPHELIA

My lord, as I was sewing in my closet,
Lord Hamlet, with his doublet all unbraced;
No hat upon his head; his stockings foul'd,
Ungarter'd, and down-gyved to his ankle;
Pale as his shirt; his knees knocking each other;
And with a look so piteous in purport
As if he had been loosed out of hell
To speak of horrors, – he comes before me.

Hamlet, II. i. 75–82

Once again, read it out loud a couple of times. It is important to commit to speaking aloud as the voice, the body and the brain respond differently from when you read silently. The energy necessary to deliver a Shakespearean line out loud somehow engages you directly with the language and the emotional and intellectual life of the character. So, aloud!

What do you notice? How does it differ from Richard's speech? Don't worry if you cannot put it into words as this book will teach you to analyse and articulate what's going on in the text. At this point simply try to get a feel for the language. The images that are conveyed are just as vivid, just as emotionally potent, but the expression feels different, doesn't it? The rhythms are more complex, more jazz-like; there is more variety, the passage feels denser. There is an intensity and concentration of language that perfectly communicates Ophelia's situation and the young, vulnerable personality that will lose her mind and commit suicide.

LATE

Let's move straight on to The Tempest, Shakespeare's penultimate play, probably written ten years after Hamlet, in 1611. Ariel is an airy spirit who attends on Prospero, the shipwrecked Lord of this remote island. Here he describes to his master how he has conjured a terrible storm.

ARIEL

I boarded the king's ship; now on the beak,
Now in the waist, the deck, in every cabin,
I flamed amazement: sometime I'ld divide,
And burn in many places; on the topmast,
The yards and bowsprit, would I flame distinctly,
Then meet and join. Jove's lightnings, the precursors
O' the dreadful thunder-claps, more momentary
And sight-outrunning were not; the fire and cracks
Of sulphurous roaring the most mighty Neptune
Seem to besiege and make his bold waves tremble,
Yea, his dread trident shake.

The Tempest, I. ii. 197–207

Now this is brilliant, but tricky. Again, say it aloud; try and get the sense and then try and communicate that sense, perhaps to an imaginary person in your room. It's much more difficult than the Henry VI and the Hamlet, so don't worry if you can't master it. What are the differences? There are even more rhythmic variations than in the Ophelia speech. If that was jazz, then this is modern jazz! Look at these three lines out of context:

Then meet and join. Jove's lightnings, the precursors
O' the dreadful thunder-claps, more momentary
And sight-outrunning were not;

Don't worry about the meaning; just get a sense of the different rhythms. The rhythms in the first half of line one are completely different from those in the second half; I would call these 'cross rhythms'. The type of words he uses is completely different in the second half of that line from the first; simple and monosyllabic becomes complex and polysyllabic. The rhythms of the next lines are quite percussive and the images are created by clusters of words such as 'sight-outrunning'. The word order sometimes seems strange. The whole speech has a lot more full stops and semicolons placed in the middle of the lines than in the earlier plays. These complexities, juxtapositions and variations impart volumes to the listener but require a high level of skill from the performer.

I have shown you three snapshots from a man's work, taken at approximately ten-year intervals. The contrasts are dramatic and revealing. They represent a clear, organic development in his art that would have been matched step by step by his actors. It is usually the writers in any society that set the agenda; it is the writers that illuminate the past and pose the vital questions for the future. Their art develops in indivisible accord with their response to the outside world and in a continuous dialogue with their inner self. Shakespeare's company of actors were his first interpreters and with the arrival of each new play would have had to refine their technique to deal with the fresh demands placed upon them. Our task is clear: as actors or students living in the twenty-first century, we have to equip ourselves as well as possible to continue that process of interpretation. That's what we'll do in this book. We won't be proceeding chronologically through the plays, but will build up a body of knowledge that will hold you in good stead for any of Shakespeare's works, early, middle or late.

2

APPOSITION

Setting word against word, phrase against phrase

What is the most famous speech in all literature?

No prizes here, it's probably Hamlet's soliloquy 'To be or not to be'. The utter simplicity of the language on the one hand and the intellectual and emotional reverberation on the other hand have given these words a unique place in our culture. Dozens of authors have sourced the titles of their books and films from within the speech. Articles, commentaries and mighty tomes have been written about this speech. Philosophers have pondered its meaning and significance. Actors rehearsing the part have woken bolt upright in the middle of the night, sweating, in fearful anticipation of having to perform the speech in front of audiences that could probably recite along to many of the words, in karaoke style.

So let's look at how it's done. Let's read it.

HAMLET

To be, or not to be: that is the question:
Whether 'tis nobler in the mind to suffer
The slings and arrows of outrageous fortune,
Or to take arms against a sea of troubles,
And by opposing end them? To die: to sleep;
No more; and by a sleep to say we end
The heart-ache and the thousand natural shocks

That flesh is heir to, 'tis a consummation
Devoutly to be wish'd. To die, to sleep;
To sleep: perchance to dream: ay, there's the rub;
For in that sleep of death what dreams may come
When we have shuffled off this mortal coil,
Must give us pause: there's the respect
That makes calamity of so long life;
For who would bear the whips and scorns of time,
The oppressor's wrong, the proud man's contumely,
The pangs of despised love, the law's delay,
The insolence of office and the spurns
That patient merit of the unworthy takes,
When he himself might his quietus make
With a bare bodkin? who would fardels bear,
To grunt and sweat under a weary life,
But that the dread of something after death,
The undiscover'd country from whose bourn
No traveller returns, puzzles the will
And makes us rather bear those ills we have
Than fly to others that we know not of?
Thus conscience does make cowards of us all;
And thus the native hue of resolution
Is sicklied o'er with the pale cast of thought,
And enterprises of great pith and moment
With this regard their currents turn awry,
And lose the name of action.

Hamlet, III. i. 58–90

There is so much that we could talk about in this speech but here I want to
concentrate on one single aspect: apposition. Apposition is the juxtaposition
of one word with another, one phrase or sentence with another or one idea
with another. Apposition is the key to how to perform this speech.

Shakespeare starts with the simplest of juxtapositions: 'To be or not to be'.
Six monosyllabic words express the question the character is considering.
Simple. Try it yourself: on the one hand 'To be', on the other 'Not to be'.
Imagine a pair of scales and weigh up the options of 'To be' or 'Not to be'. Try
not to be too heavy handed with it. You will find that you can quite easily bias
the weight of each phrase in your pair of imaginary scales towards one side or
the other: 'TO BE' or 'Not to be' or vice versa 'To be' or 'NOT TO BE'. You don't
have to decide now, just be aware that you have here a choice that will reveal
something about how your character is thinking in this moment of time.

Hamlet's dilemma is set out absolutely clearly in this first line: 'To be or not to be: that is the question'. He lays it out, as if on a white tablecloth, or (perhaps more appropriately) on a mortuary slab. He is frighteningly honest with himself and with us, and I think this act of self-exposure is what makes this speech terrifying to our actor and fascinating to our audience. Let's carry on and see how the character dissects his problem with the use of apposition. He lays out one option:

> Whether 'tis nobler in the mind to suffer
> The slings and arrows of outrageous fortune

He balances this option with another:

> Or take arms against a sea of troubles,
> And by opposing end them?

Try this for yourself; try and place one thought against another. Using your imaginary scales, balance one whole clause with another whole clause. Create a counterpoint. For the moment, don't worry about interpreting it, just try and get the feel in your mouth, the weight of each argument. Try it in as many different ways as you like, but hold on to the notion of setting one idea against another. Notice that he concludes the second clause with four simple words: 'To die, to sleep'. This is another apposition, deceptively simple, but in this context, so powerful that it leads Hamlet onto the next phase of his exploration.

> No more; and by a sleep to say we end
> The heart-ache and the thousand natural shocks
> That flesh is heir to, 'tis a consummation
> Devoutly to be wish'd. To die, to sleep;
> To sleep: perchance to dream: ay, there's the rub;

Hamlet picks up the word 'sleep' and takes the argument through to a repetition of the same idea, 'To die, to sleep.' He then repeats the word 'sleep' at the beginning of the next line and juxtaposes it with 'perchance to dream.' Continuously through this speech, one word or phrase is being set against another. Point/counterpoint. By grasping this idea you will appreciate how Shakespeare has written this speech and it will give you the building blocks to proceed.

And, crucially, these building blocks are concrete! Don't think of 'To be or not to be' as a wishy-washy expression of a young man's general unhappiness. It is a specific, dialectical problem that must be resolved and deserves the full attention of the audience while he is doing it!

I have directed Hamlet twice in my life, firstly at the Royal Shakespeare

Company with Kenneth Branagh in 1993 and then in Stratford, Ontario fifteen years later with a young Canadian actor called Ben Carlson. In England we did the full, uncut, four-hour text and Branagh, one of our greatest Shakespearean actors, created an unforgettable portrait of a young man: highly romantic, volatile and very much at the mercy of the emotions swirling around inside him. The second time round I sought a more politically

Kenneth Brannagh as Hamlet and David Bradley as Polonius at the Royal Shakespeare Theatre, 1993. Photo: Reg Wilson © Royal Shakespeare Company

alert interpretation of the play. I had never worked with Canadian actors before and I was hugely impressed by their ability to create real people in real situations on the stage. Perhaps this was because of their background in the North American method tradition. They were also keen to embrace a regime of verse-speaking that not only do I believe in as the best way of doing Shakespeare, but seemed to me particularly appropriate to this more political reading. So I encouraged every member of the cast to really take on board all the appositions, antitheses and contrasting arguments in the play. It was a revelation. The whole play immediately became argumentative, full of debate and sharp political thinking. Hamlet was not a sad lad in the corner, but the central problem in a fast-changing political world. His emotions and his existential explorations were both the cause of the debate going on in every corner of the court and the result of the changes going on around him. So there was a correlation between his trauma and the political traumas associated with the regime change. The proof of the pudding is in the eating, as they say, so I was mighty pleased when the audiences responded with alertness and a quick-mindedness that gave a real buzz to the occasion. And the root of this work lay entirely in a systematic focusing on the appositions in the play. It immediately made the characters articulate and the play intelligent. It helped to create an intellectual world for the characters to exist in.

This rubbing together of words and ideas is a characteristic of all Shakespeare's plays. It gives energy to the language. It is a basic tool that he seemed to alight upon right at the beginning of his career and continued developing until he retired to Stratford-upon-Avon. It is a characteristic that distinguishes him from his contemporaries. Marlowe did not write like this, nor did Ben Jonson. It is a feature that is both utilitarian, in so far as it helps the actor to communicate and the audience to understand, and artistic, giving rhythm, elegance and intelligence.

The more I work on the plays, the more I am convinced that this is the most important idea to get hold of. By immediately seeking out the appositions, you will straight away get a handle on the shape of even the most complicated of speeches. Consequently, it is the quickest way to transform the way you do Shakespeare.

Let's go on and consider another well-known speech in another well-known play. Here is the moment in *Romeo and Juliet* when we first meet Friar Laurence:

FRIAR LAURENCE

The grey-eyed morn smiles on the frowning night,
Chequering the eastern clouds with streaks of light,
And flecked darkness like a drunkard reels
From forth day's path and Titan's fiery wheels:

Now, ere the sun advance his burning eye,
The day to cheer and night's dank dew to dry,
I must up-fill this osier cage of ours
With baleful weeds and precious-juiced flowers.
The earth that's nature's mother is her tomb;
What is her burying grave that is her womb,
And from her womb children of divers kind
We sucking on her natural bosom find,
Many for many virtues excellent,
None but for some and yet all different.
O, mickle is the powerful grace that lies
In herbs, plants, stones, and their true qualities:
For nought so vile that on the earth doth live
But to the earth some special good doth give,
Nor aught so good but strain'd from that fair use
Revolts from true birth, stumbling on abuse:
Virtue itself turns vice, being misapplied;
And vice sometimes by action dignified.
Within the infant rind of this small flower
Poison hath residence and medicine power:
For this, being smelt, with that part cheers each part;
Being tasted, slays all senses with the heart.
Two such opposed kings encamp them still
In man as well as herbs, grace and rude will;
And where the worser is predominant,
Full soon the canker death eats up that plant.

Romeo and Juliet, II. iii. 1–30

These are the first words that Friar Laurence speaks and it's most likely to be the first time the audience sets eyes on him. The character occupies a crucial position in the play and decisively alters the course of events. The actor playing the part has to arrest the audience's attention and make them listen. At the same time, he must give the audience some idea of the sort of person he is. How does he do it?

A quick glance at the speech will tell you that it's absolutely littered with appositions and antitheses. This is obvious even if you don't fully understand everything that's being said. Here's the first line: 'The grey-eyed morn smiles on the frowning night'. He's telling us it's dawn. But by beginning with a double antithesis (morn/night and smiles/frowning) he creates an immediate energy and a very strong picture. He continues with two more visual contrasts between 'clouds' and 'streaks of light' and then between 'darkness' and 'day'. All this is wrapped up inside a series of brilliant metaphors, which both serve the antitheses and are strengthened by them. We will be dealing with metaphors and similes in the next chapter, so start to appreciate how all the different techniques interrelate and are mutually supportive. Read the next four lines:

> Now, ere the sun advance his burning eye,
> The day to cheer and night's dank dew to dry,
> I must up-fill this osier cage of ours
> With baleful weeds and precious-juiced flowers.

Look straight for the appositions. You have 'The day to cheer' and 'night's dank dew to dry' and 'baleful weeds' and 'precious-juiced flowers'. Try saying these phrases out loud. Try balancing them in your imaginary pair of scales. Try using your two hands as the pans of each scale. Contrast the words 'baleful' and 'precious-juiced'. Do they have different weights? Do you have a different emotional reaction to 'baleful' as opposed to 'precious-juiced'? Try emphasising different words. What you are doing is interpreting the text. You are beginning to make choices about how the character expresses himself, how he communicates. Now try saying all four lines out loud. Notice that the first and the third lines (beginning 'Now, ere the sun' and 'I must') have a different rhythm from our pair of balanced, contrapuntal lines. It's as if their energy flows through to the ends of the lines in one sweep, whereas lines two and four, because of the appositions, are choppier and have a strong point of balance or fulcrum in the middle. Practice this a few times. In this case, by recognising the appositions and playing the counterpoint, you get a pretty good steer as to the rhythm and shape of this section.

You also get an insight into the purpose and the context of the speech, in other words, what it contributes to the play as a whole. Here are the next two lines:

> The earth that's nature's mother is her tomb;
> What is her burying grave that is her womb.

So, the earth is the tomb and the burying grave is the womb. This is a startling truth, given extra emphasis and authority by the rhyme (of which much more later). Recognising the appositions will tell you what you might stress or, more likely, what not to stress. The plumbing of these two lines flows from earth to tomb and from grave to womb. Get this right and the rest will fall into place. What is also emerging in this speech is a sense of mortality, the presence of death and the danger to life. This is expressed through numerous antitheses (fair use/abuse, virtue/vice, etc.). Then Shakespeare does something quite inspired. Friar Laurence holds up a tiny flower that he has picked. The audience will hardly be able to see it from the back and he says:

> Within the infant rind of this small flower
> Poison hath residence and medicine power.

This delicate, beautiful flower is both dangerous and life enhancing; the scent is cheering but the taste is deadly. The paradox is expressed with a devastating finality in the Poison line. The antitheses that run through this whole speech express more fully than anything else the perilous, contradictory nature of our lives, which provides the true context for the tragedy of Romeo and Juliet. Their love is doomed from the very start, but it burns so brightly that it has lit up the imaginations of actors and audiences for hundreds of years.

Getting to grips with the counterpoint also has the effect of making the language more muscular. Take that last line: 'Poison has residence and medicine power'. First of all, you have to get your brain round what it means. It is very condensed and precise. It's like a bomb waiting to go off. Then you have to get the movement through the thought: poison into residence, medicine into power. There are four hefty words in this line and each of them needs to be delivered, to be landed on by the speaker. Try it out loud. Use your imaginary scales. See how the 'P' in 'Poison' and the 'p' in 'power' bookend the line and give it extra authority – this is what I mean by muscularity. By playing the counterpoint, you will automatically inhabit the contrasting and opposing thoughts. Don't slide over them; engage with them.

Let's now look at another example, this time from an early, popular comedy, The Taming of the Shrew. This is Petruchio speaking to the audience. He is planning how to woo Kate, a notorious firebrand, the 'shrew' of the title. She has a violent temper and has sent many men packing who have come to woo her for her large fortune.

PETRUCHIO

I will attend her here,
And woo her with some spirit when she comes.
Say that she rail; why then I'll tell her plain
She sings as sweetly as a nightingale:
Say that she frown, I'll say she looks as clear
As morning roses newly, wash'd with dew:
Say she be mute and will not speak a word;
Then I'll commend her volubility,
And say she uttereth piercing eloquence:
If she do bid me pack, I'll give her thanks,
As though she bid me stay by her a week:
If she deny to wed, I'll crave the day

When I shall ask the banns and when be married.
But here she comes; and now, Petruchio, speak.
>   *The Taming of the Shrew*, II. i. 166–179

What we have here is not so much the antithesis of word on word, but the counterpoint of phrase on phrase or idea on idea. It's almost a catechism of question and answer. How does it work?

First of all, he tells the audience what he intends to do, then he tells them how he's going to set about doing it: 'Say that she rail', why then I'll do this; 'Say that she frown', why then I'll do that. He engages the audience by conjuring up an imaginary situation, a series of snapshots of Kate in a variety of foul moods; he then juxtaposes this with a preposterous response. The audience can certainly appreciate this humour, but in some ways the joke is on Petruchio, for we have already seen Kate in action, tying up her sister and abusing her and know full well that she can more than handle herself. So we look forward to the fight.

The speech only works if you try and engage the audience, and the appositions give you the tool you need. Take the first example:

> Say that she rail; why then I'll tell her plain
> She sings as sweetly as a nightingale:

First of all, try and balance the two halves of the sentence. This may feel odd at first because the first section has just four words and the second section has thirteen words. Practice it a couple of times by putting the first phrase in your left hand and the second in your right. A simple physical gesture will often help you to speak. Now imagine you are talking to someone, a friend, maybe. You will find that the energy of the first phrase goes towards the word 'rail', a strong word, and that the energy of the second phrase goes all the way through to the word 'nightingale'. The key thing to remember when dealing with these appositions is that it's not just a question of emphasis; it's much more to do with juxtaposing two thoughts. Counterpoint. And always try and play a thought right through to the end, in this case the songbird. This does not mean that you can't emphasise something en route or colour a word or phrase. Just don't lose sight of the bigger picture.

Try the next couplet:

> Say that she frown, I'll say she looks as clear
> As morning roses newly, wash'd with dew;

This time, take the energy towards 'frown', the strong word, as before. Then, under your breath, ask yourself the question, 'What would I do?', then answer it: 'I'll say she looks etc. etc.' In other words, invent the second half of the apposition yourself. Still play the energy through as far as 'dew', but give it the freshness of a new thought.

Straight on:

> Say she be mute and will not speak a word;
> [*Question: what would I do?*
> *Answer:*]
> Then I'll commend her volubility,
> And say she uttereth piercing eloquence:

Here in the first line, the energy goes through to 'mute' and then onto 'word' at the end of the line. The answer to the question is two whole lines, so you have to play through to 'eloquence'. The apposition is one whole line balancing two. Try it again, this time thinking the question 'What would I do?' in a split second. This is an important habit to get into because the audience has to believe that you are having the thoughts for the very first time, indeed that no one on earth has ever had these thoughts before. We can call this inventing the text or coining the text. You will need to do this in a split second, because often you will have to invent right in the middle of the line and you don't want to keep breaking up the rhythm (of which more later)! But in real life, thoughts come into our heads in a flash, so all we are doing is imitating life.

Let's finish this text:

> If she do bid me pack, [*Question*] I'll give her thanks,
> As though she bid me stay by her a week:
> If she deny to wed, [*Question*] I'll crave the day
> When I shall ask the banns and when be married.

Shakespeare very neatly takes the speech right up to the notion of marriage, which is precisely what Petruchio wants and Kate is keen to avoid. And at this point she enters. The appositions have given a clear structure to the speech, which the actor can quickly grasp: a short introduction, then a series of two line appositions, with a three-liner in the middle. There's a musical shape. The speech is very neatly packaged; every contingency has been catered to in Petruchio's mind. You could deduce from this that he's rather self-satisfied at this point. In addition, the actor has the opportunity to engage directly with the audience, which is important if you are playing a leading role and critical if the character goes on to do some pretty unpleasant things to Kate.

Let's continue thinking about character for the moment and further examine how a powerful, antithetical speech can lead you towards an understanding of whom you are playing. Richard of Gloucester, later King Richard III, is one of the most fascinating and charismatic villains in Shakespeare. The fact that Shakespeare played fast and loose with the historical facts and was partly writing a crude piece of Tudor propaganda need not concern us here. During the course of the play he addresses the audience frequently and at great length. He describes in great detail, and often very wittily, what he is about to do, then he does it and then he dissects it with the audience. There is an awful satisfaction to be gained from sharing the intimate thoughts of one so appalling! But the consequence is that we are complicit in the action. Here is the beginning of the play, when Richard, not yet king, settles upon his course.

GLOUCESTER

Now is the winter of our discontent
Made glorious summer by this sun of York;
And all the clouds that lour'd upon our house
In the deep bosom of the ocean buried.
Now are our brows bound with victorious wreaths;
Our bruised arms hung up for monuments;
Our stern alarums changed to merry meetings,
Our dreadful marches to delightful measures.
Grim-visaged war hath smooth'd his wrinkled front;
And now, instead of mounting barded steeds
To fright the souls of fearful adversaries,
He capers nimbly in a lady's chamber
To the lascivious pleasing of a lute.
But I, that am not shaped for sportive tricks,
Nor made to court an amorous looking-glass;
I, that am rudely stamp'd, and want love's majesty
To strut before a wanton ambling nymph;
I, that am curtail'd of this fair proportion,
Cheated of feature by dissembling nature,
Deformed, unfinish'd, sent before my time
Into this breathing world, scarce half made up,
And that so lamely and unfashionable
That dogs bark at me as I halt by them;
Why, I, in this weak piping time of peace,
Have no delight to pass away the time,
Unless to spy my shadow in the sun
And descant on mine own deformity:
And therefore, since I cannot prove a lover,
To entertain these fair well-spoken days,
I am determinèd to prove a villain
And hate the idle pleasures of these days.

Richard III, I. i. 1–31

This is fabulous stuff! It is a speech so powerful, so dangerous that in the hands of a great actor, the audience can be gripped by a quite extraordinary sense of fear and excitement in equal measure. Laurence Olivier achieved this in 1944 at the Old Vic. Antony Sher had a spectacular success at Stratford in 1984. Sher played Richard as a 'Bottled spider', deformed and savage, on a pair of crutches that he hid from the view of the audience until the line 'But I, that am not shaped for sportive tricks', at which point the crutches appeared like wings and he leapt forward to the front of the stage and delivered the remainder of the speech prowling up and down the footlights like an animal. I was present at the press night and the audience, not knowing what to expect, quite literally screamed out loud. It was one of those performances that shift the theatrical tectonic plates for a generation.

Let's examine the material that Shakespeare gave these two mighty actors. Let's examine the situation. We learn that peace has arrived after decades of bloody civil conflict, the War of the Roses. The Yorkist king, Edward IV, is now firmly on the throne and is giving close attention to his new wife, Queen Elizabeth. The first thirteen lines, from 'Now . . .' to 'The lascivious pleasing of a lute' give Richard's view on this state of affairs. He sets out his stall with a vivid antithesis in the opening couplet:

> Now is the winter of our discontent
> Made glorious summer by this sun of York.

So winter has become summer. Place these two words carefully and you appear to have a neat, compact view of the world. We get a clue to Richard's sense of irony with his choice of the word 'discontent', a bit of an under-statement, considering that the bloodiest battles ever to take place on English soil occurred during the recent civil war. You should counterpoint the whole of the next line, 'And all the clouds that lour'd upon our house', with the whole of the fourth, 'In the deep bosom of the ocean buried'.

These are appositions that require you to strongly visualize the imagery. Olivier added a chilling irony here, by pausing just before the word 'buried', and glancing at the ground. We get a glimpse into the character's mind and a foretaste of what is to come. Shakespeare then repeats the opening word, 'Now', and follows on with four one-line appositions:

> Now are our brows bound with victorious wreaths;
> Our bruised arms hung up for monuments;
> Our stern alarums changed to merry meetings,
> Our dreadful marches to delightful measures.

You can give this a terrific energy. The brows are bound with wreaths (a useful alliteration on the letter B). The arms become monuments; the alarums, meet-

"Now is the Winter. . ." Anthony Sher as Richard III at the Royal Shakespeare
Theatre, 1984. Photo: Reg Wilson © Royal Shakespeare Company

ings; and the dreadful marches, delightful measures (again, helpful alliteration). Speak it through for yourself. Really work the appositions. You will find
that, because the second, balancing word is always placed at the end of the line,
the verse gets a strength and muscularity. The degree to which this is ironic is,
of course, dependent on your interpretation of the role, but it has to be
delivered with a certain strength and grip, because it's written that way. The
next line is interesting: 'Grim-visaged war hath smooth'd his wrinkled front'.
The antithesis is striking here. It's important that you visualize these images
fully. Consider, as you practice, the weight and texture of the words. 'Grim',

'visaged' and 'war' are quite heavy words, so Shakespeare is suggesting to you that you start with three strong stresses; this contrasts with the liquid quality of the word 'smooth'd'. I'd like you to get into the habit of following the language and seeing where it leads you; allow it to teach you, if you like. To achieve this, it's always necessary to speak the words out loud. I've said before that something happens if you commit yourself and really vocalize. It allows the lines to work on you, like a Greek mask. So allow yourself to remain open and sensitive to the language, its rhythms, its weights and its textures. At the same time, work on the basic tools that I describe in these chapters.

Onwards! Richard concludes this section of the speech with a real soldier's antithesis:

> And now, instead of mounting barded steeds
> To fright the souls of fearful adversaries,
> He capers nimbly in a lady's chamber
> To the lascivious pleasing of a lute.

Sustain each half of the apposition over the full two lines. As you balance each half in your hands, try and feel the weight of the different imagery used. There is a delicate irony in the third and fourth lines, which sit at the moment just before Richard starts talking about himself. (The moment, incidentally when Sher skittled down to the footlights, and when Olivier, in his film of the play, approached the camera in a pretty scary way.) In the following lines, Richard confronts the audience with his terrible deformity. This is perhaps the cruelest antithesis of them all – a witty, brilliant mind inside a badly deformed body.

In the last four lines, which are:

> And therefore, since I cannot prove a lover,
> To entertain these fair well-spoken days,
> I am determined to prove a villain
> And hate the idle pleasures of these days

Shakespeare places the antithesis – lover and villain – boldly at the end of the lines; this contrasts with the rather antiseptic repeated cadence of 'well-spoken days' and 'of these days'. By this time, the audience is well and truly inducted into Richard's dangerous and sly, but attractive, mind.

There are many examples throughout Shakespeare where a character's use of apposition defines the kind of person they are. I would suggest that you take a look at Polonius's advice to his son, Laertes, in *Hamlet*, I. iii. Here's a short extract:

POLONIUS

Give thy thoughts no tongue,
Nor any unproportioned thought his act.
Be thou familiar, but by no means vulgar.
Those friends thou hast, and their adoption tried,
Grapple them to thy soul with hoops of steel;
But do not dull thy palm with entertainment
Of each new-hatch'd, unfledged comrade. Beware
Of entrance to a quarrel, but being in,
Bear't that the opposed may beware of thee.

Hamlet, I. iii. 55–81

There is almost an overuse of apposition. The character is often played as a pedant and a bore that is over-fond of his own voice and much addicted to his clever word play. But at the same time, the counterpoint gives him an intellectual vigour that is a long way away from a man in his dotage. Try the speech for yourself. Use the techniques you have learnt to work the language. Set word against word, thought against thought. You'll need to be quite alert to make the most of this speech; it needs a lot of intellectual energy. Both times I have directed the play I have opted for a character that is almost over-educated, but loves his children dearly.

Angelo in *Measure for Measure* is a courtier who aspires to be a perfect, incorruptible civil servant. He is given temporary absolute power. He soon falls victim to his own lust for a young girl who comes to plead for the life of her brother, who is guilty of fornication. Look at this extract and see how his language reveals his situation and his character:

ANGELO

What's this, what's this? Is this her fault or mine?
The tempter or the tempted, who sins most? Ha!
Not she: nor doth she tempt: but it is I
That, lying by the violet in the sun,
Do as the carrion does, not as the flower,
Corrupt with virtuous season. Can it be
That modesty may more betray our sense
Than woman's lightness? Having waste ground enough,
Shall we desire to raze the sanctuary
And pitch our evils there? O, fie, fie, fie!

Measure for Measure, II. ii. 168–177

The verse here is quite complex and suggests to me not only a tortured mind, but also someone with a lawyer-like ability to analyse and dissect their own feelings. In situations like this, it's vital to hang on to the appositions because they will give a structure to the turbulent emotions that the character is experiencing. Highlight the main ones and they will give you a security as you explore the speech and try to experience some of Angelo's contradictory feelings. Look out for all the I/she, tempter/tempted appositions and try and argue them through like a lawyer. They will give you the 'grip' you need as Angelo embarks on some of his more exotic metaphors. Laid before you in this speech are two key aspects of Angelo's character: the ability to argue in a fiercely logical, contrapuntal way, even putting himself in the dock, and an imagination that comes up with some fairly ripe imagery. Note that the principal resource for character building lies in the text; Shakespeare always wrote into the text information necessary for the actor.

Shakespeare was himself an actor. He had a profound understanding of how actors worked and what they needed to fulfill their roles. He was a practical man who provided practical solutions. When I was starting out as a director at the Bristol Old Vic, I was given Shakespeare's early tragedy *Titus Andronicus* to direct. I invited Simon Callow, then still in his twenties, to play the part. Now Titus is a Roman general who undergoes almost unimaginable suffering. Most of his sons are either killed in war in service of the state or executed at the whim of the tyrannical emperor Saturninus. His daughter is raped, her hands cut off and her tongue cut out by the emperor's stepsons. Titus himself is repeatedly humiliated and cuts his own hand off in a vain attempt to save the life of one of his children. At one point in rehearsals, when yet another load of misery had been heaped on Titus's head, Simon cried out in frustration that the part was unplayable and suggested that at this point in the production an intolerably loud noise should be played over the loudspeaker system and remain there until Titus's pain had subsided. I believe Shakespeare was well aware of the difficulty facing the actor; he offers the actor a structure that allows him to deal with the extreme emotions. Here's an example from *Titus Andronicus*. He has just seen his daughter who has been violated and heard that his last son is banished. His brother Marcus counsels reason:

MARCUS ANDRONICUS

But yet let reason govern thy lament.

TITUS ANDRONICUS

If there were reason for these miseries,
Then into limits could I bind my woes:
When heaven doth weep, doth not the earth o'erflow?
If the winds rage, doth not the sea wax mad,
Threatening the welkin with his big-swoln face?

And wilt thou have a reason for this coil?
I am the sea; hark, how her sighs do blow!
She is the weeping welkin, I the earth:
Then must my sea be moved with her sighs;
Then must my earth with her continual tears
Become a deluge, overflow'd and drown'd;
For why my bowels cannot hide her woes,
But like a drunkard must I vomit them.
Then give me leave, for losers will have leave
To ease their stomachs with their bitter tongues.

Titus Andronicus, III. i. 217–232

Titus struggles to put into words that which is inexpressible. Remember that the audiences at the Globe came mainly to 'hear' a play and Shakespeare's characters always have something to say. Here Titus uses counterpoint to bind into some shape the rage, frustration and grief that he feels. In the first six lines, in a series of tightly argued appositions, he exposes the absurdity of Marcus's position: reason/miseries; limits/woes; heaven weep/earth o'erflow; winds rage/sea wax mad. We feel he is hanging on to his sanity by a thread! In the second half of the speech he releases his emotions through metaphors that express the size, the sheer volume of his grief:

I am the sea; hark, how her sighs do blow!
She is the weeping welkin, I the earth:
Then must my sea be moved with her sighs;
Then must my earth with her continual tears
Become a deluge, overflow'd and drown'd;

Again, he holds his emotions in shape by the force of counterpoint. He is trying to describe something that is beyond the frontiers of civilization; like a barrel which holds in the huge pressure of the liquid inside, so the appositions hold in the pressure of his emotions and allow the actor to communicate to the audience.

Titus Andronicus was one of Shakespeare's earliest box-office 'hits' and, directing the play, I got a real sense of Shakespeare pushing back the limits of the form. The piece is extremely violent and highly emotional, but by giving it poetic expression, the audience is emancipated from mere ghoulish pleasure and given a glimpse into an ancient, dangerous world that, we discover, is not too distant from our own. Shakespeare takes a crowd-pleasing format – the bloody revenge play – and gives it humanity and compassion. In *Titus*, we see the meeting of popular drama with high art. We see extreme emotion being given a form that allows the actor to control and cast a spell over the listener.

You can see the shaping, controlling impact of appositions throughout Shakespeare's work. It is the tool that gave form to emotion and power to his actors. It allows intelligent debate to be accessible, robust and entertaining. It is, habitually, the first thing I seek out in a speech I am tackling for the first time – which is why it is our point of departure in this voyage of discovery.

3

METAPHOR

The highway to the imagination

Why is this a good lyric?

> The Mississippi delta was shining
> Like a national guitar.

It's the opening line of Paul Simon's song 'Graceland' (1986). He's travelling south on the highway down the Mississippi towards Memphis, Tennessee, with his nine-year-old son. The simile is perfect; the river and delta look like an electric guitar catching the light; the destination is a musical shrine and the national guitar is a legend itself. Genius! It gets the song off to a fantastic start. In one stroke, it lifts the status of the journey to that of a pilgrimage.

The concern of this whole chapter is metaphor, and I will use the word metaphor as a generic term to cover all simile, imagery and allegory as well as metaphor in the usual sense. Metaphor in Shakespeare strikes me as being so important, so central to the question 'How to do Shakespeare' that I wanted you to tackle it very early on.

Why? Well, metaphor is the highway to the character's imagination, the secret to their inner self, their mystery. To state the obvious, in a dramatic situation it is the character that is inventing the language, coining the imagery. Shakespeare has this great gift of being able to inhabit each of the characters he is creating, moment by moment, and give them the expression that is perfect for that particular instant. So by recognising and understanding the metaphors a character is using, you are going a long way to understanding the character itself.

I want to start by looking at one of Shakespeare's sonnets. He wrote at least 154 sonnets, all love poems, mostly in the early 1590s. Many are written to a beautiful young man, others to a 'dark lady'. It is an elegant, concentrated form of fourteen lines which originated in Italy. Shakespeare's sonnets provide us with a perfect microscope through which to examine some of the dramatic tools that he developed in his early career. Here's Sonnet 29:

> When, in disgrace with fortune and men's eyes,
> I all alone beweep my outcast state
> And trouble deaf heaven with my bootless cries
> And look upon myself and curse my fate,
> Wishing me like to one more rich in hope,
> Featured like him, like him with friends possess'd,
> Desiring this man's art and that man's scope,
> With what I most enjoy contented least;
> Yet in these thoughts myself almost despising,
> Haply I think on thee, and then my state,
> Like to the lark at break of day arising
> From sullen earth, sings hymns at heaven's gate;
> For thy sweet love remember'd such wealth brings
> That then I scorn to change my state with kings.
>
> Sonnet 29

Read it through out loud as we have all the other texts. At the moment, don't worry about rhyme or rhythm or structure or apposition. Just look for the metaphor. I think it's a stunning piece of writing because there are nine lines in which he beweeps his outcast state and catalogues all the many reasons why he is miserable, many of which I am sure you can identify with. In the ninth line, 'Yet in these thoughts myself almost despising,' he arrives at his lowest point with the loaded word 'despising' sitting at the end of the line. Then, on the tenth line, pow!, he thinks about his lover: 'Haply I think on thee, and then my state'. At this point he delivers the *coup de grâce*, this wonderful, life enriching metaphor:

> Like to the lark at break of day arising
> From sullen earth, sings hymns at heaven's gate.

Its impact lies in the fact that he has made you wait for over two thirds of the poem; its potency lies in the inspired image. There are other things we should notice, the apposition of 'earth' and 'heaven' and the strong antithetical argument throughout, but we won't dwell on them here. The lessons to be learnt here relate to metaphor and how to handle it.

First and most important of all, try and invent the metaphor, coin it, make it up on the spot. How do I do this? The character arrives at the point in the story where 'Haply I think on thee, and then my state'. This is the point of invention, the point of inspiration. Over the end of the line he comes up with the perfect depiction of how he feels; he doesn't describe it – he probably can't describe it – but he can express it through this uplifting metaphor. It might help you to insert a 'what' under your breath at the end of the line – 'Haply I think on thee, and then my state, [what?]' – and then answer your own question with the metaphor. When preparing a text or practicing a speech, I find this method of inserting imaginary questions at the end of lines really helpful in creating a more spontaneous reading. The best position to place such questions of where, why, how and what is always at the ends of lines, which, we will discover later, are the natural breaks in thought.

Second, how does Shakespeare set the metaphor up? We have already noticed that Shakespeare makes us wait a long while before delivering the image, but have you realized that there is no full stop in this poem? It is one long sentence, one sequence of developing thoughts. Try the whole poem again straight away; don't rush it, but try and use the fact that it's one sentence. What will emerge is the overall sense, which is 'When' . . . blah, blah, blah . . . 'Haply I think on thee'. In other words, try and get the overall shape and distinguish the wood from the trees. You will realize that he has teed up the metaphor brilliantly.

Third, choose where to use colour. Imagine a large white canvas in a gallery with one single spot of red in the centre. That spot will stand out and be the focus of the painting. The same applies to speaking Shakespeare. You must choose what phrase, what word, what image you want to stand out and colour the speech accordingly. Colour can be emphasis, volume, vocal texture and emotional weight. Don't worry about those techniques for the moment. Human beings are naturally communicative and if you are clear about what you are trying to communicate, then the how usually falls into place easily. When you invent a phrase in a moment of inspiration, it will naturally have colour because the character needs that phrase. When this character invents the idea of the lark, it comes out of a moment of need. The type of need is a character question. How much does the speaker love the boy or girl? How lonely is he? Perhaps he is trying to get the boy or girl back, so the invention of the metaphor is like a gift. You have to admit it would be pretty flattering for someone to write that about you! This is a different kind of need, a different character choice. Now a word of warning: if you want that choice, that image, to stand out, beware of over-colouring elsewhere. The red spot on our canvas stands out because it is against plain white. The language of this poem could be played in an almost self-dramatising way. You can do that, but remember it's one long sentence, so don't spend too much time admiring the trees or the audience might get lost! You'll lose the power of the metaphor.

Now let's look at the use of metaphor inside a play. Here's an example from *Henry V*. The Chorus is describing the English fleet sailing for France seen from the shore:

CHORUS

O, do but think
You stand upon the rivage and behold
A city on the inconstant billows dancing.
Henry V, III. Prologue. 13–15

Imagine you are in the Globe Theatre at the first performance. There is very little scenery so the story is told principally through the power of the language. The chorus has to do three things: make the audience listen; tell the story; and engage the audience's imaginations. Shakespeare places the two imperative verbs, 'think' and 'behold', at the ends of the lines. These engage the audience and set up the fabulous metaphor, which begins the next line with 'A city'. Try this for yourself. Play the first two lines through to the verbs at the end and then after 'behold' ask yourself the question 'What?' and coin the image of what it looks like. So,

O, do but *think*
You stand upon the rivage and *behold*
[What?]
A *city* on the inconstant billows dancing.

There will inevitably be a small pause or beat after 'behold', but that's all right; it's on the line ending and so preserves the pulse. Really inhabit the metaphor. It's a perfect image that delivers exactly what Shakespeare needs at this moment. It's visually accurate but, more importantly, it's inspiring: 'A city . . . *dancing*'. Amazing!

Now let's consider one of Shakespeare's most extraordinary inventions: the teenager, Juliet. In this speech, newly wed, she is awaiting the arrival of her husband, Romeo.

JULIET

Gallop apace, you fiery-footed steeds,
Towards Phoebus' lodging: such a wagoner

As Phaethon would whip you to the west,
And bring in cloudy night immediately.
Spread thy close curtain, love-performing night,
That runaway's eyes may wink and Romeo
Leap to these arms, untalk'd of and unseen.
Lovers can see to do their amorous rites
By their own beauties; or, if love be blind,
It best agrees with night. Come, civil night,
Thou sober-suited matron, all in black,
And learn me how to lose a winning match,
Play'd for a pair of stainless maidenhoods:
Hood my unmann'd blood, bating in my cheeks,
With thy black mantle; till strange love, grown bold,
Think true love acted simple modesty.
Come, night; come, Romeo; come, thou day in night
For thou wilt lie upon the wings of night
Whiter than new snow on a raven's back.
Come, gentle night, come, loving, black-brow'd night,
Give me my Romeo; and, when he shall die,
Take him and cut him out in little stars,
And he will make the face of heaven so fine
That all the world will be in love with night
And pay no worship to the garish sun.
O, I have bought the mansion of a love,
But not possess'd it, and, though I am sold,
Not yet enjoy'd: so tedious is this day
As is the night before some festival
To an impatient child that hath new robes
And may not wear them.
Romeo and Juliet, III. ii. 1–31

This speech is jam-packed with metaphor; it's almost super-saturated! No plain canvas here. There is, however, a crucial similarity with the speaker in the sonnet. Both are passionately in love, and that seems to be the main source of inspiration on both occasions. Love and the frustration of not seeing her new husband turns Juliet into a fountain of inspired speech. It's one of the key observations to make about Juliet. Love makes her wildly, almost unstoppably, articulate. In this situation, her articulacy takes the form of metaphor upon metaphor. Let's apply the lessons from the sonnet.

There is no set up here. Juliet launches straight in with a big, full-blown image. Bang!

> Gallop apace, you fiery-footed steeds,
> Towards Phoebus' lodging: such a wagoner
> As Phaethon would whip you to the west,
> And bring in cloudy night immediately.

You need to invent and speak immediately. She is desperate for night (and her lover) to arrive. She chooses an image from mythology, which gives the speech size and resonance. She paints a startling picture that is full of drama. Try it a couple of times. Find the need to speak and inhabit the imaginary situation. Open it out by addressing the elements. Try and create the picture more vividly each time. The lines are full of energy. They are almost aggressive and show a powerful sexual desire. There is an issue of colour here. Do you paint it all with strong colours or do you try and find contrast? I think part of the attraction of Juliet is her almost over-the-top manner, so I'd keep most of it quite strong, but perhaps ease back with 'And bring in cloudy night immediately'. You could find smoothness in this line that would contrast with the earlier passage. Onwards.

> Spread thy close curtain, love-performing night,
> That runaway's eyes may wink and Romeo
> Leap to these arms, untalk'd of and unseen.

She starts with the instruction 'Spread' that echoes the first word 'Gallop'. She picks up 'night' from the previous line, but you don't need to hit it hard. The image here is more intimate and more clandestine, but still highly dramatic. The drama lies partly in the variation of rhythm between the slow action of closing a curtain and the abrupt 'Leap' at the beginning of the line. Underpinning this whole passage there is an energy which is sometimes held in check, sometimes released. She follows with a simpler, more reflective, perhaps less coloured passage that takes its cue from 'unseen':

> Lovers can see to do their amorous rites
> By their own beauties; or, if love be blind,
> It best agrees with night.

After this short respite Juliet continues with her invocation:

> Come, civil night,
> Thou sober-suited matron, all in black,
> And learn me how to lose a winning match,
> Play'd for a pair of stainless maidenhoods:
> Hood my unmann'd blood, bating in my cheeks,
> With thy black mantle; till strange love, grown bold,
> Think true love acted simple modesty.

The technique here is to invent the image – in this case a 'sober-suited matron' – and then follow the metaphor through over the next five lines. She wears black, she has the authority to teach; 'stainless maidenhoods' conjures up a contrasting pure white image; 'hood' and 'black mantle' continue the chain of reference. It's like a paper chase; you must pick up each fragment as you proceed through the speech. She conjures once more. There's something almost demonic going on here:

> Come, night; come, Romeo; come, thou day in night;
> For thou wilt lie upon the wings of night
> Whiter than new snow on a raven's back.
> Come, gentle night, come, loving, black-brow'd night,
> Give me my Romeo; and, when he shall die,
> Take him and cut him out in little stars,
> And he will make the face of heaven so fine
> That all the world will be in love with night
> And pay no worship to the garish sun.

All the imagery here relates to light and its opposite, night. 'Night' occupies four of the line endings. So, in this section, bring together the work we have done on appositions to help give you a structure. Observe that there is a three-line sentence and then a six-liner. You will need to play the thought through and also choose which of the images you should invent and colour. Juliet continues her speech with yet another metaphor: the 'Mansion'. She concludes with a very self-revealing image:

> so tedious is this day
> As is the night before some festival
> To an impatient child that hath new robes
> And may not wear them.

Practise this nice simple metaphor by inserting a silent 'How?' after 'day' and then invent the next three lines. Now try the whole thing.

Let's summarise. This is a great feast of a speech, so beware gluttony. It's very easy to over-colour because there are so many elaborate metaphors. Look out for the simpler, more naturalistic lines to give you contrast. Each metaphor needs to be invented. Follow each metaphor through to its end. Try and find the links between one image and the next.

Crucially, you need to find out why Juliet needs to speak and why she uses these particular metaphors. It's worth noting that in this speech there are twenty separate images or references to night and darkness. From this you can learn that she not only yearns for night and darkness, but that it makes her highly articulate. I believe that you will learn most about the character by immersing yourself in the language. The yearning of Juliet for Romeo is expressed in the repeated use of 'come', her impatience for him by her commands and her deep desire for an all-consuming, intimate relationship by her need for darkness. It's also important to remember that she's not yet fourteen! Love is a matter of life and death and proves to be just so for Juliet.

Love and death are often cheek-to-cheek in Shakespeare's imagery. For example, here's Rosalind describing her love for Orlando to her friend Celia, in prose, in *As You Like It*:

ROSALIND

O coz, coz, coz, my pretty little coz, that thou
didst know how many fathom deep I am in love! But
it cannot be sounded: my affection hath an unknown
bottom, like the bay of Portugal.

As You Like It, IV. i. 175–178

The Bay of Portugal is of course the Bay of Biscay, the most dangerous waters for Elizabethan sailors and the scene of much loss of life. Notice the way her thought moves. The potential for drowning is present from the beginning but not expressed. No one can 'know how many fathom deep I am in love'. This leads Rosalind into new, 'unknown' waters, and she ends up at the bottom of the Bay of Portugal, a place of death. When she begins speaking to Celia, I believe she has no idea where she is going to end up. She is trying to express feelings she has never experienced before and the very act of putting them into words leads her to a strange, frightening place. In the space of just four lines, Shakespeare has changed the key of the scene into minor. Rosalind leaves the scene lost in her own thoughts, at the threshold of womanhood, bewildered and excited in equal measure. This speech, along with Juliet's, is a wonderful example of a metaphor leading a character on a voyage of self-discovery. Metaphor, I believe, often springs out of the character's unconscious; the character is trying to articulate something about himself, and the choice of metaphor is invariably highly enlightening. I would argue that the metaphor must come from a place of inspiration, not a place of deliberate, conscious thought. I think we can all understand this in our own lives; thoughts frequently just pop into our minds in an involuntary way. Playing parts like Juliet or Rosalind requires you open yourself to the full journey of the character. It is a highly exposing undertaking that demands great imagination, great courage and great technique.

You will find that a character in Shakespeare uses a metaphor when there is nothing else to do or say. An explanation or description of what you are feeling is inadequate. Here's Antipholus in *The Comedy of Errors*. He has spent years searching for his lost twin and now despairs of ever finding him.

ANTIPHOLUS

I to the world am like a drop of water
That in the ocean seeks another drop,
Who, falling there to find his fellow forth,
Unseen, inquisitive, confounds himself.
                    The Comedy of Errors, I. ii. 35–38

Antipholus searches his imagination for a metaphor that has the dimension to fully express the hopelessness he feels. The key to fulfilling these lines is not just to invent the image, but to pursue the thoughts that flow from that image as far as 'confounds himself'. It is as if he is cornered and can only express himself in a heightened way.

As we have observed, the metaphor itself will often open up a new realm for the speaker to explore. In his first scene, Hamlet is required to endure the spectacle of his mother and her new husband, his uncle Claudius, holding court. He finds the whole situation suffocating and intolerable. He is left alone and says:

HAMLET

O, that this too too solid flesh would melt
Thaw and resolve itself into a dew!
Or that the Everlasting had not fix'd
His canon 'gainst self-slaughter! O God! God!
How weary, stale, flat and unprofitable,
Seem to me all the uses of this world!
Fie on't! ah fie! 'tis an unweeded garden,
That grows to seed; things rank and gross in nature
Possess it merely. That it should come to this!
                    Hamlet, I. ii. 129–137

He can only express what he feels through metaphor. He comes up with this inspired but horrific image of self-annihilation. As with Juliet's speech, this absolutely has to be coined in the moment, possibly even just before the word 'melt'. Try the first two lines, inventing the image at that point. Now try to create the whole image before you speak. Either way is valid. The key is to find the need to invent and then to act upon it. That way the image will leap out at the audience and grab their imaginations. It is perforce a colourful image and lays the ground for all of Hamlet's contemplation of death. It's followed by a description of life in Denmark that is deliberately flat, plain and without colour:

> How weary, stale, flat and unprofitable,
> Seem to me all the uses of this world!

(Use the relentless regularity of the 'How' line.) Then the perfect image comes into his head: ' 'tis an unweeded garden'. It's vivid and memorable. In just a few lines Hamlet has given us a window into his own state of mind and his perception of Denmark. In other words, the metaphors have created an interior and an exterior landscape. This is a crucial idea to get hold of, particularly when you remember that Shakespeare was writing for an essentially non-scenic theatre. We have seen that in *Romeo and Juliet*, both Friar Laurence and Juliet herself introduce ideas of death – here Hamlet does the same. In both cases these contribute to what can be described as 'atmosphere'. The point to remember is that atmosphere emanates from the imagination of characters in specific moments, although, of course, Shakespeare is carefully and cleverly weaving a fabric that will give the whole play, or a section of the play, a mood or atmosphere.

Take a look at Macbeth, for example. Quite independently, Lady Macbeth and Macbeth come up with chillingly similar evocations to night:

LADY MACBETH

> Come, thick night,
> And pall thee in the dunnest smoke of hell,
> That my keen knife see not the wound it makes,
> Nor heaven peep through the blanket of the dark,
> To cry 'Hold, hold!'
>
> *Macbeth*, I. v. 49–53

MACBETH

> Come, seeling night,
> Scarf up the tender eye of pitiful day;
> And with thy bloody and invisible hand
> Cancel and tear to pieces that great bond
> Which keeps me pale!
>
> *Macbeth*, III. ii. 47–51

These are good speeches to practice taking an image or metaphor and tracking it over several lines to see how it develops. As with 'Gallop apace', Shakespeare makes much use of apposition and imagery of darkness and light. When I first directed the play in Stratford-upon-Avon, I agreed with the actors that their ambition, coupled with their inability to have children, created a diabolical bond between them. They shared an intimacy and passion, which manifests itself in a shared imagery. Any two actors playing these roles have to find much common ground in their imaginations.

We will now look at how other couples in Shakespeare share imagery and how it is passed on from one actor to another like the baton in a relay race. Let's look at some comedies. We'll return to best friends Rosalind and Celia in *As You Like It*. Rosalind has fallen head over heels in love with Orlando, who has just triumphed at the court wrestling competition. The two friends are left alone, Rosalind on fire with her new passion.

CELIA

Why, cousin! why, Rosalind! Cupid have mercy! not a word?

ROSALIND

Not one to throw at a dog.

CELIA

No, thy words are too precious to be cast away upon
curs; throw some of them at me; come, lame me with reasons.

ROSALIND

Then there were two cousins laid up; when the one
should be lamed with reasons and the other mad without any.

CELIA

But is all this for your father?

ROSALIND

No, some of it is for my child's father. O, how
full of briers is this working-day world!

CELIA

They are but burs, cousin, thrown upon thee in
holiday foolery: if we walk not in the trodden
paths our very petticoats will catch them.

ROSALIND

I could shake them off my coat: these burs are in my heart.

CELIA

Hem them away.

ROSALIND

I would try, if I could cry 'hem' and have him.

As You Like It, I. iii. 1–16

This is a useful passage to examine because you don't just learn about each individual character; you discover a huge amount about their relationship. And the great thing is that it's all in the text. Notice the way they pick up on each other's words and imagery. If possible, practice this passage with a friend or relative.

First of all, Celia asks a straightforward question (with a little 'Cupid' dig thrown in). The dog image in Rosalind's reply leads onto 'cast away', 'throw' and the inspired idea of laming 'with reasons' and then its antithesis, 'mad', which is what Rosalind clearly is. Indeed she soon lets slip her secret wish: 'some of it is for my child's father'. I think there is a direct visceral connection between this confession and the 'briers' metaphor that follows. You can invent this in the 'blush moment' as soon as she has told her friend what she really wants. Celia catches this metaphor in mid-air and plays with it and develops it (with 'burs' and 'walk not in trodden paths'). Celia throws it back to her friend, who takes it further. Rosalind then throws it back to Celia. It is finally resolved by Rosalind with the emphatic 'have him'. This is, of course, banter, but the metaphor is apt for the way Rosalind feels: 'these burs are in my heart'.

In this dialogue, Rosalind is the originator of the imagery, throwing things at dogs and briers. Her invention probably comes from the fact that, of the two friends, she is the first to arrive at that moment of flux when you fall in love and nothing is the same ever again. She is changing emotionally and chemically. Celia responds with great wit and intelligence, underpinned by huge affection. Human relationships shift and change according to circumstances, so it's important to note precisely where these two friends are at this moment.

To play this section, follow the trail of the imagery, as described above. At first it is probably best to stress or even over-stress the words and ideas that are being passed on. Try and become more and more playful with the language. Imagine it's a ball being thrown between the two of you or it's a tennis match only with words. Invent your own game that gives you a sense of the movement of word to word, image to image. Then you should lighten it and make it more conversational. Create different situations to play the scene in – perhaps over a drink in a bar or on a walk through the park. But always retain the pleasure of inventing an image or transforming an idea you have been tossed. How you deal with an idea thrown at you defines, to a degree, the kind of character you are. Celia, for example, could be very bookish, someone who hides their emotions behind a torrent of wit. It's

Juliet Stevenson as Rosalind and Fiona Shaw as Celia in *As You Like It* at the Royal Shakespeare Theatre, 1985. Photo: Joe Cocks Studio Collection © Shakespeare Birthplace Trust

often a good idea to set your character as long an emotional journey in the play as possible. Accentuating the drier, ironic aspects of Celia's character might be wise, given what happens to her when she meets Oliver, Orlando's brother. Here's Rosalind's description:

ROSALIND

There was never any thing so sudden but the fight of two rams
and Caesar's thrasonical brag of 'I came, saw, and
overcame:' for your brother and my sister no sooner
met but they looked, no sooner looked but they
loved, no sooner loved but they sighed, no sooner
sighed but they asked one another the reason, no
sooner knew the reason but they sought the remedy;
and in these degrees have they made a pair of stairs

> to marriage which they will climb incontinent, or
> else be incontinent before marriage: they are in
> the very wrath of love and they will together; clubs
> cannot part them.
>
> *As You Like It,* V. ii. 28–40

This is an inspired description, brought alive by the two images: rams fighting and Caesar. Rosalind follows this with a whole series of counterpoints ('looked', 'loved', etc.), which give her the idea of the stairway. She resolves with another image of combat. We should remember that Rosalind is, at this point, dressed as a boy. There is an extravagance, a swagger about the text and the metaphors she uses, giving the actress a real sensation of the disguise Rosalind has adopted. Notice also a point I made earlier: situations and events often make Shakespeare's characters more fluent and articulate. For me, this is one of his most brilliant insights into human nature, and also one of his most optimistic, for it presumes the possibility of change. We will deal with it fully in a later chapter.

Let us look at one last example of shared metaphor that cleverly advances the story and helps define relationships. In *Twelfth Night,* Viola, dressed as a young man, is sent by her master to woo Olivia, a rich and beautiful young woman. She bursts into Olivia's private rooms where we pick up the conversation after Viola has managed to offend just about everybody:

OLIVIA

Yet you began rudely. What are you? what would you?

VIOLA

The rudeness that hath appeared in me have I
learned from my entertainment. What I am, and what I
would, are as secret as maidenhead; to your ears,
divinity, to any other's, profanation.

OLIVIA

Give us the place alone: we will hear this divinity.
Exeunt MARIA and Attendants

Now, sir, what is your text?

VIOLA

Most sweet lady, –

OLIVIA

A comfortable doctrine, and much may be said of it.
Where lies your text?

VIOLA

> In Orsino's bosom.

OLIVIA

In his bosom! In what chapter of his bosom?

VIOLA

To answer by the method, in the first of his heart.

OLIVIA

O, I have read it: it is heresy. Have you no more to say?

VIOLA

Good madam, let me see your face.

Twelfth Night, I. v. 203–217

As you work on this, it's crucial to remember that Viola is disguised as a man, for it gives the situation not only comic opportunities, but also an eroticism that Shakespeare exploits fully. Viola is like a breath of fresh air in Olivia's household, which is still in mourning. Shakespeare plays on the fact that we, the audience, know Viola's secrets, but Olivia is intrigued by the statement:

> What I am, and what I would, are as secret as maidenhead; to your ears, divinity, to any other's, profanation.

It's the counterpoint of divinity and profanation that Olivia picks up on. This provides her with the conceit that we can track through the next six lines. She sets up Viola's speech as a holy text and quizzes her accordingly. Viola eventually joins in the game, with 'the first of his heart', but Olivia tops this with 'O, I have read it: it is heresy'.

If you follow her metaphor in a nice, disingenuous way, you can get a good laugh after 'heresy', which I am sure Shakespeare intended, because, at this point, he changes the subject. In the passage we have just read, it is Olivia who drives the metaphor; it is Olivia who throws down the challenges to Viola. We learn later that this is fuelled by a sexual attraction towards this 'boy'. As so often in Shakespeare, the sexual attraction is manifest in word play. Viola wants a more direct encounter so asks Olivia to lift her veil. In this exchange we see a quite sophisticated, multi-layered use of language with metaphor at its very heart.

I think to be successful at playing Shakespeare, you have to love language because he obviously did, and we must assume that his audience did as well. This is explained partly by the fact that it was essentially a non-scenic art form (although even here one could argue that it was non-scenic *because* it was a language-based form). But it goes beyond theatrical convention. In Shakespeare, language is a fundamental expression of self, and communication through language is as joyful and essential as eating and drinking. Shakespeare's use of metaphor is the key to that expression of self because it has the capability of vaulting everyday exchanges and landing the listener in a very special place: the world of the imagination. The exploration of this world is a source of enormous satisfaction to the actor. It is essential, I believe, to why audiences love Shakespeare.

4

METRE AND PULSE

The rhythm section

I remember when I was a small boy there was an old-fashioned radio in the kitchen that lit up when you turned it on. Printed on the dial were exotic sounding place names from around the world. I would sit and twiddle the knob and listen to a stream of different languages, each with its distinctive cadence, rhythm and chatter. The purpose of this chapter is to help you to tune in to the rhythms and cadence of Shakespeare's language. We will learn how to recognise different rhythms and how to be sensitive to variations. We will look at the nuts and bolts of metre. We will examine why, at any moment, Shakespeare used a particular effect and learn how to create energy from it. We will consider what rhythm tells us about character. We will try to identify the musical structure of a speech and of a play. We will need to use a few technical terms to make discussion and demonstration easier. But technical terms in themselves are of no importance whatsoever; what counts is that you experience the rhythms and the metre for yourself and that you understand the verse from your guts rather than from your head. As we look at these somewhat technical aspects, we will continuously relate them to the meaning, to the emotion and to the situation. We will learn a considerable amount about character as well.

We will start with pulse. Every line has a pulse; every speech has a pulse. Sometimes a whole play has a distinctive pulse. The pulse is the heartbeat of the speech. Pursue the analogy a little. At first, it can be hard to identify your own pulse, but with practice it gets much easier. The same is true of a Shakespeare play. I find it hard to feel my pulse in the wrist, but quite easy if I locate a place in my neck. If I run hard for ten minutes, my pulse races; if I lie down, my pulse slows; if I get angry, my pulse quickens. We use words such as 'strong' or 'weak'. Our heartbeat adjusts in response to different physical and emotional circumstances, as does the verse in a Shakespeare play. Your pulse will tell your doctor volumes about your health; a practiced eye can read volumes into the changing pulse of a character's speech in different situations. And I can assure you, none of this is too difficult. Shakespeare didn't write in a foreign language. He wrote in English, the language we speak, and the rhythms and cadences he used in his plays are the rhythms and cadences he heard every day. He did not develop a special language with a special vocabulary that has to be approached as an alien form. One of the great strengths of English literature, and drama in particular, is that there is no great divide between the literary and the common language, as is certainly true to a considerable degree in French. In Shakespeare's day, English was a relatively young, rapidly developing language that he himself did much to shape. Probably more than any other human being, Shakespeare contributed to the vocabulary, to the phraseology, to the cadence and to the rhythm of our language. Think back to the Globe Theatre. As we have observed, the actors shared one space with an audience consisting of every sort, condition and class of person. And the language they heard was their own; the language was bounced back and reformed through Shakespeare's genius, but still, essentially, their own.

Back to pulse. For the most part, Shakespeare used five beats to the line of verse. Sometimes he would use six beats and this gives an almost overfull, stuffed feeling. Sometimes he would use three or four beats and this gives a particular style especially effective in comedy. But mostly five. The form of verse Shakespeare used for most of his plays is known as the iambic pentameter. Iambic is a rhythm consisting of one short, unstressed syllable and one long, stressed syllable: De Dum. Pentameter means five feet or five beats. So an iambic pentameter is De Dum, De Dum, De Dum, De Dum, De Dum. Easy! Here's one:

ORSINO

If music be the food of love, play on.
                    Twelfth Night, I. i. 1

This is the opening line of *Twelfth Night*. Orsino, passionately in love with Olivia, shares his feelings with his friends. If you work out the rhythm of a line of poetry, you say you are scanning it. So this line scans like this:

Ĭf músĭc bé thĕ fóod ŏf lóve, plăy ón.

Try it for yourself out loud. De Dum, De Dum, De Dum, De Dum, De Dum. At first, stress every one of the strong beats: mu, be, food, love and on. Try tapping your fingers or clapping your hands on the beat. It will, of course, sound absurd. Never mind, just try and feel the rhythm. Do this a couple of times, then ease up and play it much lighter. Keep the pulse alive, but don't hit it hard. Focus on playing through to the end of the line. Feel how the energy flows to the end of the line quite naturally. What you have just experienced is an iambic pentameter. It's useful to notice that when you focus on the pulse, you automatically get a firm, almost insistent quality, which is quite useful for getting the audience's attention.

Try another line. This is Romeo commenting on Mercutio's teasing:

> Hĕ jésts ăt scárs thát névĕr félt ă wóund.
> *Romeo and Juliet*, II. ii. 1

Use the same method. De Dum, De Dum, etc. At first, stress each strong beat, and then ease back. Imagine yourself in Romeo's situation and look out for the apposition (scars/wound). You will soon find that you can phrase the line in a quite naturalistic manner, while at the same time keeping a light sense of the pulse. And since, in the next moment, Juliet appears up at the balcony, it's probably a good idea if this line is almost throwaway, contrasting with the next line, when he sees her:

> But, soft! what light through yonder window breaks?
> *Romeo and Juliet*, II. ii. 2

The reply to the question is, of course, one of the great metaphors in drama:

> It is the east, and Juliet is the sun.
> *Romeo and Juliet*, II. ii. 3

Try these lines one after the other. As you practice, you will find the pulse becoming more and more part of you. But be light with it; don't bash it. The three lines reveal a sort of awakening in Romeo. At first, a man hidden and feeling different from his pals; then a man awakening; finally, a man dazzled by this woman's light. As you work, keep asking yourself: Is it real? Do people speak like this? Make the adjustments; retain the underlying pulse, but phrase it in a real way, using the work you have done in earlier chapters. It might help to think of the pulse as the rhythm section in a band. You are not always aware of the drums or the bass, and usually they should not attract attention to themselves, but they are always there, lending support and, crucially, giving a forward motion to the music. Incidentally, you will also discover that Shakespeare clearly intends the name 'Juliet' to have the stress on the first syllable and not on the second, as is often heard.

All three lines are written with our regular pulse, but what a contrast of effect from the one to the other! Demonstrably, using an iambic pentameter doesn't automatically mean that the language has to sound heightened or formal. It can do, but it can also present totally naturalistic speech within a split second, the one or the other. I think it is the flexibility of the form, it's ability to move swiftly from effect to effect that attracted Shakespeare. He didn't invent the iambic pentameter; it was originally a Greek form, developed in England by the Earl of Surrey several decades before Shakespeare's birth. Other playwrights also used the form, but none with the effortless brilliance of Shakespeare. He began using it right at the beginning of his career and continued with it for the rest of his working life. He found it was a tool capable of developing in tandem with his own extraordinary experiments in dramatic form.

But I hope you have already got a glimmer of something even more important than all this. This verse line is somehow the perfect conduit for thought and expression in the English language. It has a strong forward motion but at the same time can merely lightly underscore a line; it has a good length to allow expression of thought; and it can contain an almost infinite amount of variety, as we will see. But, crucially, it seems to most accurately represent the way the language expresses itself.

Let's go back to the beginning of Shakespeare's career and take an example from *Henry VI Part II*. The play takes place during the bloody Wars of the Roses and here is the Duke of York, who believes he has a stronger claim to the throne than King Henry:

YORK

From Ireland thus comes York to claim his right,
And pluck the crown from feeble Henry's head:
Ring, bells, aloud; burn, bonfires, clear and bright,
To entertain great England's lawful king.

Henry VI, Part II, V. i. 1–4

This is a full-blooded speech with a very strong pulse. York has just landed from Ireland along with his army and is full of self-confidence and certainty. That certainty is expressed in a powerful rhythm. Try it for yourself. Read the first two lines aloud and give them a very strong De Dum pulse. I think you will find straight away that the speech gives back to you a sense of York's power. Try them a couple of times, perhaps imagining that you are addressing your troops. Allow the strong, regular beat to empower you. York isn't going to allow anyone to get in his way! Then a wonderful thing happens in the third line. The rhythm is broken. You can try and scan the line De Dum, De Dum, etc., but you will find it very odd. Both the sense and the rhythm suggest a series of strong beats, perhaps six or even seven strong beats: 'Ríng, bélls, ăloúd; búrn, bónfiřes, cléar ănd bríght'. This is a line you can really enjoy. It's a line that cries out for a series of strong punchy beats. The words can be fully coloured and the alliteration on the letter 'b' give useful fuel. The pictures it conjures up are vivid and the impact of the change of rhythm is made startling by preceding and following the line with a regular pulse. Try all four lines for yourself. Play the first two lines through to their ends with an insistent but not over-strong pulse. Sense the strength in the words 'pluck the crown' and contrast them with the weaker 'feeble Henry's head'. Relish the series of strong beats in the third line, then return to a regular rhythm in the last line: 'To entertain great England's lawful king'.

The rhythm gives this line a sense of satisfaction and inevitability. Notice also that York contrasts himself ('England's lawful king') at the end of the fourth line with Henry ('feeble Henry's head') at the end of the second line. These four lines tell us a lot about York. They reveal a huge self-confidence and an ability to use rhetoric to inspire other people, which is an essential quality in a leader. The pulse and the rhythm do most of the work for you. They empower you.

In Stratford-upon-Avon, in 1988, I directed the three parts of *Henry VI* and *Richard III* condensed into three evenings under the title *The Plantagenets*. We had a large company of actors to play the hundreds of parts; some actors were highly experienced and some were embarking on their very first job. We had a six-month rehearsal period and quite soon realized that these plays had a very distinctive pulse that somehow characterized their raw, dangerous energy. So, every morning before rehearsals, we spent half an hour in what we somewhat inelegantly called a 'pulse workshop'. In it we sought out not only the rhythm of a particular speech, but the pulse that seemed to underpin the whole endeavour. The actors not only practiced their own lines, but also continuously heard other people's. Over the weeks, the company became saturated in the language of these early Shakespeare plays and the pulse seemed to become the very heartbeat of the group. I want to emphasise that the beat was not overstated, but the text always had a strong pulse, which lent a particular style to the whole event. In this case, we did not seek a naturalistic conversational delivery, but followed the imperative of the text, which lead us to a slightly heightened reading. It seemed to have the right sound, the right cadence for the story of one of the bloodiest, most impassioned episodes in English history.

Now let us take another speech in which there is much more variation of rhythm and learn how to tackle it. It's time to take a look at the opening

Chorus of *Henry V*. It's a wonderful speech to work on, all the more so because it contains a whole philosophy about the importance of language in theatre. Just read it through first of all.

CHORUS

O for a Muse of fire, that would ascend
The brightest heaven of invention,
A kingdom for a stage, princes to act
And monarchs to behold the swelling scene!
Then should the warlike Harry, like himself,
Assume the port of Mars; and at his heels,
Leash'd in like hounds, should famine, sword and fire
Crouch for employment. But pardon, gentles all,
The flat unraised spirits that have dared
On this unworthy scaffold to bring forth
So great an object: can this cockpit hold
The vasty fields of France? or may we cram
Within this wooden O the very casques
That did affright the air at Agincourt?
O, pardon! since a crooked figure may
Attest in little place a million;
And let us, ciphers to this great accompt,
On your imaginary forces work.
Suppose within the girdle of these walls
Are now confined two mighty monarchies,
Whose high upreared and abutting fronts
The perilous narrow ocean parts asunder:
Piece out our imperfections with your thoughts;
Into a thousand parts divide one man,
And make imaginary puissance;
Think when we talk of horses, that you see them
Printing their proud hoofs i' the receiving earth;
For 'tis your thoughts that now must deck our kings,
Carry them here and there; jumping o'er times,
Turning the accomplishment of many years
Into an hour-glass: for the which supply,
Admit me Chorus to this history;
Who prologue-like your humble patience pray,
Gently to hear, kindly to judge, our play.

Henry V, I, Prologue, 1–34

In *Henry V*, Shakespeare told the story of a great national hero. The play is fascinating. On the one hand, it celebrates Henry's achievements (he reconquered France and married the daughter of the French king, thereby securing the territory). On the other hand, it offers a critique of war and the human suffering that attends it. In this play, Shakespeare uses the device of the Chorus, who addresses the audience directly at several junctures in the action. Shakespeare fills in the gaps in the story and comments on what has just taken place and what is about to happen. In this speech the Chorus, standing on the bare stage of the Globe Theatre, the 'wooden O', sets the scene and invites the audience to participate in the event by using their ears and their imaginations.

Remember, there might be up to three thousand people crammed into the theatre so the actor playing the Chorus has got to grab their attention. He does this by starting with a strong beat of Dum de, rather than a De Dum. This is known as a trochee, a stressed syllable followed by an unstressed one. It is the opposite of an iambic. The remainder of this line is regular iambics, so it scans thus: 'Ó fŏr ă Múse ŏf fíre, thăt wóuld ăscénd'.

Try it for yourself. Perhaps start by saying the whole line with an iambic rhythm. Of course, the first few words sound absurd. So do it again, this time starting with the strong trochee and then finding your regular rhythm. Notice that Shakespeare not only starts against the rhythm, but he also uses the open vowel 'O'. This gives the actor a powerful tool to control the audience and shut them up if necessary. He can make the 'O' as loud and as long as he likes! Try it.

The speech continues:

> O for a Muse of fire, that would ascend
> The brightest heaven of invention,
> A kingdom for a stage, princes to act
> And monarchs to behold the swelling scene!

For the time being, I would advise that you start by continuing the speech using your De Dum method (scanning). You'll quite soon be able to dispense with it, but it does help to get you into the pulse. At the same time, it highlights the variations that Shakespeare brings into play. For the most part, this is regular iambic pentameter, but can you spot the variation? In the third line, 'princes' has to be spoken as a trochee: Dum De. This gives the line an attractive counter-rhythm and also provides a contrast to the fourth line ('And monarchs to behold the swelling scene!'), which has a regularity appropriate to its meaning. What Shakespeare is doing here, writing at the height of his powers, is to provide opportunities for the actor to make the audience listen. This is Shakespeare at his most practical. The audience would be unaware of most of these variations but they help to keep the ear alert.

Onwards:

Then should the warlike Harry, like himself,
Assume the port of Mars; and at his heels,
Leash'd in like hounds, should famine, sword and fire
Crouch for employment. But pardon, gentles all,

Again, scan the lines for yourself. Where does he change the rhythm and why? As in the first line, he starts with a trochee, 'Then'. This gives you an edge which you can use lightly or in an attacking way. Either way, you will find there is no need to bang out the pulse of the rest of the line, just keep it ticking along under the text. The next line is regular, which prepares us for the highly energetic rhythm of:

Léash'd ĭn líke hóunds, shŏuld fámĭne, swórd ănd fíre
Cróuch fŏr ĕmploýmĕnt. Bŭt párdŏn, géntlĕs áll,

Each line starts with a trochee or off-beat. This somehow tips the energy towards the strong words of 'famine, sword and fire' in the case of the first line. It also sets up an expectation in the second line, which the Chorus can undercut with the regular, almost understated apology. Practice these changes of rhythm. They are the dramatic equivalent of hairpin bends, sometimes tricky to negotiate, but very exciting when achieved. They always keep the audience alert and the excitement building.

Let's take a short diversion off the highway to note the advice Hamlet gives to the players:

HAMLET

Speak the speech, I pray you, as I pronounced it to
you, trippingly on the tongue.

Hamlet, III. i. 1–2

'Trippingly'. Later in the same speech Hamlet talks of 'smoothness'. These are useful hints when you are dealing with issues of metre and pulse. The lesson is not to be too heavy-handed on the wheel.

The next section of the Chorus is quite regular up to 'On your imaginary forces work'. Scan it, and then play it through for practice, quite lightly, looking out for the ironies and understatements. What I want you to focus on next is the way, in the last section of the speech, Shakespeare uses variations in rhythm to drive home his declared intention, to work on the audience's 'imaginary forces'. The choice of verb 'work' is also noteworthy, lying at the end of the line in a powerful position. It's a doing word that is active and contains energy. The Chorus is trying to bring about change on the audience; he is being transitive. This is something I believe in quite passionately about

Shakespeare: his words should engage with the imagination of the audience and not just be consumed by them as a commodity. The French have a helpful phrase; they describe attending a performance as '*assister à*'. Isn't that heavenly!

Read the passage through from 'Suppose' to the end. Look out for the variations in rhythm.

> Suppose within the girdle of these walls
> Are now confined two mighty monarchies,
> Whose high upreared and abutting fronts
> The perilous narrow ocean parts asunder:
> Piece out our imperfections with your thoughts;
> Into a thousand parts divide one man,
> And make imaginary puissance;
> Think when we talk of horses, that you see them
> Printing their proud hoofs i' the receiving earth;
> For 'tis your thoughts that now must deck our kings,
> Carry them here and there; jumping o'er times,
> Turning the accomplishment of many years
> Into an hour-glass: for the which supply,
> Admit me Chorus to this history;
> Who prologue-like your humble patience pray,
> Gently to hear, kindly to judge, our play.

Note particularly the sequence of verbs placed at the beginning of lines: 'Piece', 'Think', 'Printing', 'Carry' and 'Turning'. Add to these 'Jumping' and you have six trochees, each one a change of rhythm which gives an energy and a drive to the line. It's like a tennis player suddenly starting to volley the ball. The energy and excitement level in the court immediately goes up. With lines like these, give a strong impulse on the verb at the beginning of the line, but make sure you then play through to the line ending.

Try these lines:

> Think when we talk of horses, that you see them
> Printing their proud hoofs i' the receiving earth;

Challenge the audience with the verb 'Think', but play the thought through to 'see them'. Just follow the sense: 'Think . . . you see them'. Then, next line, bang! The first word is 'Printing' and, almost immediately, another two strong stresses back to back with 'proud' and 'hoofs': Dum de de Dum Dum. You can see what Shakespeare is doing here; he's creating a sound picture of hooves on the earth. He reinforces the effect with the alliteration of 'p'. Try it and start to enjoy the changes of rhythm. Think back to the band analogy.

There is a continuous pulse, but different instruments are creating cross rhythms. It's like jazz!

Look at this line: 'Into a thousand parts divide one man'. It scans De de de Dum de Dum. 'Into a thousand parts'. Try it. Remember, trippingly on the tongue. It has the chatter of a chopping knife on a block. De de de Dum. It's a witty line because the counterpoint of this choppy rhythm is the two lone words 'one man'. To complete the thought, perhaps these words need to be scanned 'óne mán'.

This whole section, from 'Suppose' to the end, is full of dramatic and verbal energy. The verbs challenge our imagination and thrust us into the future. We are made to think of the exciting possibilities in store if only we can imagine. When I directed the play in 1984 with Kenneth Branagh as the king, I started with the full company on stage gathered around Ian McDiarmid, who was playing the Chorus. When he got to the word 'work', he delivered it with real relish and the whole company swept off stage. This in itself created great energy onstage, but it left Ian alone to really conjure the audience with all those imperative verbs we have been working on. It was one man working the audience with language.

In this speech, there are many other techniques that Shakespeare employs to deliver his effects that we have either examined in previous chapters or will do later in the book. But there are a couple of other points we should deal with at this stage. You have probably found that some lines only scan as pentameters if certain words are pronounced in the way that Shakespeare intended. An example is the word 'puissance'. The original Chorus would have pronounced this word 'pu-i-ssance', three syllables. This, of course, makes the line scan in a regular fashion. The same is true of the word 'upreared', which would have been pronounced 'upreared'. What you do here comes down to a question of taste. In my own productions, I encourage the actors to add the extra syllable to maintain the pulse, but not to make too much of it. I know other directors can't bear old-fashioned pronunciations, but it doesn't worry me. Occasionally you will come across a line that appears to have an extra foot or at least extra syllables, as in: 'The perilous narrow ocean parts asunder.' Here there are twelve syllables but only five beats. The word 'perilous' is best pronounced with just one stress. This syncopation, this cramming in of syllables is, I'm sure, deliberate on Shakespeare's part, for it demonstrates the image he is describing. Again, it's best to deal with it lightly and practically.

I have found that in rehearsals I very rarely use technical terms when talking to actors. This is not because they are unaware of the vocabulary, but because it is usually better to identify the thought, the emotion or the intention behind a line rather than just analyse the technical aspects. However, you need a thorough understanding of the plumbing in order to support the imaginative work you are engaged in. So as we progress through these chapters, consciously try and cross-refererence the subjects. Try to see how your understanding of metaphor or apposition is supported by a grasp of metre and pulse. So, for example, the metre will tell you how a line is scanned, but it will not necessarily tell you which words to stress. Your understanding of metaphor and Shakespeare's technique of writing contrapuntally will certainly tell you much more. Look at this line:

O, what a rogue and peasant slave am I!
Hamlet, II. ii. 552

It's Hamlet, chastising himself. Now, where do you place the stress in this line? On any or all of 'O', 'rogue', 'peasant', 'slave' or 'I'? There's a funny character in Dickens's *Nicholas Nickleby* who thought all the editors had got Shakespeare's punctuation wrong, and that in this case there should be an exclamation mark after 'what' and a question mark after 'I'. Try it for yourself. It gives a wonderfully eccentric reading. But wrong!

Now back to the problem. He starts with an exclamation, 'O', a strong beat. 'Rogue' and 'peasant' are very colourful words, so you could certainly use these, especially if the character was consumed with self-loathing. Strictly speaking, the apposition is 'slave' and 'I', so perhaps there is a way through here. By counter-pointing these two words you certainly take the energy through the line and avoid any self-indulgence. Remember, your first responsibility to the audience is to tell the story; some actors worry far too much about what they are feeling themselves and not quite enough about what the audience is feeling. So in this case, I'd probably opt for the apposition of 'slave' and 'I', and not stress much else. By stressing too many words in a line, you can give the audience too much information. However, it's important to learn that there is no single solution to how to stress a line, but, hopefully, this will give you a methodology that will help inform your choices.

Let's look at this question of stress or emphasis in a slightly different way. By now you will certainly have noticed that most of the lines you have been working on fall naturally into two sections. There is a fulcrum point somewhere in the line. This is not always smack in the middle; sometimes it is after one beat, sometimes after three, sometimes even after four. Occasionally it's hard to identify one at all. But usually there is a break point, sometimes even a tiny pause, in every line. It's called a caesura. It helps to give shape to the line, it helps the audience to get the sense of the line and, in Shakespeare's hands, it helps to confer the cadence of everyday speech. Read this speech of Claudio in *Measure for Measure*. He has been condemned to death for fornication, and his sister, Isabella, has told him of the deal Angelo has offered: if she sleeps with him, Claudio will be spared. Claudio is revolted by this idea, but frightened of death:

CLAUDIO

Ay, but to die, and go we know not where;
To lie in cold obstruction and to rot;
This sensible warm motion to become
A kneaded clod; and the delighted spirit
To bathe in fiery floods, or to reside
In thrilling region of thick-ribbed ice;
To be imprison'd in the viewless winds,
And blown with restless violence round about
The pendent world; or to be worse than worst
Of those that lawless and incertain thought
Imagine howling: 'tis too horrible!
The weariest and most loathed worldly life
That age, ache, penury and imprisonment
Can lay on nature is a paradise
To what we fear of death.

ISABELLA

Alas, alas!

CLAUDIO

Sweet sister, let me live:
Measure for Measure, III. i. 118–134

First of all, just read it out loud. Now go through and lightly mark with a pencil where you think the caesuras may fall. It's mostly common sense. Remember, only one caesura per line! Now read it again and see what difference it makes. You will probably find it has become a bit stilted. That's all right; you are going through a process of work. Eventually you will want to be less heavy-handed with it, but we will arrive there in good time. For now I want you to recognize the way Shakespeare is shaping the rhythm and how the rhythm is following the thought. I would identify the caesuras as follows:

1. Ay, but to die, . . . and go we know not where;
2. To lie in cold obstruction . . . and to rot;
3. This sensible warm motion . . . to become
4. A kneaded clod; . . . and the delighted spirit
5. To bathe in fiery floods, . . . or to reside
6. In thrilling region . . . of thick-ribbed ice;

7. To be imprison'd . . . in the viewless winds,

8. And blown with restless violence . . . round about

9. The pendent world; . . . or to be worse than worst

10. Of those that lawless . . . and incertain thought

11. Imagine howling: . . . 'tis too horrible!

12. The weariest . . . and most loathed worldly life

13. That age, ache, penury . . . and imprisonment

14. Can lay on nature . . . is a paradise

15. To what we fear of death.

Observe in line 1 how the first half of the line is developed in the second half. 'And go we know not where' is an idea that developes from 'to die'. This is what I mean by the movement of thought. Try it again, developing the thought in the second half of the line. The same applies to the second line: again there's a development of thought after the caesura. The energy moves forward towards the ends of the lines. This is so important in playing Shakespeare. In line 3, the verb 'become' at the end of the line links the apposition of 'sensible warm motion' with 'kneaded clod' at the top of line 4. Here there is a semicolon, but Claudio's mind moves forward to the vivid contrast of 'delighted spirit' and on to the next apposition at the beginning

"Ay but to die. . ." Juliet Stevenson as Isabella and John Nolan as Claudio in *Measure for Measure* at the Barbican, 1984. Photo: Joe Cocks Studio Collection © Shakespeare Birthplace Trust

of line 5. Again, Claudio's mind restlessly moves on to 'reside'. This is truly a man with an unquiet spirit, which is expressed not just in the content of his statements, but in the rhythm and progress of his thoughts. It's an example of the text teaching you.

You will find, if you go back and scan these lines, that there is a regular pulse with some subtle emphases given by light changes of rhythm (e.g. strong beats on 'warm' and 'motion' which help set up the apposition 'kneaded clod'). On the whole, the rhythm is regular, but the quickening of the pulse tends to happen in the second half of the line, after the caesura, in response to the progress of his imagination. Continue the process for yourself. Remember, the caesura is not a pause. It can be, but mostly it's a tiny moment of balance; it's as if the line hovers for a split second. As you proceed, you will find that some lines, such as line 8, seem to have no caesura at all. I would follow your instincts on this. Perhaps the imagery of 'restless violence' can allow no interruption at all, no matter how brief. This is all the better to lead us onto 'the pendent world'. An amazing image! But poor Claudio cannot rest here; his mind moves on, as in a nightmare, to 'be worse than worst'. Line 10 can hardly take a delay in it, but rather pitches straight on to the horror of 'imagine howling' in line 11. Again, he can't rest here, it's 'too horrible'. The rhythms, in this case revealed by the caesuras, betray a man on an unstoppable roller coaster of terror as he stares at death.

His speech begins and ends in a monosyllabic line. I always find, for reasons I'll go into in another chapter, that it's best to slow up on monosyllabic lines. These lines of Claudio have such simplicity and resonance that it's not surprising that Shakespeare suggests a pause after he has spoken. Isabella does not speak immediately. Claudio's speech is only three beats long; there could be a pause of at least two beats before she replies. This is important: a regular rhythm not only highlights the variations the character makes, but it highlights the silence that occurs when no one is speaking. This can be readily understood from music. Composers of rock songs and classical symphonies both employ the same technique: the rock band or the orchestra goes silent or tacit, but the beat carries on in the audience's head. And bang! it returns to create some effect or other. So if you see a short line or 'half-line' as it is sometimes called, then Shakespeare is suggesting a pause. If, of course, you have imposed all sorts of pauses in the previous speech, then you will get no value from the half-line pause. So discipline yourself in the use of pauses. Earn them! In a parallel way, the full line of inverse rhythm ('Never, Never') when King Lear holds the dead body of his beloved daughter is only potent because the verse preceding it is regular.

KING LEAR

And my poor fool is hang'd! No, no, no life!
Why should a dog, a horse, a rat, have life,
And thou no breath at all? Thou'lt come no more,
Never, never, never, never, never!

King Lear, V. i. 281–284

If the three preceding lines are not played as straight iambic pentameters, then you've blown the impact of the great, simple line 'Névěr, névěr, névěr, névěr, névěr!'. And there's not much more can be said over the dead body of your child.

We have glimpsed the way that rhythm and metre affect not just the speaker, but the listener as well. Let's now look at a piece of text in which the rhythm is shared between two characters for a substantial passage. I love the play *Macbeth* and have directed it three times for the Royal Shakespeare Company (RSC). I have mentioned earlier that the two characters Macbeth and Lady Macbeth have a shared imagery. Look at these lines and see how interdependent they are on each other's rhythms:

MACBETH

1. I have done the deed. Didst thou not hear a noise?

LADY MACBETH

2. I heard the owl scream and the crickets cry.
3. Did not you speak?

MACBETH

When?

LADY MACBETH

Now.

MACBETH

As I descended?

LADY MACBETH

4. Ay.

MACBETH

5. Hark!
6. Who lies i' the second chamber?

LADY MACBETH

Donalbain.

MACBETH

7. This is a sorry sight.
Looking on his hands

LADY MACBETH

8. A foolish thought, to say a sorry sight.

MACBETH

9. There's one did laugh in's sleep, and one cried 'Murder!'
10. That they did wake each other: I stood and heard them:
11. But they did say their prayers, and address'd them
12. Again to sleep.

LADY MACBETH

There are two lodged together.

MACBETH

13. One cried 'God bless us!' and 'Amen' the other;
14. As they had seen me with these hangman's hands.
15. Listening their fear, I could not say 'Amen,'
16. When they did say 'God bless us!'

LADY MACBETH

Consider it not so deeply.

MACBETH

17. But wherefore could not I pronounce 'Amen'?
18. I had most need of blessing, and 'Amen'
19. Stuck in my throat.

LADY MACBETH

These deeds must not be thought
20. After these ways; so, it will make us mad.

Macbeth, II. ii. 14–32

The situation is highly charged: it is the middle of the night and Macbeth has just murdered King Duncan. On leaving the king's bedroom he comes face to face with his wife, who has entreated him to commit the crime. Different editors lay out this passage in different ways on the page, but I

Derek Jacobi as Macbeth and Cheryl Campbell as Lady Macbeth at the
Royal Shakespeare Theatre, 1993. Photo: Malcolm Davies Collection
© Shakespeare Birthplace Trust

prefer this version as it interweaves the metre and the drama most plausibly.
So let's look at the way that the metre is used to heighten the dramatic tension.

Here, the same rules apply as before. It is written in iambic pentameters
that are sometimes shared between the two characters. Shakespeare cleverly
creates suspense in Macbeth's first line: 'I have done the deed. Didst thou not
hear a noise?' So we understand that he has committed murder, but, without
a pause, he carries straight on and asks if his wife has heard anything. This
immediately makes the audience sit up and listen, rendering them sensitive
to the rhythms and silences that are to follow. Line 3 is shared between the
two characters and it should be delivered as a pentameter; the actors have to
say their lines in a strict rhythm. Try this with a friend. It can be tricky at first,
but it will create a real build-up to the silence that follows the next line, 'Ay'
line 4. A single beat on a whole line. This is followed by another, 'Hark', on
line 5. So if you follow the strict pulse that Shakespeare gives you, you will
automatically get the silences that characterize this appalling situation. But
they are dynamic silences because the audience is straining to hear along
with the Macbeths. Line 6 is a shared line and line 7 is a short line, which
allows the full horror of his bloody hands to register. Again, allow a short
pause after it. The pulse then carries on quite consistently, with shared lines
on 12, 16 and 19, leading up to the resonant word 'mad' at the end of line

20. The dynamic between the two characters is interesting because at first they are quite interwoven with, perhaps, Lady Macbeth trying to stay in control. But after line 9, 'There's one did laugh in's sleep, and one cried 'Murder!'', Macbeth is unremitting in his need to express his horror at what happened to him in the death chamber. The rhythm is very regular – try and spot the variations – and the language contains a high number of monosyllables, both of which suggest a determination to tell the tale, the significance of which is certainly not lost on Lady Macbeth. If Alfred Hitchcock is the master of suspense in film, then Shakespeare more than equals him in this extraordinary exposition of terror. Never once does Shakespeare describe what actually happened in the room. He leaves this to our imagination. What he does is refer to events around the action and, by a skillful use of rhythm and silence, builds an atmosphere of fear that is not just witnessed, but 'assisted' by the audience, to borrow from the French. But don't forget, as you play it, try not to add in lots of other pauses because the impact of Shakespeare's tight rhythm will be dissipated. This is hard to achieve, because in rehearsal, quite properly, you will want to imagine the situation, and then speak as you think. This is all part of a healthy process. Your final aim is to speak as you think – not think, pause, speak – and to embrace the rhythms that Shakespeare has offered you. We will talk about this later, but it is called 'speaking on the line'.

I want to finish this chapter on a lighter note and examine a speech from *A Midsummer Night's Dream*. In this play, Shakespeare is restless and exuberant in his experiments with verse form. This is, of course, appropriate because so many of the characters are immortals. Read these gorgeous lines:

Enter, from opposite sides, a Fairy, and Puck

PUCK

How now, spirit! whither wander you?

FAIRY

> Over hill, over dale,
>> Thorough bush, thorough brier,
> Over park, over pale,
>> Thorough flood, thorough fire,
> I do wander everywhere,
> Swifter than the moon's sphere;
> And I serve the fairy queen,
> To dew her orbs upon the green.
> The cowslips tall her pensioners be:
> In their gold coats spots you see;

> Those be rubies, fairy favours,
> In those freckles live their savours:
> I must go seek some dewdrops here
> And hang a pearl in every cowslip's ear.
> Farewell, thou lob of spirits; I'll be gone:
> Our queen and all our elves come here anon.
> A *Midsummer Night's Dream*, II. i. 1–17

I have indented the two-beat lines and the four-beat lines and left the pentameters against the margin. The moment the Fairy speaks we know we are in a strange territory. There is a wildness about these first four lines:

> Over hill, over dale,
> Thorough bush, thorough brier,
> Over park, over pale,
> Thorough flood, thorough fire.

The rhythm is that of a horse cantering. Try it. Enjoy it. It should have a very strong pulse. It heralds a whole new dimension in the play and it is achieved entirely through sound. (Although, when I directed the play in Stratford-upon-Avon in 1994, I had the pair of them swinging in mid-air, fifteen feet off the ground, clutching umbrellas. I wanted to explore a dimension wholly different from the earth-bound demesne of the mortals.) Then she/he/it suddenly changes rhythm:

> I do wander everywhere,
> Swifter than the moon's sphere;

We're into four beats. It's childlike; she changes on a sixpence. She continues to rhyme, but adopts a different pattern. No longer a b a b but aa bb. The key here is playfulness. It's interesting that the last line of Peter Brook's seminal work *The Empty Space* is 'A play is play'. Very good. And not surprising that he wrote this book just after he directed the *Dream* at Stratford. We can learn a lot from this statement. Shakespeare adapts the metre and pulse according to the dramatic needs of the moment. We should observe any changes carefully and embrace them joyfully.

A final word: do not regard metre and pulse as just literary devices; think of them as the heartbeat of the play. It is my belief that a sense of pulse and rhythm are inborn in every human being. Pulse is the sound of your mother's heart beating before you were born. A feel for rhythm is as natural as breathing and does not need to be learnt; it is already inside you.

5

LINE ENDINGS

Giving shape to the thought

The purpose of this chapter is to examine one particular aspect of Shake-speare's writing: line endings. Or more particularly, line endings in verse. This is called prosody. I want to devote a chapter to it, partly because it is an aspect of his writing that many young actors find hard to deal with, but mostly because, once you master it, you gain an immense freedom and authority. And the great news is that it's very straightforward.

Let's start with another aural art form: music. The measure of music is the bar. Beethoven's music is notated using bars; so is John Lennon's; so is Benjamin Britten's; so is Eminem's. When a violinist picks up a Beethoven score, he will know pretty much what the composer intended from what's on the page. Likewise, if you open a book of Lennon songs at, say, the page marked 'Imagine', there will be enough information in the score to play and sing the song. It won't make you a great musician or a pop star, nor will it show you how to interpret it, let alone make it yours, but, assuming you can read music, you will have a very good idea of what the composer wanted to hear. You can, of course, ignore this. You could, for example, turn 'Imagine' into a rap song. That is not the business of this chapter. Here I want to help you to read what Shakespeare intended and to show you what opportunities this gives you.

Shakespeare's measure is the verse line. We have already gained an understanding of this in the previous chapter; we'll now look at how he used his 'bars' to reveal more about how the character thinks, and how we can use them to empower us as we speak them.

We'll start with an example from an early play, *Henry VI Part III*. One of the bloodiest battles of the Wars of the Roses is raging nearby. The king has been told by his wife and advisers to stay away because his presence disheartens the troops.

KING HENRY VI

1. This battle fares like to the morning's war,
2. When dying clouds contend with growing light,
3. What time the shepherd, blowing of his nails,
4. Can neither call it perfect day nor night.
5. Now sways it this way, like a mighty sea
6. Forced by the tide to combat with the wind;
7. Now sways it that way, like the selfsame sea
8. Forced to retire by fury of the wind:
9. Sometime the flood prevails, and then the wind;
10. Now one the better, then another best;
11. Both tugging to be victors, breast to breast,
12. Yet neither conqueror nor conqueréd:
13. So is the equal of this fell war.
Here on this molehill will I sit me down.
To whom God will, there be the victory!
For Margaret my queen, and Clifford too,
Have chid me from the battle; swearing both
They prosper best of all when I am thence.
Would I were dead! if God's good will were so;
For what is in this world but grief and woe?
O God! methinks it were a happy life,
To be no better than a homely swain;
To sit upon a hill, as I do now,
To carve out dials quaintly, point by point,
Thereby to see the minutes how they run,
How many make the hour full complete;
How many hours bring about the day;
How many days will finish up the year;
How many years a mortal man may live.
When this is known, then to divide the times:
So many hours must I tend my flock;
So many hours must I take my rest;
So many hours must I contemplate;
So many hours must I sport myself;
So many days my ewes have been with young;
So many weeks ere the poor fools will ean:

So many years ere I shall shear the fleece:
So minutes, hours, days, months, and years,
Pass'd over to the end they were created,
Would bring white hairs unto a quiet grave.

Henry VI, II. v. 1–40

To me, this is one of the most beautiful speeches in Shakespeare, all the more so because it is so simple. I remember quite clearly, Ralph Fiennes sitting on an upturned shield, which represented the molehill in my production of *The Plantagenets* for the RSC. He delivered the speech with simplicity and poise; there were no tricks or gimmicks. He gave the character a quiet authority that held the house spellbound. It was a perfect marriage of thought and form.

Let's start this section with a quick recap of what we've learnt so far. As usual, start by reading the lines out loud. You will find that the verse is very regular; there are one or two variations that you'll be able to identify quite instinctively. For example, there appears to be a natural change of rhythm on the sequence of 'So many . . . So many'. Experiment with these rhythmical changes, relish them. Now focus on the many appositions and counterpoints throughout the speech. Remember, there's no need to bash them. If you think them, then it's most likely that you will communicate them. That's what this chapter is all about: thought and form. Get your mind round the metaphors. He starts with one: 'This battle fares like to the morning's war'. This single image sustains his imagination for the next thirteen lines; it is a series of improvisations on one metaphor, mostly executed through apposition. Notice that there is a perfect harmony between form and content. If you are going to describe a conflict, then counterpoint is a pretty basic tool, and given the almost unimaginable horror, metaphor becomes a necessity. Following this, he moves into quite conversational language, beginning 'Here on this molehill will I sit me down'. He talks to us in a very straightforward way, as confidantes. He then embarks upon his contemplation of the blessings of a simple shepherd's life:

O God! methinks it were a happy life,
To be no better than a homely swain,

He sustains his thought through to the end. It is a good speech to practice and recap on because, although it appears simple, it is masterly.

The aspect I want you to concentrate on now is the way in which the thought matches the lines. You will find that in line after line, with the possible exception of lines 3 and 4, the thought is exactly the same length as a single line. This does not mean that one thought does not develop out of another or is not qualified by another – it does and we have already noticed how the whole first movement is born out of the single opening metaphor. But each line is occupied by a single clause, which represents a thought. To understand better what I mean, take the first thirteen lines up to 'So is the equal of this fell war'. Speak the lines through as far as the line ending and then give yourself a small pause before you carry on to the next line. Try and sense the way the thought moves. One thought takes you to the end of line 1, which is then qualified by the thought in line 2. Line 3 seems to want to run onto line 4. That's okay, follow it through. The thought that singly occupies line 5 is developed in line 6. The same pattern is repeated in lines 7 and 8. Line 9 contains a single thought that gives birth to the clauses that occupy the next three lines, one after the other. After the full, polysyllabic line 12, a short mostly monosyllabic line concludes this sequence: 'So is the equal of this fell war'. It has an appropriate finality about it. The rhythm differs from the preceding passage and the monosyllables allow you to slow down if you wish, leading to 'thís féll wár'.

Repeat the exercise on the first thirteen lines, again with tiny pauses. You will find that you can breathe at the end of every single line, if you wish, and not lose the sense. Try it. It works because each line contains one clause. Also, by now, I'm sure you have become conscious of the rhymes and repetitions that sit at the line endings: 'light/night', 'sea/sea', 'wind/wind' and 'best/breast'. Don't be scared of these; they help to deliver up the thought and they tell us a lot about Henry. He has great wisdom, but it is contained within almost childlike parameters. Furthermore, the rhyme has the effect of drawing you towards the line ending. This is an important lesson to learn. There was a great Shakespearean actress called Edith Evans who once said that she drew the line ending towards her like a golden thread. That's a good image. What we are talking about here is being conscious of the line endings. It doesn't mean that you have to stress them, but just be aware of them and alight upon them. This awareness will also help you avoid the trap that so many poor or inexperienced actors fall into, which is to 'drop' the ends of the lines or give them a downward inflexion, which means there is no ongoing energy. It is also a sure-fire way to send an audience to sleep. By alighting upon the line endings of, for example, 'sea/sea', you will find you get a much stronger purchase on the first words of the next lines, 'Forced/Forced', with their powerful counter-rhythm.

Settle all this in your mind by reading on to the end of the speech just taking tiny pauses. You will sometimes want to run on over the line endings. Just follow your instincts. This is an early play and the character has a beautiful innocence about him; the form is appropriate to his thought.

We will now take a look at a speech from *As You Like It*. Again, there is a degree of formality in the speech, but we will see how Shakespeare uses the line endings to accommodate more complex thought. This is Jaques, who is in exile in the Forest of Arden, talking to the Duke:

JAQUES

All the world's a stage,
And all the men and women merely players:
They have their exits and their entrances;
And one man in his time plays many parts,
His acts being seven ages. At first the infant,
Mewling and puking in the nurse's arms.
And then the whining school-boy, with his satchel
And shining morning face, creeping like snail
Unwillingly to school. And then the lover,
Sighing like furnace, with a woeful ballad
Made to his mistress' eyebrow. Then a soldier,
Full of strange oaths and bearded like the pard,
Jealous in honour, sudden and quick in quarrel,
Seeking the bubble reputation
Even in the cannon's mouth. And then the justice,
In fair round belly with good capon lined,
With eyes severe and beard of formal cut,
Full of wise saws and modern instances;
And so he plays his part. The sixth age shifts
Into the lean and slipper'd pantaloon,
With spectacles on nose and pouch on side,
His youthful hose, well saved, a world too wide
For his shrunk shank; and his big manly voice,
Turning again toward childish treble, pipes
And whistles in his sound. Last scene of all,
That ends this strange eventful history,
Is second childishness and mere oblivion,
Sans teeth, sans eyes, sans taste, sans everything.
As You Like It, II. v. 139–166

The speech is known as the 'Seven Ages of Man' and is rightly celebrated. First of all, just read it through for sense. What I'm going to do now is to write down the last word of each line:

stage
players
entrances

parts
infant
arms
satchel
snail
lover
ballad
soldier
pard
quarrel
reputation
justice
lined
cut
instances
shifts
pantaloon
side
wide
voice
pipes
all
history
oblivion
everything

It looks a bit like a poem from the 1950s American Beat generation, written by e.e. cummings perhaps. What is interesting for us is that if you read those words through, you can more or less follow the sense, or at least the story outline, of the original speech. This gives us a measure of the sheer amount of information carried in the line endings. It's a useful and simple exercise to do when approaching a speech for the first time. Flip back and do the same on the *Henry VI* passage.

Now what I want you to notice in this speech is that on the introduction of six out of the seven 'characters', he begins a new sentence half-way through the line. Why has Shakespeare done this and what are the implications for speaking it?

Perhaps the answer lies in one of the earlier chapters. Jaques is a great observer of humanity, and here he makes a quite startling proposition: 'All the world's a stage', a metaphor. He then proceeds to substantiate his claim. I talked about the need to invent a metaphor, the need to create in the moment. So perhaps Jaques invents the metaphor and then improvises the rest of the

speech. So at the beginning, he doesn't know exactly where he is going to
end up. Let's test this hypothesis.

We know Jaques invents the metaphor in the moment because he completes Duke Senior's previous half-line (not shown); this is why I have
printed the first line in the middle of the page. There is no pause between the
Duke and the reply. It is a sudden flash of inspiration: 'All the world's a
stage'. This he pursues with three lines, each containing one clause/thought:

> And all the men and women merely players:
> They have their exits and their entrances;
> And one man in his time plays many parts,

After this comes another wonderful moment of invention: 'His acts being
seven ages.' Now if you follow the pulse, you should not stop after 'ages'. The
pentameter continues: 'At first the infant . . .' And then on to the next line.
The temptation is obviously to pause after the word 'ages', have a bit of a
think, then carry on when you have got the first idea. What Shakespeare
actually writes is much more interesting. The idea of the infant comes precisely on the spur of the moment. You have to think and speak at the same
time (as, of course, we do in real life). Try this whole line for yourself a
couple of times: 'His acts being seven ages. At first the infant'. Try it with a
pause after 'ages' and then try it without. If you opt for the latter, you could
try a quickening towards the end of the line, which takes the energy forward
to the first example, the 'infant'. So you would have a steady rhythm on 'His
acts being seven ages'. And then a burst of energy as the next idea comes to
you. I think this path is much more exciting. It makes complete sense if you
think of the character inventing the whole speech, coining the ideas, one
after the other. You will also get more involvement from the audience
because they are witness to, what appears to be, a piece of real life, off the
cuff, brilliant dramatic invention.

As we have noticed before, a good strong line ending gives you an excellent purchase on to the start of the next line; here it's 'mewling', a juicy
word, against the iambic rhythm. Now look forward through the speech. The
second age of man, the schoolboy, is introduced at the beginning of the line
but the lover, the soldier, the justice, the pantaloon and the senile man are all
placed on the half-line after a full stop. The pentameter, the 'bar', is complete
even though it contains two thoughts. Try all these and see if you can play
them through without a pause half-way through the line. The way to do it is
to have the idea of the lover, the soldier, etc. in the moment; think and speak
at the same time! Practice it a few times so it feels natural.

It is worth reflecting here for a moment. At first reading, you might think
that the most natural way of doing this speech would be to play it slowly,

pausing and considering before each new character is introduced. And I believe that this is often how the speech is delivered. However, in my judgement, this goes against Shakespeare's intentions for the speech and the character. If he wanted pauses, he would have written it differently; he would have introduced each new idea on a new line. In addition, we get a clue about the exiled court of Duke Senior. Perhaps they pass the long hours in the forest entertaining each other, either with song – the play is full of music – or, as in this case, with highly entertaining and provocative speeches. If you go down the improvisation route, then the speech appears to be more fun, which is perfect because it allows the actor to really turn the tables at the end as he takes us into very bleak territory. Here I must acknowledge a debt to Alan Rickman who played Jaques for my production and gave one of those performances that makes everyone rethink a role.

Just a couple of practical points now. Where do you breathe and where do you pause? My answer is that you can pause anywhere you like, for as long as you like, so long as it's at the end of a line. And if you pause, then you can breathe! Here's a quick example from *Henry V*. The situation is the morning of the Battle of Agincourt. Everyone is terrified. The king overhears one of his followers:

WESTMORELAND

> O that we now had here
> But one ten thousand of those men in England
> That do no work to-day!

KING HENRY V

> What's he that wishes so?
> My cousin Westmoreland? No, my fair cousin:
> If we are mark'd to die, we are enow
> To do our country loss; and if to live,
> The fewer men, the greater share of honour.
>
> *Henry V*, IV. iii. 16–22

First of all, the king completes Westmoreland's half-line with the question, 'What's he that wishes so?'. So, no pause, straight in on cue. After this, Henry can pause as long as he likes. He has everyone's attention; they are waiting to see how he will react. Will he lose his temper? Will he agree, which would send out a dangerous signal to the troops? Or perhaps he will move straight on and answer his own question with 'My cousin Westmoreland'. The pulse carries on, 'No, my fair cousin'. No break till the end of the line. You can pause there if you like, though it might get a bit ponderous. There follows a counterpoint of 'to die' and 'to live'. You probably want to run over the line ending of 'enow', and move the next line straight through to 'live', to complete the apposition, not pausing at the semicolon. Then you *can* pause which allows the troops to speculate on the prospect of 'to live'. Then you give them the really positive signal: 'The fewer men, the greater share of honour'. So the pauses and the breathing can be used dynamically to aid the drama. It makes the other characters and the audience want to know what comes next. So, of course, they listen more intently.

It might be worth listening to seasoned politicians when they address a meeting or make a speech. The British House of Commons is more like a bear pit than a debating chamber with frequent interruptions and heckling from colleagues and opposing members alike. There, like in Shakespeare's Globe, you have to make people listen. A technique you will often hear used is for a politician to start the next sentence the moment he has finished the first, thereby allowing no room for hecklers to interrupt. He can then take a pause, a breath, in the knowledge that he is unlikely to be interrupted because the audience are curious to know what he is about to say. It's a way of controlling the House, and Shakespeare uses this technique frequently, especially in scenes in which a character is addressing a large crowd. Here is Caius Martius, known as Coriolanus, a brilliant but arrogant soldier, addressing a mob of angry, hungry Romans. It's a dazzling display of rhetoric and a master class in how to rub people up the wrong way.

MARTIUS

1. He that will give good words to thee will flatter
2. Beneath abhorring. What would you have, you curs,
3. That like nor peace nor war? the one affrights you,
4. The other makes you proud. He that trusts to you,
5. Where he should find you lions, finds you hares;
6. Where foxes, geese: you are no surer, no,
7. Than is the coal of fire upon the ice,
8. Or hailstone in the sun. Your virtue is
9. To make him worthy whose offence subdues him
10. And curse that justice did it. Who deserves greatness
11. Deserves your hate; and your affections are
12. A sick man's appetite, who desires most that
13. Which would increase his evil. He that depends
14. Upon your favours swims with fins of lead
15. And hews down oaks with rushes. Hang ye! Trust Ye?
16. With every minute you do change a mind,
17. And call him noble that was now your hate,
18. Him vile that was your garland. What's the matter,
19. That in these several places of the city

20. You cry against the noble senate, who,
21. Under the gods, keep you in awe, which else
22. Would feed on one another? What's their seeking?

Coriolanus, I. i. 165–185

This play, *Coriolanus*, was written towards the end of Shakespeare's writing career. The use of verse seems a world away from the one-line/one-clause speech of *Henry VI*. Furthermore, if you try the e.e. cummings-style exercise of listing the final word of each line, you will get little clue as to content after the first two lines. 'Flatter' and 'curs', is a pretty good guide to his attitude, but afterwards there is not much to go on. You could argue that this is just prose cut up into pentameters, and conclude that we should ignore the line endings and just play the sense from full stop to full stop. If this were the case, why would the playwright, at the height of his powers, bother to put it into verse? There is plenty of prose in the play and plenty of examples throughout the canon where aristocrats speak in prose.

I think we should start as if he had written in prose. Read the speech a couple of times, ignoring the line endings, playing the sense from one full stop to the next. This will help you get comfortable with the meaning. The clue to the meaning, as is very often the case, lies in his first statement:

He that will give good words to thee will flatter
Beneath abhorring'.

So flattery is off the menu. Now read it through trying to identify the appositions. There are many in this speech and they do much to give it a sinewy, compact flavour. They are all comparisons that are unfavourable to the citizens. Most of them pretty savage. Let's just look at the first few lines. There is 'peace' and 'war' and their reactions to them on lines 3 and 4. They are 'hares' not 'lions', 'geese' not 'foxes'. Continue the list for yourself. Just notice how uncompromising they are. Martius lashes them with the power of his arguments. As you practice, give yourself an imaginary audience and 'work' on them, to use the Chorus's word. This will make the speech more dynamic, more *transitive*, a quality I would define as bringing about change in other people.

I think you will have found that it works quite well as prose, so the questions I would pose are, first, as you speak it from full stop to full stop, do you find that at times the line endings are just perfectly placed? And, second, are there any benefits we can gain from the structure that the verse gives it? Let's examine it.

I'm certain that the word 'flatter' has a good ring to it, so you will quite naturally give yourself a line ending. There is a period half-way through line 2, at which you could pause, but it would be unwise because the citizens might interrupt. So you might be best to carry on to 'curs', at the end of line 2, also a good strong word, full of disgust. We have already noticed that the apposition in line 3 is developed into line 4, but 'you' at the end of the line is not a good word to alight on; the obvious word is 'affrights'. This is quite natural, because this line has what is called a 'feminine' ending, which means that there is an extra syllable, eleven instead of ten. You do not need to stress it. In fact, you are best to ignore it. (You have come across this before: 'To be or not to be, that is the question' has a feminine ending.) Now look on down the speech and see where there is a period or a colon in the middle of the line. Now look at how he completes the line. I'll list them for you:

> He that trusts to you
> You are no surer, no
> Your virtue is
> Who deserves greatness
> He that depends
> Hang ye! Trust Ye?
> What's the matter?

All of these possess two characteristics. First, each of these half-lines immediately follows one of Martius's damning comparisons. I think Shakespeare, like our canny politician, suggests that the character does not pause after he's delivered an insult in case he loses control to the crowd. So in the line 6, 'Where foxes, geese: you are no surer, no,', Martius wouldn't hang around after he's called them geese; he quickens to the end of the line, thus retaining control. I've never directed this play, but I'm sure that this scene should be highly volatile, with a constant danger that the crowd will run riot. This makes Martius's speech all the more reckless because he seems to be continuously throwing petrol on the flames. The actor playing the part needs all the help he can get to stay on top of the situation and finish what he wants to say.

Second, each of these half-lines introduces the next idea, so the speech has a forward momentum, with the audience wanting to know what he's going to say next. It's a version of the technique used in the 'Seven Ages of Man' whereby he introduces a new subject at the end of the line. This gives a structure to the speech that is helpful to both actor and audience.

So with this speech, I wouldn't take any pauses after full stops in the middle of lines. Play through and invent the remainder of the line in the moment, what I call 'quickening', where the new thought makes the words come a bit quicker. Whether you should mark the line endings is a different matter; and where you should breathe needs careful consideration in a speech like this. In my view, it would be rather unnatural to end stop or point up every line ending. For example, try and play through the line ending after 'Your virtue is' on line 8 with only the lightest of indications that a new measure is about to start. If you do this, and also play through the period on line 10, then you are certainly going to need to pause at the line ending after 'greatness' to give yourself a breath. Perhaps you don't want to do this, but you are going to need to breathe somewhere. Try not to do it in the middle of the line. As I've said before, I think you can pause anywhere you like, so long as it is at the line ending. This is really where you enter the world of interpretation. The first step is always to understand the structure; how has he written it and why has he written it like that. But there will come a moment when you will want to decide how your Coriolanus phrases his speeches. That will be different from person to person. I would argue that your personal interpretation should emanate from a clear understanding of the rules that, paradoxically, are not restricting, but empowering. Shakespeare gives you a form that allows you to inhabit the situation fully. So as you work on these somewhat technical matters, always refer back to the basics: the who, the why and the where.

For example, Coriolanus is an arrogant and aggressive soldier who deliberately provokes the crowd; it's almost as if he's looking for a fight. The crowd hates him and everything he stands for. Add these two ingredients together and you have an explosive situation. So look out for ways where the verse can empower you. But most important of all, remember that Coriolanus is improvising. He doesn't know what he's going to say next, so look for opportunities in the verse where you can build in the hesitations and the spurts of energy that characterize a creative mind in a highly charged situation.

Perhaps one of the most difficult skills to acquire at this stage is to be able to mark the line endings without always emphasizing them. There are several occasions in this speech when you might run over the line ending, but you should never lose touch with the underlying rhythm. Even if you don't use it, you should always know where the bar ends. You can't worry about this in performance, but you should be conscious of it when you are preparing. Think of it like driving down the motorway. The exit signs flash past you; you don't necessarily 'clock' each one, but you know that you are passing them. Try this line:

. . . He that depends
Upon your favours swims with fins of lead

Start by just saying it straight, no inflexion. Now say it again; this time be aware of the change of line. Practice it a couple of times; don't allow yourself to hit 'depends' too hard, just be aware that you are moving over the line ending. And now ensure you are playing right through the next line as far as 'lead'. So the energy is in the second half of the line; it keeps moving forward.

Let's look at one more speech, this time from a late play, *The Winter's Tale*. Hermione, the Queen of Sicily, is on trial for treason. She is accused of adultery and the child she has given birth to just hours before is taken away from her. She pleads in her defence:

HERMIONE

Since what I am to say must be but that
Which contradicts my accusation and
The testimony on my part no other
But what comes from myself, it shall scarce boot me
To say 'not guilty:' mine integrity
Being counted falsehood, shall, as I express it,
Be so received. But thus: if powers divine
Behold our human actions, as they do,
I doubt not then but innocence shall make
False accusation blush and tyranny
Tremble at patience.

The Winter's Tale, III. ii. 21–31

First of all, look at these final words:

that
and
other
me
integrity
express it
divine
do
make
tyranny.

I find these very revealing. They tell their own story; not a narrative as we find with Jaques, but a story nevertheless. The first four words are quite weak, but with the word 'integrity' she seems to gain strength, then continues in this vein with words starting with strong consonants: 'd's and 't's. There is a great clue here for the actress playing the part. She starts weak and unconfident but gets strong, with the idea of 'integrity' as the transition. She hasn't got her freedom, but she's got her integrity!

Try this speech for yourself. Read it through for sense, and then take it through, giving yourself the tiniest of pauses at the line endings as we did with the *Henry VI*. Now some of these you will want to dispense with and others you will want to keep. The first four and a half lines seem to run as prose, so play over these line endings, but try to keep a sense of the bar, as described above. She then arrives at 'not guilty'. Interestingly, Shakespeare does not put this at the end of the line; the suggestion is that you run on to 'integrity'. Now that makes sense for a woman of Hermione's character. The next period is after 'received', but, again, this is placed in the middle of the line and Hermione moves forward to 'powers divine'. This is matched at the end of the next line by 'as they do', a strong affirmative statement. She then makes a powerful declaration of her innocence in lines full of weighty polysyllabic words.

There are two things to practice here. First, try to deliver the first four lines in a realistic way, while at the same time keeping the rhythm ticking along underneath. Use the same method as above: first speak it with no inflexion and then repeat being aware of the line endings. This should give you a subliminal feeling of the pulse. Allow this to happen. It's good; it's Hermione's pulse, however weak. The fact that the first line is written in monosyllables might help you here, because, to me, it suggests a deliberate, careful delivery. Second, as she gains in confidence, try and find how the energy moves to the second half of the line. Again, an awareness of this will do most of the work for you.

Earlier, I used the word 'realistic'. This was to remind you of the reality of her situation. She has just given birth, her new baby has been taken from her, she has been publicly accused of adultery, her little boy has been kept from her and she has to stand up and give a speech in a courtroom in her defence. No wonder she begins a little hesitantly. Interestingly, when I directed the play for the RSC, Samantha Bond, the actress playing the role, made a wonderful connection between a method approach and a verse-based approach. We realized that, having just given birth, she would have lost a lot of blood and would hardly be able to stand up. So she began very slowly and deliberately, and when she reached the end of the first line, she stopped. She nearly fainted. She closed her eyes, waited until she regained her strength and then continued through the second line at the end of which she stopped again, this time for a shorter period. She then carried on, getting stronger and stronger as her body found strength and the verse found a strong forward pulse. The pauses at the ends of the first two lines were electric; they were accurate from a realistic point of view and they totally respected the rhythm of the verse. This is often such a creative area: to observe the formal structure of the verse and then match it to an imaginative reading of the scene. It's a theme we will return to later.

I know that some actors feel that to mark the line endings will result in a rather artificial or stilted reading of the text. This can, indeed, be the result, but only if you are too heavy-handed or do not match the character's thoughts with the verse lines. As we have seen, the thought often runs over the end of one line into the next, so it is not necessary to impose a pause at every line ending. In these circumstances, play the sentence straight through or, better still, just mark the line ending with the slightest of inflexions so you can maintain the metre. (An actor once described this to me as the equivalent of using the pedal on a piano; the melody carries on, but it is given a small inflexion.) When you are working on a speech, always ensure that you know where the line endings fall, even if you choose not to observe them. Whatever you do, don't ignore them as they shape the sward of thought.

6

WORD PLAY

'All for your delight . . .'
A Midsummer Night's Dream, V. i. 114

High above the Swan Theatre in Stratford-upon-Avon there is a majestic rehearsal room that commands sensational views down river towards Holy Trinity Church, where Shakespeare is buried. I named it the Ashcroft Room after the great RSC actress Dame Peggy. She never rehearsed there but loved the space. When she died it seemed fitting to honour her memory, so I decided to rename this beautiful room where actors go about their daily business.

One summer morning in 1994, the call went out over the loudspeaker system, 'Midsummer Night's Dream Company to the Ashcroft Room, please'. This was the Press Night of my production, the night when all the national newspaper, radio and TV critics assembled to deliver their verdict on our work. It's always a tricky problem to know what to do on such a day. Do you run the play? That might tire everyone out. Do you give reams of detailed notes? Not a good idea as the actors would probably spend the evening concentrating on the notes they have just received rather than freely playing the play. Trudging up the stairs from my office, I had an idea. Let's examine, as a group, one single aspect of the play: rhyme. That shouldn't be too daunting to anyone! Stage management kindly magicked coloured marker pens for everyone out of thin air, and we set about our task. We would work right through the play and highlight the rhyming word in each line, using a different colour for each category of rhyme. We picked our way carefully through Act I, Scene i. At first there was very little. A bit of repetition (night/night, eyes/eyes) and not a lot else. Then towards the end of the duologue between Hermia and Lysander, something happened. Here is the speech. Hermia responds to his proposal to elope:

HERMIA

My good Lysander!
I swear to thee, by Cupid's strongest bow,
By his best arrow with the golden head,
By the simplicity of Venus' doves,
By that which knitteth souls and prospers loves,
And by that fire which burn'd the Carthage queen,
When the false Troyan under sail was seen,
By all the vows that ever men have broke,
In number more than ever women spoke,
In that same place thou hast appointed me,
To-morrow truly will I meet with thee.
A Midsummer Night's Dream, I. i. 168–178

This is, of course, the speech in which the dramatic gears engage and the plot zooms away. Hermia, desperate to avoid the arranged marriage to Demetrius proposed by her father, seeks to assure Lysander emphatically that she will elope with him. She swears to him, she reinforces this with metaphors, then significantly she rhymes 'doves' with 'loves' and we are away; rhyme after rhyme follows, dozens and dozens of them right through this scene. The first mechanical's scene comes next, written in prose, then Puck and the Fairy, all in rhyme, and so on through the play, scene after scene, all in different patterns of rhyme. By the time we reached the end, our copies of the script had become multi-coloured, a testament to Shakespeare's dazzling powers of invention. Although we had of course rehearsed thoroughly for six weeks, this visual display somehow pointed us towards the meaning of the play or, at the very least, set the agenda for that important day. This was a play as *play*. There was fun to be had from inventing the rhymes; it somehow made the characters into creative human beings, which is vital in a play that is, to a large degree, a rite of passage for the young lovers, a crazy, frightening improvisation that leads to the final rituals of the play, the blessing of their marriages.

So we set about rediscovering the rhymes. Do this for yourself with the speech above. The action is to make Lysander believe you. Start out by swearing to him, now invent the three images of 'bow', 'arrow' and 'doves', then start the fifth line, 'By that which knitteth souls and prospers loves,' not knowing how you are going to complete it. Try and discover the final idea with its rhyme, 'loves'. I think Shakespeare intends it to be satisfying for

Hermia when she alights upon this rhyme. I think the feeling of fulfillment continues with the powerful image, 'And by that fire which burn'd the Carthage queen'. It's as if he sets up the final word, 'queen', in expectation of a rhyme to come. And along it comes: 'When the false Troyan under sail was seen,'.

Again, don't worry if you are searching for the rhyme; it's part of the thought process of the character and part of the excitement she is feeling at the prospect of elopement. Indeed, the rhyme tells you about the character's inner life, and how to play her. Take the next two lines:

> By all the vows that ever men have broke,
> In number more than ever women spoke.

Play these two lines by challenging yourself to set up and then fulfill the rhyme. The situation is deadly serious, but she is playing a game with herself and her boyfriend. After all the misery and frustration of the last few days, there is a sense of release in the rhyme. This is crucial to understand. At first you might think that rhyming couplets are a somewhat formal, restrictive medium; here we see them used in an exuberant, an almost celebratory way. Hermia clinches the bargain with a final couplet:

> In that same place thou hast appointed me,
> To-morrow truly will I meet with thee.

By neatly pairing 'me' with 'thee' she perfectly expresses how she would like their relationship to end up. We found that if you make the choice that Hermia moves into rhyme as a conscious act, not just as a writer's device, then this opens up a whole vocabulary for the actors for the rest of the play. Word play in general, and rhyming in particular, provided the evening with an injection of intelligent fun, at times dizzying and effervescent.

This is at the core of what this chapter is about. We started the book by observing that language was the principal means of communication in Shakespeare's theatre and that the Elizabethan audience clearly relished language in a way that is far removed from our twenty-first-century experience. But herein lies the joy and the challenge of doing Shakespeare. An audience does not have to be highbrow to enjoy Shakespeare's language, but the actor has to serve up the language or they simply won't follow what's being said. Shakespeare's characters have fun with words, and this is infectious. So the key instruction here is to enjoy it!

Let us take a look at another example from later in the same play, where Shakespeare displays an almost extravagant use of word play and rhyme. This is Titania, the Fairy Queen, who has fallen violently in love with Bottom, a weaver, who has been transformed into an ass. Oberon, her lord, has streaked her eyes with juice, to 'make her full of hateful fantasies'. Here she gives instructions to her helpers:

TITANIA

Be kind and courteous to this gentleman;
Hop in his walks and gambol in his eyes;
Feed him with apricocks and dewberries,
With purple grapes, green figs, and mulberries;
The honey-bags steal from the humble-bees,
And for night-tapers crop their waxen thighs
And light them at the fiery glow-worm's eyes,
To have my love to bed and to arise;
And pluck the wings from Painted butterflies
To fan the moonbeams from his sleeping eyes:
Nod to him, elves, and do him courtesies.

A Midsummer Night's Dream, III. i. 142–152

Titania is clearly enthralled with her lover and the language she uses is sensuous and luxurious. In the first line she tells them what to do; in the subsequent ten lines she tells them how to do it. At first, as you read through, move lightly from verb to verb. 'Hop', a trochee, starts the line. Read on to 'gambol'. 'Feed', another strong beat, starts the next line and gives rise to a list of gorgeous food. Read on through 'steal', then 'crop', then 'light', then 'arise', then 'pluck', then 'fan' and then 'nod'. The verbs make the speech active, they give it energy. Although she is delivering instructions to the fairies, the real purpose of the speech is to woo Bottom, and the sexual overtones are unmistakable. Now that you have identified the energy and the action of the speech, concentrate on the rhymes. It is remarkable that, after the introductory line, almost every line has the same rhyme: 'eye'. Do the speech again, maintaining a light energy on the verbs, but now play through to the rhymes. As usual, I would counsel against hitting the rhymes too hard; it is, after all, a love scene, albeit with an animal. Be conscious of the rhymes and alight upon them. This should give you the shape of the speech, the action of the speech and something in addition: a playful quality that is, of itself, quite seductive. Furthermore, Shakespeare has Titania repeat the critical word 'eye'. It's an extraordinary seduction scene, but it's also a masterful piece of dramaturgy. Shakespeare feeds one of the key themes of the play: the way infatuation distorts perception.

Just before we move on, recap our methodology. We began by identifying what the character is doing; we then focused on what it is that carries the action, in this case the verbs; we then added the unusual feature of this speech, the 'mono rhyme'. I think the mistake in this speech would be to over-colour all the nouns and adjectives; it could easily become overindulgent. To me, it is the verbs that carry the story.

Now I want to look at what happens when more than one character is responsible for creating the rhyme. Shakespeare, like Mozart, seemed to display brilliance from his earliest works (though not at such a tender age as the composer). This is an extract from his early play *The Comedy of Errors*. Adriana is complaining to her unmarried sister, Luciana, that her husband is late home yet again:

ADRIANA

Neither my husband nor the slave return'd,
That in such haste I sent to seek his master!
Sure, Luciana, it is two o'clock.

LUCIANA

Perhaps some merchant hath invited him,
And from the mart he's somewhere gone to dinner.
Good sister, let us dine and never fret:
A man is master of his liberty:
Time is their master, and, when they see time,
They'll go or come: if so, be patient, sister.

ADRIANA

Why should their liberty than ours be more?

LUCIANA

Because their business still lies out o' door.

ADRIANA

Look, when I serve him so, he takes it ill.

LUCIANA

O, know he is the bridle of your will.

ADRIANA

There's none but asses will be bridled so.

LUCIANA

Why, headstrong liberty is lash'd with woe.
There's nothing situate under heaven's eye
But hath his bound, in earth, in sea, in sky:
The beasts, the fishes, and the winged fowls,

Are their males' subjects and at their controls:
Men, more divine, the masters of all these,
Lords of the wide world and wild watery seas,
Indued with intellectual sense and souls,
Of more preeminence than fish and fowls,
Are masters to their females, and their lords:
Then let your will attend on their accords.

ADRIANA

This servitude makes you to keep unwed.

LUCIANA

Not this, but troubles of the marriage-bed.

ADRIANA

But, were you wedded, you would bear some sway.

LUCIANA

Ere I learn love, I'll practise to obey.

ADRIANA

How if your husband start some other where?

LUCIANA

Till he come home again, I would forbear.

ADRIANA

Patience unmoved! no marvel though she pause;
They can be meek that have no other cause.
A wretched soul, bruised with adversity,
We bid be quiet when we hear it cry;
But were we burdened with like weight of pain,
As much or more would we ourselves complain:
So thou, that hast no unkind mate to grieve thee,
With urging helpless patience wouldst relieve me,
But, if thou live to see like right bereft,
This fool-begg'd patience in thee will be left.

LUCIANA

Well, I will marry one day, but to try.
Here comes your man; now is your husband nigh.
                    The Comedy of Errors, II. i. 1–43

I love this scene; it's so funny, well observed and beautifully constructed. I remember I had a joyous time when I directed the play with wonderful, highly skilled actors and an inspired design by Ultz. In some respects it's highly artificial, but the whole story is underpinned by great humanity.

Read it through. Adriana is climbing up the wall with impatience; Luciana is maddeningly even-tempered, as is reflected in her very regular rhythms. You will notice that the first two speeches are unrhymed; it is Luciana's plea for patience that spurs Adriana on. She asks a question; Luciana replies with a rather smug rhyme. By completing the rhymes, Luciana comes across as the person in charge, which she reinforces with her speech beginning: 'Why, headstrong liberty is lash'd with woe'. Adriana tries to take back the initiative with her next line, but Luciana again answers with a rhyme. She invents, she controls. Adriana's final outburst, beginning 'Patience unmoved', is the first time that Adriana is responsible for completing her own rhymes. A single, witty line of Luciana answers her; the rhyme is only completed when she sees Antipholus arrive. We should note that the completion of a scene in Shakespeare is invariably marked by a rhyme. The power play between the sisters and their differing philosophies is perfectly demonstrated by the use of rhyme. Their humanity is not diminished, but increased, by the formality. There is a comic ceremony enacted here that tells us much about their household and provides sheer delight for the audience.

Let us leave rhyme for the time being and look at some dazzling use of language in a totally different context. In the first chapter, we left Petruchio, in The Taming of the Shrew, another of Shakespeare's early plays, planning how to woo Kate. This is part of the scene that follows:

PETRUCHIO

Good morrow, Kate; for that's your name, I hear.

KATHERINE

Well have you heard, but something hard of hearing:
They call me Katherine that do talk of me.

PETRUCHIO

You lie, in faith; for you are call'd plain Kate,
And bonny Kate and sometimes Kate the curst;
But Kate, the prettiest Kate in Christendom
Kate of Kate Hall, my super-dainty Kate,
For dainties are all Kates, and therefore, Kate,
Take this of me, Kate of my consolation;
Hearing thy mildness praised in every town,
Thy virtues spoke of, and thy beauty sounded,

Yet not so deeply as to thee belongs,
Myself am moved to woo thee for my wife.

KATHERINE

Moved! in good time: let him that moved you hither
Remove you hence: I knew you at the first
You were a moveable.

PETRUCHIO

                    Why, what's a moveable?

KATHERINE

A join'd-stool.

PETRUCHIO

                Thou hast hit it: come, sit on me.

KATHERINE

Asses are made to bear, and so are you.

PETRUCHIO

Women are made to bear, and so are you.

KATHERINE

No such jade as you, if me you mean.

PETRUCHIO

Alas! good Kate, I will not burden thee;
For, knowing thee to be but young and light –

KATHERINE

Too light for such a swain as you to catch.

PETRUCHIO

Come, come, you wasp; i' faith, you are too angry.

KATHERINE

If I be waspish, best beware my sting.

PETRUCHIO

My remedy is then, to pluck it out.

KATHERINE

Ay, if the fool could find it where it lies,

PETRUCHIO

Who knows not where a wasp does wear his sting?
In his tail.

KATHERINE

In his tongue.

PETRUCHIO

Whose tongue?

KATHERINE

Yours, if you talk of tails: and so farewell.

PETRUCHIO

What, with my tongue in your tail? nay, come again,
Good Kate; I am a gentleman.

KATHERINE

That I'll try.

She strikes him
The Taming of the Shrew, II. i. 182–217

Remember, the audience has been awaiting this scene for most of the play. It is like a world heavy-weight boxing contest at Las Vegas in that the expectations are very high. We have already heard Petruchio brag of his certain success; Katherine's family have warned him of his likely failure. So Shakespeare has set himself a massive challenge. Let's see how he delivers.

First of all, a few definitions that may be useful: 'alliteration' means starting two or more words with the same letter or sound, for example 'the lovely leafy lane'; 'assonance' means the repetition of two or more vowel sounds, for example 'the proud crowd'; 'pun' means a word or phrase that has more than one meaning, for example 'the vicar told the curate and the curate tolled the bell'. Now read the passage through a couple of times for the sense. If you can work on this scene with a partner, so much the better. Try to get a feel for the rhythm and the way the ball is batted back and forth between the two players. It really is a contest with each opponent determined to win. You need to be mentally alert with your wits razor sharp. We'll start by looking at the sound and the rhythm. I have a hunch that were an alien from outer space to hear this dialogue, it would be pretty sure of what was taking place!

Petruchio, seemingly the perfect gentleman, immediately irritates Katherine by calling her by the wrong name. How many of us get sore if we are misnamed? Katherine replies: 'Well have you heard, but something hard of hearing'. She picks up on his 'hear' and instantly conveys her displeasure through the repeated 'h's of 'heard', 'hard' and 'hearing'. You need vocal attack to deliver these words. Fifteen-love to Katherine. Petruchio responds using her misnomer no less than ten times in the next six lines. It's a name that has a hard cracking sound to it. For good measure he adds in several words with the same attacking sound: 'curst', 'Christendom' and 'consolation'. Play it thus far and really relish tormenting her with these sounds. Petruchio now performs a one-hundred-and-eighty-degree handbrake turn and shifts from harsh-sounding words to soft, soothing consonants and smooth rhythms for the next four lines, all of which need to be played through to the line ending. He might effect this change because Kate is about to burst into flames with frustration. The sound game continues with her reply. She picks up his word 'move', a word to which you can apply masses of vocal energy and elongate the vowel if you wish, and then uses it four more times, ending by laying a trap for Petruchio on the half-line:

Moved! in good time: let him that moved you hither
Remove you hence: I knew you at the first
You were a moveable.

Which, of course, Petruchio falls into out of sheer curiosity: 'Why, what's a moveable?' Katherine wins the next point with her reply of 'A join'd-stool', but Petruchio is too quick for her and tops her half-line, with 'Thou hast hit it: come, sit on me'. This is brilliant verbal sword play. To fulfill it, you need to be sharp and quick with the rhythms, particularly the changes of rhythm, and bold and clear with the alliteration and assonance. There is something physical about the use of language here, and at this stage in the process you should certainly indulge yourself with the word play; you can always pull back later. The trap of the scene is that sometimes directors add in so much physical knockabout humour that the verbal energy gets dissipated.

The dialogue continues with a series of one-liners, each with a similar rhythm, each character seizing upon the other's words and changing the meaning. For example, the word 'bear' means to carry a load but also to bear children. Practice this section from 'I knew you at the first' down to 'Too light for such a swain as you to catch'. Concentrate on picking up each other's rhythms and vocabulary, but also on delivering each other a good cue. A tennis match is dull unless the players return each other's balls with vigour. Similarly, this dialogue, and many others, demands that pleasure be taken in the playing. The characters are challenging each other to defend themselves;

their lines demand a reply. So beware of dropping the ends of lines; no downward inflections here! The final section is even more challenging. That ball just zings over the net. Each character is determined to win. Their replies are sharp; it's important to think on the line, you can't pause, think and then answer. You have to respond in the split second or else your opponent will get the better of you. The rhythm hots up:

PETRUCHIO

Who knows not where a wasp does wear his sting?
In his tail.

KATHERINE

      In his tongue.

PETRUCHIO

            Whose tongue?

KATHERINE

Yours.

You have to be perfectly on the rhythm here and bite the alliteration on 'tail', 'tongue' and 'tongue'. Furthermore, the sexual temperature is rising as many of these lines have double meanings. Throughout this exchange, Katherine more than holds her own, concluding this passage with a well-aimed blow to his head.

This material is fun to play, it's fun for the audience and it speaks volumes about their relationship. It is certainly going to be fiery and volatile but, just as important, they do seem to be well matched. There is parity in their use of language; their rhythms seem to be inter-dependent. They are clearly as intelligent as each other. I would say that they inspire one another. Crucially, for the play, the audience will want to know what is going to happen next.

Shakespeare frequently used comparable exchanges when establishing important relationships. We have already seen an example from *As You Like It* when we first meet Rosalind and Celia. Such exchanges are first and foremost witty. So what is the difference between wit and comedy? Wit is a clever and often ingenious association of words that reveals a nimble and lively mind. It is often funny, but is not necessarily so. Significantly, it engenders a mental alertness in the audience, which is critical to the success of the play. Wit engenders wit. Falstaff has a great comment in *Henry IV Part II*: 'I am not only witty in myself, but the cause that wit is in other men.' Wit is central to Shakespeare's exploration of love and sexual attraction. This was partly because boy players took on the women's roles, limiting the opportunities for physical engagement. But, more importantly, he seemed to be fascinated by the circuitous routes that men and women take to arrive at their desired destination. He was intrigued by the rituals of courtship and often took a wry, ironical perspective on love and marriage. Remember the whole love story of *Romeo and Juliet* is seen through the lens of dramatic irony, because the chorus tells us right up front that they are going to die: 'A pair of star-cross'd lovers take their life'.

Word play is central to such relationships. Read this passage from *Much Ado about Nothing* when Beatrice and Benedict meet for the first time in many years:

BEATRICE

I wonder that you will still be talking, Signior Benedick: nobody marks you.

BENEDICK

What, my dear Lady Disdain! are you yet living?

BEATRICE

Is it possible disdain should die while she hath such meet food to feed it as Signior Benedick? Courtesy itself must convert to disdain, if you come in her presence.

BENEDICK

Then is courtesy a turncoat. But it is certain I am loved of all ladies, only you excepted: and I would I could find in my heart that I had not a hard heart; for, truly, I love none.

BEATRICE

A dear happiness to women: they would else have been troubled with a pernicious suitor. I thank God and my cold blood, I am of your humour for that: I had rather hear my dog bark at a crow than a man swear he loves me.

BENEDICK

God keep your ladyship still in that mind! so some gentleman or other shall 'scape a predestinate scratched face.

BEATRICE

Scratching could not make it worse, an 'twere such a face as yours were.

BENEDICK

Well, you are a rare parrot-teacher.

BEATRICE

A bird of my tongue is better than a beast of yours.

BENEDICK

I would my horse had the speed of your tongue, and
so good a continuer. But keep your way, i' God's
name; I have done.

BEATRICE

You always end with a jade's trick: I know you of
old.

Much Ado about Nothing, I. i. 110–138

These two people are clearly destined for each other! But the journey to
marriage is likely to be long and stony. It's as if Beatrice and Benedick are
addicted to wit; they can't escape it and, at times, it seems that they bring out
the worst in each other. This makes them outsiders and lends a melancholy to
the play. A bittersweet quality suffuses through most of Shakespeare's comedies. It's fascinating that at the end of *Love's Labour's Lost*, Mercade, a court
messenger, arrives to announce the death of the king of France, casting a
profound shadow over the proceedings. Rosaline requires Berowne, a notorious wit, to pass a year visiting the 'speechless sick', trying to 'enforce' a
smile, before she will marry him.

Wit is not exclusive to the comedies. If you take the above definition of
wit, 'a clever and often ingenious association of words that reveals a nimble
and lively mind', then this, of course, could apply to a host of characters
throughout the plays. The important question is: How does a character use
language in a situation? I would argue that Juliet's 'Gallop apace' speech,
which we have already examined, is very witty. Her imaginative use of language reveals an enormous amount about her mental processes and the
suppleness of her mind.

Here is Edmund, the Duke of Gloucester's illegitimate son and brother to
Edgar, in *King Lear*. Hitherto, he has been an almost silent presence on the
stage. Here he is alone.

EDMUND

Thou, nature, art my goddess; to thy law
My services are bound. Wherefore should I
Stand in the plague of custom, and permit
The curiosity of nations to deprive me,

For that I am some twelve or fourteen moon-shines
Lag of a brother? Why bastard? wherefore base?
When my dimensions are as well compact,
My mind as generous, and my shape as true,
As honest madam's issue? Why brand they us
With base? with baseness? bastardy? base, base?
Who, in the lusty stealth of nature, take
More composition and fierce quality
Than doth, within a dull, stale, tired bed,
Go to the creating a whole tribe of fops,
Got 'tween asleep and wake? Well, then,
Legitimate Edgar, I must have your land:
Our father's love is to the bastard Edmund
As to the legitimate: fine word, – legitimate!
Well, my legitimate, if this letter speed,
And my invention thrive, Edmund the base
Shall top the legitimate. I grow; I prosper:
Now, gods, stand up for bastards!

King Lear, I. ii. 1–22

This is a ferocious speech that is full of anger, full of humour and full of passion, all of which is expressed with an irresistible wit. Edmund proves to be a highly dangerous man, but he's attractive at the same time. And I think his attraction lies in his wit. It's a very clever strategy on Shakespeare's part to make the villain likeable. He does it magnificently with *Richard III*; he does it to a lesser extent with Iago in *Othello*; and here, in a world dominated by old men, is a young man determined to claim his birthright and, in doing so, to sweep aside the old laws and privileges. And he's witty.

This is a great speech to work on at this stage because it brings together a number of techniques that we have been occupied with. Here we will primarily be looking at word play but we will also think about the line endings. We will start by asking what Edmund is doing? By this I don't mean is he standing, sitting, cooking breakfast or whatever, but what is his action? I suggest that you always seek a transitive action, one that effects change in yourself or another person. He's alone, so he's clearly not addressing anyone other than the audience. And I think that's the clue. He's arguing through his claim with the audience. He is justifying himself. It's fascinating; the subject of the speech is law and Edmund argues his case like a seasoned lawyer. So, let's argue it!

Start by saying aloud the final words of each line one after the other. Some of this is interesting and some isn't. Law is the subject of the speech and 'law' is the first line ending. 'Law/I/permit/me' is revealing. 'Prosper/

bastards' at the end is a pretty clear signal as to his intentions! The repetition of 'base' and the use of other 'b' words on the line endings are also telling.

Now play through the speech aloud, respecting the line endings and avoiding stopping mid-line even when there is a full stop or question mark. So in the second line, you do not come to a halt on 'bound'; the thought moves forward towards the line ending and into the question.

> Thou, nature, art my goddess; to thy law
> My services are bound. Wherefore should I
> Stand in the plague of custom, and permit
> The curiosity of nations to deprive me,
> For that I am some twelve or fourteen moon-shines
> Lag of a brother? Why bastard? wherefore base?

And when you arrive at 'Lag of a brother?', the thoughts move restlessly on to two more questions. If you don't pause after each question, you will get a powerful percussive impact on 'bastard' and 'base'. You will only achieve this if you have taken a good breath earlier, probably after 'deprive me'. You can judge for yourselves which of the earlier line endings you want to play and which you want to mark; the key is to really ask the questions. Don't make them rhetorical; ask them. And if you do ask them, you will automatically get forward drive.

What is already emerging here is a series of questions supported by strong, percussive alliterations. Look at the next four lines:

> When my dimensions are as well compact,
> My mind as generous, and my shape as true,
> As honest madam's issue? Why brand they us
> With base? with baseness? bastardy? base, base?

The same pattern. A question posed on the half-line, followed by the rat-tat-tat of the 'b's. This is a totally different form of word play, but it's word play just the same. Its root is a mighty sense of injustice; he's a bastard, but he could just as well be black, be gay, be out of work, be disabled . . . it's a long list. The word 'base' could easily be a taunt he heard in the school playground when the other kids discovered his parents were not married. It's most instructive that the verb he employs is 'brand'; it's a word that conjures heat, pain and violence. This is where you need to marry an empathy with the character with your technique. These insults can be spat out from a volcano of resentment, but they need to be delivered alliteratively and rhythmically in order to make maximum impact. So far in the speech there are ten 'b' words. Now read on:

Who, in the lusty stealth of nature, take
More composition and fierce quality
Than doth, within a dull, stale, tired bed,
Go to the creating a whole tribe of fops,
Got 'tween asleep and wake? Well, then,
Legitimate Edgar, I must have your land.

Here is a question that is four and a half-lines long, so play it through, but don't miss the humour. The vivid picture he paints and the heavy, the suggestive rhythm of 'dull, stale, tired bed' and the series of questions in the speech are finally answered by 'Legitimate Edgar, I must have your land'. There is a lightness here that is underlined by the introduction of a new alliteration of 'l'. There is a laughing, mocking tone in the 'l's, repeated through the remainder of the speech:

Our father's love is to the bastard Edmund
As to the legitimate: fine word, – legitimate!
Well, my legitimate, if this letter speed,
And my invention thrive, Edmund the base
Shall top the legitimate. I grow; I prosper:
Now, gods, stand up for bastards!

So the ten 'b' words give way to eight 'l' words. Read this last section through out loud. Shakespeare invites you to roll the words round in your mouth; he invites you to share Edmund's scorn for Edgar and his legitimacy. He makes a final comparison between 'base', a strong, masculine word, and 'legitimate', a light, effeminate word. But 'legitimate' is not the last word on the line; the energy moves forward with 'I grow; I prosper'. Edmund is unstoppable. Finish by attempting the whole speech. Argue your case. Seek out all the alliterations and tap into Edmund's anger and his humour. To a large degree, the movement of sound affected by the repetitions and multiple alliterations tells the story. If you follow the word play, you will discover that Edmund is both savage and charming in the same speech. A lethal cocktail!

We have already seen a ceremony of comedy in The Comedy of Errors. Shakespeare sometimes used the repetition of words and cadence to create a ceremony of death. There is a scene in Richard III when Queen Margaret and Queen Elizabeth meet along with the Duchess of York and share their grief for their children and husbands that Richard has slaughtered.

QUEEN MARGARET

If sorrow can admit society,
Tell o'er your woes again by viewing mine:
I had an Edward, till a Richard kill'd him;

I had a Harry, till a Richard kill'd him:
Thou hadst an Edward, till a Richard kill'd him;
Thou hadst a Richard, till a Richard killed him;

DUCHESS OF YORK

I had a Richard too, and thou didst kill him;
I had a Rutland too, thou holp'st to kill him.

QUEEN MARGARET

Thou hadst a Clarence too, and Richard kill'd him.
From forth the kennel of thy womb hath crept
A hell-hound that doth hunt us all to death.

Richard III, IV. iv. 38–48

In this passage, Shakespeare creates a ritual by the repetition of words, rhythms and cadence. There is a ceremonial quality which, on the one hand, dignifies their grief and, on the other hand, underscores the horror of Richard's actions. These women who have been bitter enemies during the nightmare of the civil war are united in grief by the simple repetition and echo of each other's words. As I hear these words in the twenty-first century, I am transported away from our comfortable, civilized society to realms of terrible conflict, either in former times or across the world to contemporary scenes of carnage. And it is created by the simplest, most economic of means. Queen Margaret completes the lament with a terrifying metaphor, which is both destructive and deadly accurate.

7

VOCABULARY

'Words, words, mere words'
Troilus and Cressida, V. iii. 111

Staring down at me from the shelf above my work desk is a hefty copy of the *Shorter French Dictionary*, or more precisely the *Shorter English/French, French/English Dictionary*. It has long fascinated me that the English/French section is a full centimetre and a half fatter than the French/English section. There are thousands upon thousands more words in the English language than in the French. It is thought that, to a considerable extent, the French language was limited in size and scope by the institution of the Académie française in 1635 with the express purpose of defining vocabulary and laying down rules for grammar.

Shakespeare had no restrictions whatsoever on his use of language beyond Coleridge's definitions of prose as 'words in their best order' and poetry as 'the best words in the best order'. Shakespeare employed a vast number of words in his plays and invented a fair few of them himself. He used language like an artist uses paint or a sculptor uses stone; it was his medium and he created with it and controlled it. He was sometimes extravagant with it and sometimes frugal. He was endlessly inventive and drew abundantly from the well of language that formed in London at the end of the sixteenth century.

During Shakespeare's lifetime there was no dictionary, in the modern sense of the word, to consult. It was not until nearly one hundred and fifty years after his death that Samuel Johnson published his great *Dictionary of the English Language* in 1755. English, like most modern languages, was a mongrel tongue; a lot of Germanic words, a lot of Latin words and a smattering of

French, the first language of the English court for hundreds of years. In many respects, the language that Shakespeare heard in the streets of London was a young language, a rapidly developing language that had absorbed many rich cultures and continued to incorporate various patois. During Queen Elizabeth's reign, London became the fastest-growing metropolis in the world. Walking past Queen Hythe to cross the Thames at London Bridge on his way to the Globe Theatre, he would certainly have heard a myriad of tongues spoken by the sailors and merchants from the Hanseatic ports, from Spain, France and the Mediterranean. It is likely that the whole of London was a Babel of different accents and regional dialects. Shakespeare certainly brought with him the sound, the phrases and the common wisdom of his native Warwickshire. At the centre of society was a court that was educated, sophisticated and cosmopolitan, with a love of music and poetry. The language he had at his disposal had the earthiness of its Anglo-Saxon roots, the intellectual breadth that characterised its Latin vocabulary and the sophistication that accompanied the French influence. In short, it was energetic, pluralistic and adaptable.

When you are approaching a character, it is well worth examining the vocabulary they use because this will give you important clues as to the type of person you are playing and how to play them. Vocabulary is the raw material of character building, so it is important to recognise the ingredients that Shakespeare uses. In some respects, your character *is* your vocabulary. We will start with a clear example of vocabulary defining character. *Love's Labour's Lost* is a very beautiful play, and it is much concerned with the ways in which people express themselves. For me, its overall theme is education, both in the formal sense of academic learning and in the broader sense of preparation for life. As in most of the comedies, the lovers undergo playful rites which teach them about themselves and lead them down the road towards matrimony. In this play, as we have seen earlier, death proves to be the most important teacher of all. There is a wonderful canvas of characters, each with a different level of education. Here is Holofernes, a schoolmaster, conversing after dinner with his friend Sir Nathaniel, a curate. The conversation is silently witnessed by Antony Dull, the Constable.

Enter HOLOFERNES, SIR NATHANIEL and DULL
HOLOFERNES

Satis quod sufficit.

SIR NATHANIEL

I praise God for you, sir: your reasons at dinner
have been sharp and sententious; pleasant without
scurrility, witty without affection, audacious without

impudency, learned without opinion, and strange without
heresy. I did converse this quondam day with
a companion of the king's, who is intituled, nominated,
or called, Don Adriano de Armado.

HOLOFERNES

Novi hominem tanquam te: his humour is lofty, his
discourse peremptory, his tongue filed, his eye
ambitious, his gait majestical, and his general
behavior vain, ridiculous, and thrasonical. He is
too picked, too spruce, too affected, too odd, as it
were, too peregrinate, as I may call it.

SIR NATHANIEL

A most singular and choice epithet.
Draws out his table-book

HOLOFERNES

He draweth out the thread of his verbosity finer
than the staple of his argument. I abhor such
fanatical phantasimes, such insociable and
point-devise companions; such rackers of
orthography, as to speak dout, fine, when he should
say doubt; det, when he should pronounce debt, – d,
e, b, t, not d, e, t: he clepeth a calf, cauf;
half, hauf; neighbour vocatur nebor; neigh
abbreviated ne. This is abhominable, – which he
would call abbominable: it insinuateth me of
insanie: anne intelligis, domine? to make frantic, lunatic.

SIR NATHANIEL

Laus Deo, bene intelligo.

HOLOFERNES

Bon, bon, fort bon, Priscian! a little scratch'd,
'twill serve.

Love's Labour's Lost, V. i. 1–29

You'll be pleased to know that we won't attempt to work this passage in
great detail. However, as we go along, I will give you one or two pointers to
bear in mind. Few members of a modern audience are likely to understand
every word that is being spoken and I believe the same would have been true
of Shakespeare's original audience. What is fascinating is that people will
still laugh, but at the character's pomposity, their self-absorption and their

hypocrisy. Nevertheless, if you are planning to perform this material, you will need to know precisely what every word means. It's best to get hold of a copy of the play with first-rate notes; the Arden edition is superb, as is the New Cambridge edition. Let's examine the vocabulary and then consider the implications for character. The speeches are stacked full of polysyllabic words, which usually means they are of Latin origin. Many words are actually in Latin and a few are in French. You will find that polysyllabic words can be spoken surprisingly fast, as long as you have done a bit of work on your diction and your brain is in gear. When you see a monosyllabic line or phrase, it usually means you can slow it down and stretch it out a bit. We'll look out for examples of this.

Holofernes, the schoolmaster, sometimes referred to as the Pedant, opens the conversation in Latin. His friend, Sir Nathaniel, flatters him, at the same time showing off his own learning with a string of appositions – too long a string, for it makes him absurd. As we saw earlier, it's important to work the appositions and to play through to the end of the sentence, in this case to 'heresy'. It's essential not to attempt to explain what you are saying as, paradoxically, this will make it harder for an audience to understand! Furthermore, listen out for the music of the speech. Sir Nathaniel uses a classical vocabulary, but he also uses classical sentence forms that have elegance and balance. He moves the conversation on with 'I did converse this quondam day with a companion of the king's, who is intituled, nominated, or called, Don Adriano de Armado'. Ask yourself why he would use a Latin word, 'quondam', when it is not really necessary. Perhaps to show off or ingratiate himself or to flatter the listener or possibly to amuse Holofernes. There are a number of options here and to avoid just playing a two-dimensional cut-out, it's helpful to examine all the choices. And there is no need to find three different words for 'called'. It's funny and revealing. His friend replies with an even more formidable vocabulary, again using elegant sentence construction. You will need to be very vocally nimble with these characters; the danger lies in making them heavy and ponderous. The text suggests a precision of touch, which requires lightness. Let the text lead you towards characterisation and not the other way around.

Holoferne's speech solicits more praise. Then, brilliantly, Shakespeare has Holofernes criticize Don Armado for verbosity, the very fault of which he himself is guilty: 'He draweth out the thread of his verbosity finer than the staple of his argument'. You might think these characters are too educated for their own good, but as I read them, I can't help but sense Shakespeare's affection for their foibles – they certainly contribute to the through debate about education. Shakespeare cleverly has their conversation witnessed by Constable Dull, who needs little more introduction than his name. At the end of the scene there is this exchange:

HOLOFERNES

Via, goodman Dull! thou hast spoken no word all this while.

DULL

Nor understood none neither, sir.

Love's Labour's Lost, V. i. 142–144

Huge laugh. Perfect! But if there was any danger of the audience dismissing these two learned gentlemen as a pair of walking dictionaries, Shakespeare comes up with a master stroke in the final scene of the play when the lovers mock Holofernes, who is trying his best to perform in a simple play for them. He chastens them with a dignified: 'This is not generous, not gentle, not humble.' I think Shakespeare wants you to find the humanity and the dignity behind the façade of the language. Shakespeare asks you not to judge these men in the same way that they should not judge Dull for his lack of learning. Wisdom is important, as well as education.

Let us now look at two contrasting characters from the same play, Troilus and Cressida. This is part of a speech of Ulysses arguing for discipline in the Greek camp in the context of a stalled military campaign.

ULYSSES

The heavens themselves, the planets and this centre
Observe degree, priority and place,
Insisture, course, proportion, season, form,
Office and custom, in all line of order;
And therefore is the glorious planet Sol
In noble eminence enthroned and sphered
Amidst the other; whose medicinable eye
Corrects the ill aspects of planets evil,
And posts, like the commandment of a king,
Sans cheque to good and bad: but when the planets
In evil mixture to disorder wander,
What plagues and what portents! what mutiny!
What raging of the sea! shaking of earth!
Commotion in the winds! frights, changes, horrors,
Divert and crack, rend and deracinate
The unity and married calm of states
Quite from their fixure! O, when degree is shaked,
Which is the ladder to all high designs,
Then enterprise is sick! How could communities,
Degrees in schools and brotherhoods in cities,
Peaceful commerce from dividable shores,

The primogenitive and due of birth,
Prerogative of age, crowns, sceptres, laurels,
But by degree, stand in authentic place?
Take but degree away, untune that string,
And, hark, what discord follows! each thing meets
In mere oppugnancy: the bounded waters
Should lift their bosoms higher than the shores
And make a sop of all this solid globe:
Strength should be lord of imbecility,
And the rude son should strike his father dead:
Force should be right; or rather, right and wrong,
Between whose endless jar justice resides,
Should lose their names, and so should justice too.
Then every thing includes itself in power,
Power into will, will into appetite;
And appetite, an universal wolf,
So doubly seconded with will and power,
Must make perforce an universal prey,
And last eat up himself.
Troilus and Cressida, I. iii. 84–124

Read this speech carefully. It is a great example of speech as argument. Ulysses is precisely arguing a case with the express intention of winning. The speech is transitive; he intends to make the Greek generals see things his way. The stakes in war could not be higher: victory or defeat. To this end, Ulysses marshals his case carefully and builds his argument with all the rhetorical skills he can muster. He deploys a substantial vocabulary – again much of it Latin in origin – and constructs powerful lines of reasoning.

First, as you read it through, get a sense of the weight of the words. Try these aloud:

Observe degree, priority and place,
Insisture, course, proportion, season, form,
Office and custom, in all line of order.

These are weighty words both in meaning and delivery. Each word commands respect; each word demands a certain style of delivery, meaning that each of these lines will probably have several stressed words. The heavy nouns are followed by the lighter phrase 'in all line of order', a contrast of weight and a contrast of rhythm. Reading on, you will notice many more substantial polysyllabic words: 'eminence', 'enthroned', 'commandment', 'commotion', 'deracinate', 'communities', 'primogenitive' . . . the list is long. The choice of these words not only gives a precision to his argument, but also reveals what a formidable opponent Ulysses is. Look at this passage:

> . . . but when the planets
> In evil mixture to disorder wander,
> What plagues and what portents! what mutiny!
> What raging of the sea! shaking of earth!
> Commotion in the winds! frights, changes, horrors,
> Divert and crack, rend and deracinate
> The unity and married calm of states
> Quite from their fixure!

The choice of vocabulary here is deadly! Line after line is filled with highly energized words: 'plagues', 'portents', 'raging', 'shaking', 'commotion', 'frights', 'changes', 'horrors', 'divert', 'crack', 'rend' and 'deracinate' all have a savagery about them that you must match in the delivery. Shakespeare helps you with a strong pulse and some startling changes of rhythm. And then the speech emerges into calmer waters with the regular

> The unity and married calm of states
> Quite from their fixure!

Even the vocabulary seems calmer. You could also consider slowing right up when you get to the monosyllabic words on the last line.

Second, notice in this passage the use of lists (of words and phrases). Read on through the whole speech and you will realize that lists are a central part of his technique. Use them. He builds up a weighty edifice of argument that is pretty hard to oppose.

Finally, observe how long the sentences are. This indicates a kind of person who can hold complex arguments in the air for considerable periods of time. He is highly intelligent and demands an intelligent response. As with the sonnet we looked at earlier, the performer must play through the whole sentence without gabbling or getting lost in the detail. This is a great speech for practicing these important skills of rhetoric.

Let's now look at a contrasting character from the same play. Thersites is a scurrilous Greek and, in many respects, the fool of the play. In this prose speech he sees Agamemnon and Menelaus coming; the former is the head of the Greek army, the latter is his brother, the cuckolded husband of Helen, the cause of the war.

THERSITES

Here's Agamemnon, an honest fellow enough and one
that loves quails; but he has not so much brain as
earwax: and the goodly transformation of Jupiter
there, his brother, the bull, – the primitive statue,
and oblique memorial of cuckolds; a thrifty
shoeing-horn in a chain, hanging at his brother's
leg, – to what form but that he is, should wit larded with
malice and malice forced with wit turn him to?
To an ass, were nothing; he is both ass and ox: to
an ox, were nothing; he is both ox and ass. To be a
dog, a mule, a cat, a fitchew, a toad, a lizard, an
owl, a puttock, or a herring without a roe, I would
not care; but to be Menelaus, I would conspire
against destiny. Ask me not, what I would be, if I
were not Thersites; for I care not to be the louse
of a lazar, so I were not Menelaus! Hey-day!
spirits and fires!

Troilus and Cressida, V. i. 47–63

Like most of Thersites's monologues, this is packed with animal imagery.
The sheer quantity and savagery of that imagery marks him out from all other
Shakespearean characters. Although he is extremely witty, the constant references to beasts and insects make his frequent commentaries uncomfortable
listening. They reduce mankind to a thing of flesh and bone; there seems
small space for human dignity in Thersites's world view. Consequently, he is
the perfect commentator on a battlefield. He is the outsider who sees through
the pomp, hypocrisy and lies that are common currency in wars since time
began. This follows Shakespeare's purpose, for the play takes the great heroes
from Homer and gives them a human face, warts and all. Thersites exposes
their vanities and follies in the cruelest way.

The vocabulary that he uses also follows this purpose. There is the reduc-
tive juxtaposition of man with beast. Most animals are Anglo-Saxon words,
earthy and rustic; they have a different flavour from the more elaborate Latinate
words we found in Ulysses. At first, he affords Agamemnon some dignity: he
is 'an honest fellow enough.' Straightaway he reduces him to a rudimentary
level: he 'loves quails'. Here he describes the cuckold Menelaus:

the goodly transformation of Jupiter
there, his brother, the bull, – the primitive statue,
and oblique memorial of cuckolds

He uses grander, polysyllabic words, but to ironic effect. He debunks the myth.

You can approach this speech using similar techniques to those used in the Ulysses' speech. First, get a sense of the weight or, in this case, the flavour of the language, which is much more Anglo-Saxon and earthy. Ask yourself: What does this tell you about the speaker? Where might he have heard such language? (No prizes here because he has spent a long while around military camps.) Second, look out for the lists. Finally, notice the length of the sentences. If you play from full stop to full stop or full stop to question mark, there are only four sentences here. Play the thought through.

I now want to look at some much plainer speech and see how Shakespeare used the vocabulary and rhythms of his native Warwickshire to create some of his most memorable characters. Touchstone, a court fool, is in exile in the Forest of Arden with his mistress, Celia. Here he encounters Corin a local shepherd.

CORIN

And how like you this shepherd's life, Master Touchstone?

TOUCHSTONE

Truly, shepherd, in respect of itself, it is a good
life, but in respect that it is a shepherd's life,
it is naught. In respect that it is solitary, I
like it very well; but in respect that it is
private, it is a very vile life. Now, in respect it
is in the fields, it pleaseth me well; but in
respect it is not in the court, it is tedious. As
is it a spare life, look you, it fits my humour well;
but as there is no more plenty in it, it goes much
against my stomach. Hast any philosophy in thee, shepherd?

CORIN

No more but that I know the more one sickens the
worse at ease he is; and that he that wants money,
means and content is without three good friends;
that the property of rain is to wet and fire to
burn; that good pasture makes fat sheep, and that a
great cause of the night is lack of the sun; that
he that hath learned no wit by nature nor art may
complain of good breeding or comes of a very dull kindred.

TOUCHSTONE

Such a one is a natural philosopher.

As You Like It, III. ii. 11–31

At the heart of this dialogue lies the old debate between court and country. We have already seen another manifestation of it in *Henry VI*'s molehill speech. It is likely that Touchstone has spent his entire life in the city and that Corin has never strayed more than a few miles from his birthplace. This would have been common in Shakespeare's lifetime and was a pattern that continued across Europe until after the First World War. (My mother's family, the Midwinters, worked on the land in a small village in Oxfordshire for generations, moving to London in the late 1920s.) Here, Touchstone, the reluctant exile, unfavourably compares his present life with his past, using the rather pretentious phrase 'in respect'. It's not always clear exactly what he really feels – indeed, at the end of the play he marries a country girl, more for lust than love – which gives a restless impression to the character. This contrasts superbly with Corin, who is totally sure of his ground. His vocabulary is very simple, almost entirely monosyllabic and Anglo-Saxon. The phrasing has the charm and the certainty of an homily. It is pitch perfect. We can easily believe that Shakespeare was familiar with men like Corin in the countryside around Stratford. Reading this passage, you get a strong feeling for where his heart lay. Read the Corin speech a couple of times to get an impression of the language. There is an ease to it, a music. The same rules of apposition apply as before, with one phrase balancing another. Also beware of dropping the ends of phrases and giving too much downward inflection. Corin is clearly having fun at Touchstone's expense, so there are great opportunities for humour, but remember: it's gentle humour.

Here's a different example of two plain-speaking men: another shepherd and his son, using their native vocabulary and phrasing. In *The Winter's Tale*, the Old Shepherd is out in a terrible storm, searching for his son, known as the 'Clown'. He has come across a newborn baby, which he assumes to have been deserted by its mother. As we pick up the story, the Clown runs in with some shocking news. Read this carefully as it tells a lovely story:

CLOWN

Hilloa, loa!

SHEPHERD

What, art so near? If thou'lt see a thing to talk
on when thou art dead and rotten, come hither.
What ailest thou, man?

CLOWN

I have seen two such sights, by sea and by land!
but I am not to say it is a sea, for it is now the
sky: betwixt the firmament and it you cannot thrust
a bodkin's point.

Richard McCabe as Autolycus in *The Winter's Tale*, 1991. Photo: Malcolm Davies Collection © Shakespeare Birthplace Trust

SHEPHERD

Why, boy, how is it?

CLOWN

I would you did but see how it chafes, how it rages,
how it takes up the shore! but that's not the
point. O, the most piteous cry of the poor souls!

sometimes to see 'em, and not to see 'em; now the
ship boring the moon with her main-mast, and anon
swallowed with yest and froth, as you'ld thrust a
cork into a hogshead. And then for the
land-service, to see how the bear tore out his
shoulder-bone; how he cried to me for help and said
his name was Antigonus, a nobleman. But to make an
end of the ship, to see how the sea flap-dragoned
it: but, first, how the poor souls roared, and the
sea mocked them; and how the poor gentleman roared
and the bear mocked him, both roaring louder than the
sea or weather.

SHEPHERD

Name of mercy, when was this, boy?

CLOWN

Now, now: I have not winked since I saw these
sights: the men are not yet cold under water, nor
the bear half dined on the gentleman: he's at it
now.

SHEPHERD

Would I had been by, to have helped the old man!

CLOWN

I would you had been by the ship side, to have
helped her: there your charity would have lacked footing.

SHEPHERD

Heavy matters! heavy matters! but look thee here,
boy. Now bless thyself: thou mettest with things
dying, I with things newborn. Here's a sight for
thee.

The Winter's Tale, III. iii. 77–111

This is both funny and appalling at the same time. It's a great piece of comic
writing because the Clown is given not one but two gruesome stories to tell
at the same time, and he's not the sharpest tool in the shed. As with Corin, the
vocabulary is quite plain, but Shakespeare gives the character some gloriously
vivid imagery such as: 'Betwixt the firmament and it you cannot thrust a
bodkin's point'. Here he juxtaposes a majestic Latin word, 'firmament', with
the simplest of words, 'it'. He then completes the image with a workingman's

word for a knife. His long speech is peppered with energetic Anglo-Saxon verbs and studded with words and phrases from his local patois, like 'hogshead' and 'flap-dragoned'. When tackling a speech such as this, the most important thing is to imagine what the character has seen as clearly as possible down to the last detail. Here it would probably be useful to place one incident on your left and one on your right, so you can easily swap focus between them when you are speaking. Try and tell the story as lucidly as possible. That's what this is all about: storytelling. Use the energy and the colour in the words to bring it alive for your audience, in this case your dad. Always keep your eye out for the appositions, setting them up and playing the thoughts through.

I find it fascinating that some of the most memorable phrases in all of Shakespeare's works are the simplest and use the plainest vocabulary. The old man sums up the situation with this apposition: 'Thou mettest with things dying, I with things newborn'. This is beautiful and profound. For me, it taps directly into Shakespeare's roots in rural England. You will find many such examples throughout his work. They do not need dressing up or colouring as they have enough authority and resonance.

Another great tradition that Shakespeare drew on is the insult. Time and again, he proved himself to be the master of the noble art of abuse. In *Henry IV Part I*, Hal says 'I'll so offend, to make offence a skill'. Shakespeare could certainly have applied this aphorism to himself. His characters are often virtuoso swearers who dazzle with their insults. They are extraordinarily inventive with the English language when it comes to abuse, and Shakespeare's creative juices clearly flowed when the opportunity came along for a good bout of swearing. Here's a good example from *King Lear*. It's Kent encountering the steward Oswald, who has previously been discourteous to the king. At first, Oswald fails to recognize Kent (who is in disguise) and unwittingly offers him a gift of an opportunity:

OSWALD

Why dost thou use me thus? I know thee not.

KENT

Fellow, I know thee.

OSWALD

What dost thou know me for?

KENT

A knave; a rascal; an eater of broken meats; a
base, proud, shallow, beggarly, three-suited,

hundred-pound, filthy, worsted-stocking knave; a
lily-livered, action-taking knave, a whoreson,
glass-gazing, super-serviceable finical rogue;
one-trunk-inheriting slave; one that wouldst be a
bawd, in way of good service, and art nothing but
the composition of a knave, beggar, coward, pandar,
and the son and heir of a mongrel bitch: one whom I
will beat into clamorous whining, if thou deniest
the least syllable of thy addition.

King Lear, II. ii. 10–22

The key here is to take as much pleasure in delivering these insults as Shakespeare clearly took in writing them. They need relish and precision.

But let's go back a step. The Duke of Kent has been banished for speaking his mind and has therefore disguised himself so he can continue to serve his master. He no longer speaks in verse but in prose, and he adopts the ways and vocabulary of a 'very honest-hearted fellow and as poor as the King' (I. iv. 19). At the beginning of the play, the Duke of Kent got into trouble for speaking his mind in defence of Cordelia. Here we see his disguised persona giving the unfortunate Oswald a piece of his mind. He has completely taken on the

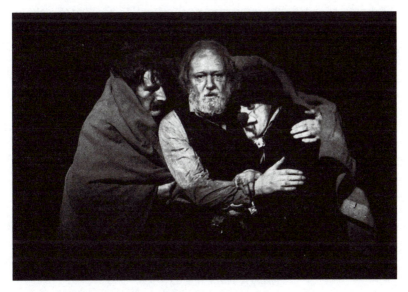

Malcolm Storry as Kent, Michael Gambon as Lear and Tony Sher as the Fool in *King Lear* at the Royal Shakespeare Theatre, 1982. Photo: Joe Cocks Studio Collection © Shakespeare Birthplace Trust

vocabulary and manner of a plain-speaking man of the soil, and here he takes his revenge on Oswald, who has insulted the king.

It's a list and the impact is cumulative. I think the best way to do this speech is to try to answer the question that Oswald poses. Listen; think about it; and then answer it. Approach the speech by attempting to define as precisely and carefully as possible this awful little creature, Oswald. Choose your words with care; search out the right insult; sometimes you might need to invent a phrase if one doesn't already exist. Remember, Kent does not set out to deliver a list of insults. He starts with just one or two insults, but they aren't sufficient to describe the cowardly Oswald. So he adds a few more and so on and so on. Start by playing through to the semicolons. At first it's just a word or two, then a phrase, then a whole list. You will find a natural music to the speech that corresponds to the way that Kent thinks, to the way that Kent invents and chooses the right words. At several moments he returns to the same word: 'knave'. You can use this. It's clearly the perfect description, so return to it with a proper sense of self-satisfaction. It's interesting to note that Oswald does not interrupt. I imagine he is spellbound by this brilliant exposition. Malcolm Storry played Kent when I directed Michael Gambon as Lear. He delivered this speech deadpan, straight out front, and he coined every insult lovingly. Oswald was so gobsmacked that he just stood there like a stunned mullet. Indeed, Malcolm paused once or twice to consider the next word and, finally, at the moment that Oswald was going to reply, he continued with his list. It was very funny and a very accurate reading of the character. So you can take your time, as long as the situation warrants it and you are inventing the language.

Hal and Falstaff are great swearers in Henry IV Part I:

PRINCE HENRY

I'll be no longer guilty of this sin; this sanguine
coward, this bed-presser, this horseback-breaker,
this huge hill of flesh, –

FALSTAFF

'Sblood, you starveling, you elf-skin, you dried
neat's tongue, you bull's pizzle, you stock-fish! O
for breath to utter what is like thee! you
tailor's-yard, you sheath, you bowcase; you vile
standing-tuck –

Henry IV Part I, II. v. 245–252

There's something hugely satisfying for an audience in a full-bodied, stand-up, no-holds-barred, slanging match. And most actors will tell you that it's equally enjoyable to play. This scene is stuffed full of choice insults, but this short exchange is especially delicious. Here is Hal, exasperated and incredulous at Falstaff's cowardice and mendacious boasting, and Falstaff, caught red-handed in a monster scam. They square up to each other like a couple of sumo wrestlers and throw great handfuls of words at each other. And it must be played with great sensuality and relish. It is a society in which mastery of language is highly prized and these two set about each other with panache and gusto. Each insult is coined, savoured and flung. Hal only loses the initiative because he chooses the brilliant image 'this huge hill of flesh', which is not only funny and deadly accurate, but requires a considerable amount of puff from the actor to fulfil the vowels in 'huge' and 'hill', which slows him down. Falstaff is straight in there with a wonderful gallery of words and imagery, conjuring the thinnest man that ever walked the earth! For good measure, Falstaff laces his cocktail with ripe sexual imagery that, in the circumstances, is irresistible. The fact that much of this vocabulary has become redundant can be used to your advantage; you should utter the words as if you are the first person on earth to use them. It is so much more satisfying to create the phrase 'bull's pizzle' than simply to regard it as a common Elizabethan term of abuse. This will help to make your character more inventive, more original.

It's a good tip to seek out sexual imagery in Shakespeare's language, like a truffle hunter. Whole books have been written on this subject and the best reference work is still Eric Partridge's *Shakespeare's Bawdy*, first published in 1947. It contains hundreds of words which would have been used with a deliberate sexual innuendo or with clear reference to bodily parts and functions. It's fascinating and highly educative to browse through the pages. You will certainly marvel at the inventiveness of Shakespeare and the contemporary language from which he drew and be astonished at the sheer magnitude of the sexual vocabulary he used. There are literally dozens of words for the male and female sexual organs (as well as a host of highly imaginative descriptions of the sexual act), for urinating and for defecating. Shakespeare, Shakespeare's characters and Shakespeare's audience clearly reveled in bawdy vocabulary. Here is a part of the opening scene from *Romeo and Juliet*:

GREGORY

The quarrel is between our masters and us their men.

SAMPSON

'Tis all one, I will show myself a tyrant: when I
have fought with the men, I will be cruel with the
maids, and cut off their heads.

GREGORY

The heads of the maids?

SAMPSON

Ay, the heads of the maids, or their maidenheads;
take it in what sense thou wilt.

GREGORY

They must take it in sense that feel it.

SAMPSON

Me they shall feel while I am able to stand: and
'tis known I am a pretty piece of flesh.

GREGORY

'Tis well thou art not fish; if thou hadst, thou
hadst been poor John. Draw thy tool! here comes
two of the house of the Montagues.

SAMPSON

My naked weapon is out: quarrel, I will back thee.
Romeo and Juliet, I. i. 18–31

We have already noted that Shakespeare took particular care at the beginning of his plays to seize the attention of the audience and especially, we must assume, the groundlings, who would certainly lack the politeness and attention generally afforded to actors by modern playgoers. This dialogue, with its considerable sexual reference, would certainly have pleased the unwashed, as would the fight that shortly breaks out between the Capulets and the Montagues. So how do you deal with it? One way is to cut it. (When I was a schoolboy, our editions of *Macbeth* and *Henry IV Part I* were carefully excised of all the parts that we called the 'dirty' bits. This, of course, sent us scurrying to the library to discover what we were missing.)

My advice: don't cut it, embrace it.

I believe you have to treat the bawdy vocabulary as you would any imagery: invent it. It's easy to say that Gregory and Sampson are just a couple of coarse oafs, which they may well be, but they are witty and inventive oafs. The vocabulary lends the scene a dangerous, volatile atmosphere. They are sparring with words, competing with each other and egging each other on. So use the words within the situation. Relish the sexual imagery, but don't illustrate it with a lot of mime (which merely treats the audience as if they were idiots). Play the scene as if the audience was intelligent and tuned in to the references. Seek out the antitheses and the alliteration; see how the baton is handed from one character to another by the repetition of words: 'Heads . . . heads . . . heads; maids . . . maids . . . maidenhead; sense . . . sense; feel . . . feel; flesh . . . fish'. Pick up the repetitions lightly; be nimble and avoid crudeness. Remember, as a performer you can do a lot to create and shape an audience; treat them with respect and intelligence and they will repay you tenfold.

Perhaps most importantly of all, have fun and allow the audience to enjoy it. Who can resist this dialogue from *The Comedy of Errors* between Antipholus of Syracuse and Dromio of Syracuse about the super-sized kitchen maid Luce?

ANTIPHOLUS OF SYRACUSE

Then she bears some breadth?

DROMIO OF SYRACUSE

No longer from head to foot than from hip to hip:
she is spherical, like a globe; I could find out
countries in her.

ANTIPHOLUS OF SYRACUSE

In what part of her body stands Ireland?

DROMIO OF SYRACUSE

Marry, in her buttocks: I found it out by the bogs.

ANTIPHOLUS OF SYRACUSE

Where Scotland?

DROMIO OF SYRACUSE

I found it by the barrenness; hard in the palm of the hand.

ANTIPHOLUS OF SYRACUSE

Where France?

DROMIO OF SYRACUSE

In her forehead; armed and reverted, making war
against her heir.

ANTIPHOLUS OF SYRACUSE

Where England?

DROMIO OF SYRACUSE

I looked for the chalky cliffs, but I could find no
whiteness in them; but I guess it stood in her chin,
by the salt rheum that ran between France and it.

ANTIPHOLUS OF SYRACUSE

Where Spain?

DROMIO OF SYRACUSE

Faith, I saw it not; but I felt it hot in her breath.

ANTIPHOLUS OF SYRACUSE

Where America, the Indies?

DROMIO OF SYRACUSE

Oh, sir, upon her nose all o'er embellished with
rubies, carbuncles, sapphires, declining their rich
aspect to the hot breath of Spain; who sent whole
armadoes of caracks to be ballast at her nose.

ANTIPHOLUS OF SYRACUSE

Where stood Belgia, the Netherlands?

DROMIO OF SYRACUSE

Oh, sir, I did not look so low.
    The Comedy of Errors, III. ii. 114–143

A few of the puns have been lost in the mists of time but, for the most part, the jokes hold up spectacularly well. Here we can see Shakespeare as the popular entertainer par excellence. This scene is great for two actors to work on almost as a party piece; it is highly enjoyable and provides the perfect raw material to practice your comic skills.

Finally, I want to examine how vocabulary can point up a situation or enhance a mood above and beyond a particular character's immediate experience. *Antony and Cleopatra* is full of occasions when Shakespeare uses vocabulary to create a special mood. Here Cleopatra commits suicide in grief at the loss of her husband, Antony. She is accompanied by her attendant, Charmian.

CLEOPATRA

                    Come, thou mortal wretch,
To an asp, which she applies to her breast
With thy sharp teeth this knot intrinsicate
Of life at once untie: poor venomous fool
Be angry, and dispatch. O, couldst thou speak,
That I might hear thee call great Caesar ass
Unpolicied!

Helen Mirren as Cleopatra and Sorcha Cusack as Charmian *in Antony and Cleopatra* at The Other Place, 1982. Photo: Joe Cocks Studio Collection © Shakespeare Birthplace Trust

CHARMIAN

> O eastern star!

CLEOPATRA

>   Peace, peace!
> Dost thou not see my baby at my breast,
> That sucks the nurse asleep?

CHARMIAN

>   O, break! O, break!

CLEOPATRA

As sweet as balm, as soft as air, as gentle, –
O Antony! – Nay, I will take thee too.
Applying another asp to her arm
What should I stay –
Dies

CHARMIAN

In this vile world? So, fare thee well.
Now boast thee, death, in thy possession lies
A lass unparallel'd.
Antony and Cleopatra, V. ii. 298–310

This is a scene of the greatest intimacy and delicacy. You could describe it as one of the first assisted suicides in English literature. These women have probably known each other all their lives. Following the death of Antony, defeat in the wars with Rome and a self-imposed 'house arrest' in her own monument, Cleopatra resolves to die. Her friend and companion, Charmian, helps to dress her and prepare her for death. It is an intensely private scene that must be shared with the whole audience. In Shakespeare's time the audience number could count several thousand. It is certainly an occasion when Coleridge's maxim 'the best words in the best order' comes into play. She applies the asp to her breast with these words:

With thy sharp teeth this knot intrinsicate
Of life at once untie

This feels like a very intricate operation and the run of monosyllabic words match the action perfectly. Remember, it is very hard to speak monosyllabic words too fast without sounding like a typewriter, so you are lead towards a measured precision, which is highlighted by the beautifully complex word 'intrinsicate'. The moment the snake bites into her flesh is probably marked by her cry of 'O' in 'O, couldst thou speak', and this heralds in a whole series of 'O' sounds from her and from Charmian: 'O eastern star!', 'O, break! O, break!' and 'O Antony!' The vowel sound is open and capable of expressing that which words simply cannot communicate. In some societies they would be a howl or a keen. Here I think they are intimate, but it is crucial that they are open and not skated over. They are key to the music of the scene and crucial in the vital process of rendering the private public. For the most part, Cleopatra's language could not be simpler; she likens the poisonous snake to a baby at her breast and employs monosyllabic words in a regular rhythm.

Peace, peace!
Dost thou not see my baby at my breast,
That sucks the nurse asleep?

Again, not only the rhythm, but, to a large extent, the speed of playing is implied by the choice of vocabulary. Try saying the above lines out loud without articulating the consonants at all. Just say the vowels in a sequence. It will go something like this:

eee eee,
oh ow oh eee aye ay ee ah ay eh,
ah uh eh urr ah ee.

Go on! Try it a couple of times. You will sound crazy, but by the end you will understand my point about monosyllabic words needing more space. Now do the lines in full, consonants and all. This exercise will give these lines more body, more presence, which is essential at this, the climactic moment of the play. Compare this with, say, the earlier line: 'With thy sharp teeth this knot intrinsicate'. Do the same thing. Just the vowels. You will find that you will need more time on the monosyllables and will be able to skip quicker through the word 'intrinsicate'. So through choice of vocabulary, supported by rhythm, Shakespeare creates an extraordinary, heightened atmosphere that is commensurate to the moment. There is a music that should not be ignored. It is soon to be shattered by the brutal arrival of Roman soldiers, which amplifies the fragile ambiance through contrast.

I hope that, in the course of this chapter, you have begun to appreciate that the choice of words used in a particular passage conveys much more than just meaning. There is sensuality to language that is of equal importance. The sound and rhythm of words communicates on a very deep level and contributes enormously to the enjoyment and meaning of a play. Allow yourself to embrace fully every aspect of vocabulary.

8

SHAPE, STRUCTURE AND MEANING

'It is shap'd, sir, like itself'
Antony and Cleopatra, II. vii. 41

Every speech tells a story.
Every speech has a beginning, a middle and an end.
Every speech starts with a headline.

Let me add an amendment:

Every speech or section of dialogue tells a story.
Every speech or section of dialogue has a beginning, a middle and an end.
Every speech or section of dialogue starts with a headline.

These are the most important lessons to be learnt in this chapter. They are key to your understanding of how to do Shakespeare. At the same time, they are the simplest and most fundamental of lessons. Why? Because storytelling is at the very heart of the actor's craft. At its most essential, theatre is one person or group of people telling a story to another person or group of people in a shared space. That's all it is!

Think back to the stories you were told as a child. They were vivid and full of incident, with clear characters and strong narrative lines. They almost certainly had a beginning, a middle and an end. They probably started 'Once upon a time . . .'. Stories remembered from childhood are, by definition, memorable. Some people are brilliant storytellers – which is somewhat different to being a good raconteur – and these are very special people. In some societies they are held in very high esteem and are even endowed with great spiritual authority as shamans or intermediaries between this world and the spirit world. In ancient societies the storyteller had a special responsibility as the holder and communicator of the history, the story of the tribe or race. I believe that Shakespeare occupies a special place in our culture and indeed, through translation and live performance, in world culture. He created, developed and popularised stories and myths that have become central to our understanding of ourselves and are powerful voices in our dialogue with ourselves.

In theatre, the responsibility for telling the story lies with both the individual and the group. On many occasions when I have been rehearsing a scene or watching a run-through of a play or even a performance, I have been struck by an inertia or lack of forward drive in the narrative. It's plain boring and dulls an audience's attention. It's like watching a soccer team passing the ball backwards and forwards with no attack. I ask my actors 'Who's got the story? Who's responsible for the narrative?' In film, this question is answered for you. The director and editor choose a sequence of shots that tell the story they wish the audience to follow. In the theatre it's different. In any given scene the responsibility will shift from character to character and sometimes to the whole group. In an ensemble situation, when a company knows one another well and has rehearsed thoroughly, the narrative will flow vigorously and without interruption. But this doesn't happen through magic or any mysterious mumbo jumbo between the actors. There are practical measures that can be learnt and real responsibilities that must be undertaken by the individual and the company. One of the objectives of this chapter is to help you to appreciate and engage with these techniques.

As always with Shakespeare, the text contains all the information you will need to make the story clear and dramatic. We will examine the shape and structure of speeches, dialogues and scenes in order to help us tell the story. It is my fundamental belief that an appreciation and command of structure empowers the actor. We have done a lot of work on this in a micro way in the chapter on line endings. Here we will look at the bigger picture and analyse in a macro way the shape of speeches, the pattern of dialogues and the structural choices Shakespeare uses to tell his tale. And perhaps most interesting of all, we will explore the implications of structure and form on meaning. For example, what does it mean if a scene is written in prose rather than verse?

As we embark on this leg of our journey, let us ponder for a moment the situation in rehearsal or performance that I referred to earlier. Although all the lines were being delivered accurately and all the moves were correct, the stage was not alive. What was not happening? First, responsibility wasn't being taken for telling the story. Second, the signals in the text were not being accurately read. We will deal with both of these issues in this chapter. But there is a third matter that you must consider, especially if you are interested in performing Shakespeare. Isaac Newton's Third Law of Motion can be paraphrased as follows: every action causes an equal and opposite reaction. We can readily adapt this law to the stage. Acting is about action and reaction: action through the text in a transitive manner, a manner that effects change on another character (e.g. I will make Shylock drop his lawsuit against Antonio); reaction to what has just been said to you or to the situation in which your character finds him or herself, in turn becoming another action. This process of action and reaction is critical to the art of acting. So perhaps there is another important question to consider: Were my actors playing an action or were they just talking? Were they trying to effect change in the other characters through the language (playing an action)? Or were they just trying to make the language sound beautiful or, worse, were they not concentrating? Both of these are undynamic. Shakespeare's characters, like all human beings, want something; what they want is specified in the text and how they set about getting it is revealed in the form.

Now let us take a look at that speech from *The Merchant of Venice* in which Portia, disguised as a male lawyer, addresses Shylock and the court during the trial of Antonio.

PORTIA

The quality of mercy is not strain'd,
It droppeth as the gentle rain from heaven
Upon the place beneath: it is twice blest;
It blesseth him that gives and him that takes:
'Tis mightiest in the mightiest: it becomes
The throned monarch better than his crown;
His sceptre shows the force of temporal power,
The attribute to awe and majesty,
Wherein doth sit the dread and fear of kings;
But mercy is above this sceptred sway;
It is enthroned in the hearts of kings,
It is an attribute to God himself;
And earthly power doth then show likest God's
When mercy seasons justice. Therefore, Jew,
Though justice be thy plea, consider this,
That, in the course of justice, none of us
Should see salvation: we do pray for mercy;
And that same prayer doth teach us all to render

The deeds of mercy. I have spoke thus much
To mitigate the justice of thy plea;
Which if thou follow, this strict court of Venice
Must needs give sentence 'gainst the merchant there.
The Merchant of Venice, IV. i. 181–202

What is Portia's action in this speech? What does she want? You play an action in order to achieve a want. Remember, actions should be transitive, they should effect change in other people. The easiest way of achieving this is to put the word 'make' before the action. I suggested earlier that her action was to make Shylock drop his lawsuit. You might suggest that her action was to make Bassanio, whom she loves, admire her. The answer to this question probably lies in the antepenultimate line: 'To mitigate the justice of thy plea'. So Portia tries to make Shylock mitigate his plea. Let's settle for this interpretation for now. Perhaps what she wants is justice or perhaps simply leniency for her friend's friend. This approach to a speech strikes me as much more dynamic than the alternatives, which might include 'to persuade' Shylock or 'to discuss' mercy. She sets out to make someone change his mind. As events turn out, she does not succeed and has to try another tack, a different action but perhaps with the same want.

You are playing Portia and you have identified the character's action from within the text. You look straight at Shylock. You know what you want to achieve. Now pause. Look at the structure. Let us apply my earlier guidelines:

Every speech tells a story.
Every speech has a beginning, a middle and an end.
Every speech starts with a headline.

What is the 'headline' of the speech? What's on the front page of the newspaper? What's in the subject box of the e-mail? With this speech, I think it's quite obvious: 'The quality of mercy'. You are going to talk about Mercy; you are going to tell a story about Mercy. And it will have a beginning, a middle and an end. Read the speech through once again and try to divide it into three parts. Mark the text lightly in pencil. They certainly don't need to be of equal length, just a beginning, a middle and an end. Understand that this is not an exact science and that the wonderful thing about rehearsal is that you can change your mind! How you divide up the speech is part of your interpretation. But you always need to be able to defend your views; you need to have good arguments. I would probably divide the speech up as follows:

1. The quality of mercy is not strain'd,
It droppeth as the gentle rain from heaven
Upon the place beneath:
                              2. it is twice blest;
It blesseth him that gives and him that takes:
'Tis mightiest in the mightiest: it becomes
The throned monarch better than his crown;
His sceptre shows the force of temporal power,
The attribute to awe and majesty,
Wherein doth sit the dread and fear of kings;
But mercy is above this sceptred sway;
It is enthroned in the hearts of kings,
It is an attribute to God himself;
And earthly power doth then show likest God's
When mercy seasons justice. Therefore, Jew,
Though justice be thy plea, consider this,
That, in the course of justice, none of us
Should see salvation: we do pray for mercy;
And that same prayer doth teach us all to render
The deeds of mercy.
                              3. I have spoke thus much
To mitigate the justice of thy plea;
Which if thou follow, this strict court of Venice
Must needs give sentence 'gainst the merchant there.

She begins by telling him what she is going to talk about; she then talks about it; she concludes by telling him why she talked about it and what she thinks he should do about it. Alternatively, you could take the first unit or 'beat' as far as 'mercy seasons justice.' She develops a proposition or hypothesis; she applies it to Shylock; she concludes. Either way, there's a formality about it that befits the character (she is disguised as an advocate) and the setting (she is in a court of law). The means are appropriate to the action and the objective.

Let's look at the story she tells. At first you might think that it is not really a story, it is not really a narrative. Well, I think it is, and I think the speech benefits from being regarded thus. The story is that a lawyer makes a brilliant argument for mercy that should close the case for the defence. She starts with a metaphor, which, like all metaphors, has the capacity to inspire the listener. Mercy is like 'the gentle rain from heaven'. She doesn't allow Shylock to dwell too long on this because she moves the argument forward, completing the half-line without a pause with: 'it is twice blest'. Then comes her proposition: 'It blesseth him that gives and him that takes'. She then argues through this idea, using many of the techniques we have already explored, especially apposition. She makes an inspirational argument about the moral supremacy of mercy on earth and its God-like attributes. If we are to plead mercy from God, then we must exercise it on earth. She concludes by telling what action she hopes he will take, while intelligently acceding that he would win the case as it stands.

Try reading Portia's speech aloud twice, using the alternative structures I have suggested and see which reading feels most comfortable.

One tip before we move onto another example: try to identify a line or phrase that sums up the whole of the speech for you. If some mad director demanded that you cut the whole speech bar one phrase, what would it be? I would probably opt for 'mercy seasons justice.' This exercise will help you to pinpoint the essence of a speech.

Twelfth Night is an iridescent, bittersweet comedy. It explores loss, unobtainable love and, like all Shakespeare's comedies, it traces the painful path to matrimony. In this scene Viola, disguised as a boy, has been sent by her master to woo, on his behalf, the beautiful Olivia. Here is a short extract:

VIOLA

If I did love you in my master's flame,
With such a suffering, such a deadly life,
In your denial I would find no sense;
I would not understand it.

OLIVIA

Why, what would you?

VIOLA

Make me a willow cabin at your gate,
And call upon my soul within the house;
Write loyal cantons of contemned love
And sing them loud even in the dead of night;
Halloo your name to the reverberate hills
And make the babbling gossip of the air
Cry out 'Olivia!' O, You should not rest
Between the elements of air and earth,
But you should pity me!

Twelfth Night, I. v. 253–265

Look at the third speech. It's clearly not something that Viola could have prepared. It's not formal, like the Portia speech; you could almost say that it was improvised in the moment. Indeed when Zoë Wanamaker played the part for the RSC, she was so full of love and passion that these lines just burst out of her like a dam breaking. So what is the structure and what is she doing? First, ask yourself what the headline is. 'Willow Cabin' I would imagine. Next, divide the speech into three. It might be as follows:

1. Make me a willow cabin at your gate,
And call upon my soul within the house;

2. Write loyal cantons of contemned love
And sing them loud even in the dead of night;
Halloo your name to the reverberate hills
And make the babbling gossip of the air
Cry out 'Olivia!'
            3. O, You should not rest
Between the elements of air and earth,
But you should pity me!

I repeat, this is not an exact science, and you might feel that the word 'gate' at the end of line 1 marks your opening section. That's your interpretation and it's valid. There is a very clear story told by Viola in this speech and the work is to create it in the moment as vividly as possible. Try it a couple of times and see if you can fresh mint each thought as it arrives. The structure you have identified will help you. Your first couple of lines are an inspired reaction to Olivia's question. You could ponder before you answer or, like Zoë, allow it to erupt in the moment. You then tell what you would do next: you would 'write', 'sing', 'halloo' and cause the hell of a noisy echo. It's very dynamic. As you practice, don't allow the energy to tail off in the lines after the strong verbs; play the thought through. She concludes with a crucial idea: you would not rest until 'you should pity me!' A beginning, a middle and an end. And perhaps that last phrase is the one you might choose if all else had to be cut: 'You should pity me!'

This speech is a good example of how a speech builds in substance and value even though the noisier part is almost certainly earlier on. A common fault in delivering speeches from Shakespeare is to play the whole speech diminuendo (starting strong and getting progressively weaker). I have already pointed out that you must play the energy right through to the end of the line. Similarly, you must play a speech right through to its conclusion, which will invariably have important content. If you glance at both the speeches we have tackled in this chapter, you will notice that there is only one full stop in each, near the end. In fact the full stop marks the beginning of the final section. Remember the sonnet we looked at earlier? It had a very long first sentence and a spectacular conclusion. The lesson we learnt then was not to become too occupied with the minutiae, but to keep an eye on the bigger picture. If you want to begin a speech with a burst of energy, great, but ensure you give its conclusion proper authority and weight. If in doubt, play a speech crescendo!

The conclusion of Hermione's trial in *The Winter's Tale* is violent and dramatic. We looked at part of the speech in which she pleads for her life. Subsequently, the Oracle at Delphi deemed her to be innocent, but her husband, Leontes, defied the judgment, at which exact moment news of the death of her only son arrives. Hermione falls in a faint and is carried off. A few moments later, Paulina, a feisty woman of the court, reenters and confronts Leontes:

PAULINA

What studied torments, tyrant, hast for me?
What wheels? racks? fires? what flaying? boiling?
In leads or oils? what old or newer torture
Must I receive, whose every word deserves
To taste of thy most worst? Thy tyranny
Together working with thy jealousies,
Fancies too weak for boys, too green and idle
For girls of nine, O, think what they have done
And then run mad indeed, stark mad! for all
Thy by-gone fooleries were but spices of it.
That thou betray'dst Polixenes, 'twas nothing;
That did but show thee, of a fool, inconstant
And damnable ingrateful: nor was't much,
Thou wouldst have poison'd good Camillo's honour,
To have him kill a king: poor trespasses,
More monstrous standing by: whereof I reckon
The casting forth to crows thy baby-daughter
To be or none or little; though a devil
Would have shed water out of fire ere done't:
Nor is't directly laid to thee, the death
Of the young prince, whose honourable thoughts,
Thoughts high for one so tender, cleft the heart
That could conceive a gross and foolish sire
Blemish'd his gracious dam: this is not, no,
Laid to thy answer: but the last, – O lords,
When I have said, cry 'woe!' the queen, the queen,
The sweet'st, dear'st creature's dead, and vengeance for't
Not dropp'd down yet.

The Winter's Tale, III. ii. 174–200

This speech is like the wrath of God! Woe betide anyone who interrupts her or gets in her way. It is powerful, poised and deadly. First, read it through a couple of times to get the sense. For information, Polixenes is Leontes' best friend, whom he accused of adultery, Camillo is his trusted servant whom he accused of treachery and the baby girl was left in the wilds (to be discovered by our friend the Old Shepherd).

I've often heard this speech come out as a splurge, so it's critical to uncover the structure and make it work for you. It's crucial to the shape and meaning of the speech that the main message lies in the penultimate line: 'The sweet'st, dear'st creature's dead'. This is the one line in the speech that cannot be cut and would certainly serve as the best possible headline. Headlines are usually early on in speeches, but this is an exception. Why? Leontes knows full well that this outburst heralds some revelation, but Paulina makes him and the audience wait in agony.

Next, find a beginning, a middle and an end. I would suggest the following:

1. What studied torments, tyrant, hast for me?
What wheels? racks? fires? what flaying? boiling?
In leads or oils? what old or newer torture
Must I receive, whose every word deserves
To taste of thy most worst?
                              2. Thy tyranny
Together working with thy jealousies,
Fancies too weak for boys, too green and idle
For girls of nine, O, think what they have done
And then run mad indeed, stark mad! for all
Thy by-gone fooleries were but spices of it.
That thou betray'dst Polixenes, 'twas nothing;
That did but show thee, of a fool, inconstant
And damnable ingrateful: nor was't much,
Thou wouldst have poison'd good Camillo's honour,
To have him kill a king: poor trespasses,
More monstrous standing by: whereof I reckon
The casting forth to crows thy baby-daughter
To be or none or little; though a devil
Would have shed water out of fire ere done't:
Nor is't directly laid to thee, the death
Of the young prince, whose honourable thoughts,
Thoughts high for one so tender, cleft the heart
That could conceive a gross and foolish sire
Blemish'd his gracious dam: this is not, no,
Laid to thy answer:

3. but the last, – O lords,
When I have said, cry 'woe!' the queen, the queen,
The sweet'st, dear'st creature's dead, and vengeance for't
Not dropp'd down yet.

In the first section, she asks a series of questions. Make these real questions, not rhetorical. Play them in order to get a response from Leontes. Put him on the spot, nail him down and try to make him answer. One of the most common faults among professional actors at all levels is the tendency to make questions rhetorical. By fully asking questions, you can often transform a scene. For example, the main task in Juliet's potion speech is to ask the questions properly. Here, ask each one of Paulina's questions for real, one after another. You will find a superb, aggressive rhythm, supported by plenty of alliteration. Of course, she does not allow him to answer because she does not pause after the final question, 'To taste of thy most worst?', but completes the line with 'Thy tyranny'. This is an answer to her questions, and it announces the subject of the whole of the middle section. It refers back to the belligerent 't' alliteration of the opening line. You can certainly take a pause after 'tyranny'. You'll need to get some breath, but you might want to allow that word to float and hang in the air. It's a brave and dangerous thing to say to an absolute ruler who is quite probably mentally unbalanced.

The middle section is the longest (which, interestingly, has been the case with every example we've examined). It is the section in which you need to pay the most attention to storytelling as it's the easiest section in which to lose your audience. Essentially, it is a list, a litany of Leontes's tyrannical acts. Highlight for yourself the subject of each episode (e.g. Polixenes, Camillo's honour, etc.) and lead the audience from one to the next, as in a story. Look out for the length of sentences and ensure not to get too bogged down in subordinate clauses. Be alert to the line endings. Full stops or semicolons frequently fall in the middle of lines. Don't let yourself pause at these points, but move forward to the line endings and allow your character to maintain control of her audience.

The final section is short and devastating and needs considerable power kept in reserve to fulfill it. Shakespeare helps by giving you the harsh, heavy pulse of the alliterated 'd's: 'dear'st', 'dead', 'dropp'd' and 'down'.

It's a virtuoso performance. So what is her action? What is she doing? Bringing the news of the child's death? If so, it's twenty-four lines too long. Try and be transitive ('to make'). The meaning will certainly lie in the structure. She pins him down with a series of savage, ironical questions. Then, she not only accuses him of tyranny, but also catalogues his faults and victims. Finally, she delivers the news and implies vengeance is waiting.

And all this in public. So perhaps her action is to make him suffer the maximum or to make him confront his crimes or possibly to make him mend his ways. It's fascinating that we learn at the end of the play that Hermione is not in fact dead and that Paulina has kept watch over a sixteen-year vigil of repentance from Leontes. In one sense, Paulina is pretending in the above speech! But her grief and anger are fuelled by very real grievances. This is an exciting meeting place of the two traditions: the Shakespearean and the Stanislavskian. In our interpretation of all the speeches so far, one tradition has informed the other.

Now let us turn to dialogue. We'll start with the passage from *Romeo and Juliet* when the lovers meet for the first time:

ROMEO

[To JULIET] If I profane with my unworthiest hand
This holy shrine, the gentle fine is this:
My lips, two blushing pilgrims, ready stand
To smooth that rough touch with a tender kiss.

JULIET

Good pilgrim, you do wrong your hand too much,
Which mannerly devotion shows in this;
For saints have hands that pilgrims' hands do touch,
And palm to palm is holy palmers' kiss.

ROMEO

Have not saints lips, and holy palmers too?

JULIET

Ay, pilgrim, lips that they must use in prayer.

ROMEO

O, then, dear saint, let lips do what hands do;
They pray, grant thou, lest faith turn to despair.

JULIET

Saints do not move, though grant for prayers' sake.

ROMEO

Then move not, while my prayer's effect I take.
He kisses her
Thus from my lips, by yours, my sin is purged.

JULIET

Then have my lips the sin that they have took.

ROMEO

Sin from thy lips? O trespass sweetly urged!
Give me my sin again.

JULIET

He kisses her   You kiss by the
book.

Romeo and Juliet, I. v. 92–109

This is a perfect piece of writing. In the Prologue, Shakespeare sets out to tell the story of 'a pair of star-crossed lovers'. The occasion of their meeting has to be pretty remarkable. The form he chooses for this scene places them square in the great literary tradition of romantic lovers. Romeo and Juliet create a sonnet between them and at the moment of the completion of the fourteen lines, their attraction is consummated with a kiss. The remainder of the scene consists of just four rhymed lines, which again result in a kiss. At this moment, the Nurse interrupts them. End of scene!

Shakespeare has to demonstrate that the lovers are the perfect fit emotionally, intellectually and sensuously. And he needs to keep it economical. So in an inspired move, he selects a formal structure: the heightened literary form of the sonnet. It's a form that they share, that they build together. It's a form that is built upon rhyme that, in this context, is very sexy. You will remember from our earlier work on rhyme that it is a form that first sets up a word, then requires that word to be answered with a rhyme. So when Romeo uses the word 'this', it's begging to be answered with 'kiss'. Juliet repeats this pattern of 'this/kiss', thus pointing the way the scene is heading. They start with four lines each, then single lines and a couplet. It's like an editor in film using shorter and shorter clips. There is a quickening, a breathlessness. They are totally reliant the one upon the other.

Romeo introduces a whopping great conceit at the beginning: Juliet is a holy shrine and he is a pilgrim. She has a straight choice: she either walks away or she joins in, which implicates her. The religious references, on the one hand, sanctify the relationship and, on the other hand, give eroticism to it. The talk is all of lips, touching and the intimacy of prayer.

Is there a story here? You bet! And it starts with a bold action from Romeo: the introduction of the sonnet. Juliet's response, the next four lines, is both a reaction and an action. The scene begins with 'If', and this single word would be my headline. The approach to Juliet is conditional! It's the perfect entry to a new relationship. For me, the greatest love song ever written is 'If I loved you' from Carousel by Richard Rodgers and Oscar Hammerstein II. It recognises the diffidence shared by all lovers and the importance of fantasy in the development of a relationship.

Another example of Shakespeare taking a highly formal structure and using it to devastating effect can be seen in Henry VI Part III. Think back to Henry VI sitting on his molehill in the middle of a bloody battle, contemplating the life of a simple shepherd. Well, this is what follows. We won't work on it, but I want you to read it.

Alarum. Enter a Son that has killed his father,
dragging in the dead body

SON

Ill blows the wind that profits nobody.
This man, whom hand to hand I slew in fight,
May be possessed with some store of crowns;
And I, that haply take them from him now,
May yet ere night yield both my life and them
To some man else, as this dead man doth me.
Who's this? O God! it is my father's face,
Whom in this conflict I unwares have kill'd.
O heavy times, begetting such events!
From London by the king was I press'd forth;
My father, being the Earl of Warwick's man,
Came on the part of York, press'd by his master;
And I, who at his hands received my life, him
Have by my hands of life bereaved him.
Pardon me, God, I knew not what I did!
And pardon, father, for I knew not thee!
My tears shall wipe away these bloody marks;
And no more words till they have flow'd their fill.

KING HENRY VI

O piteous spectacle! O bloody times!
Whiles lions war and battle for their dens,
Poor harmless lambs abide their enmity.
Weep, wretched man, I'll aid thee tear for tear;
And let our hearts and eyes, like civil war,
Be blind with tears, and break o'ercharged with grief.
Enter a Father that has killed his son, bringing in the body

FATHER

Thou that so stoutly hast resisted me,
Give me thy gold, if thou hast any gold:
For I have bought it with an hundred blows.
But let me see: is this our foeman's face?
Ah, no, no, no, it is mine only son!
Ah, boy, if any life be left in thee,
Throw up thine eye! see, see what showers arise,
Blown with the windy tempest of my heart,
Upon thy words, that kill mine eye and heart!
O, pity, God, this miserable age!
What stratagems, how fell, how butcherly,
Erroneous, mutinous and unnatural,
This deadly quarrel daily doth beget!
O boy, thy father gave thee life too soon,
And hath bereft thee of thy life too late!

KING HENRY VI

Woe above woe! grief more than common grief!
O that my death would stay these ruthful deeds!
O pity, pity, gentle heaven, pity!
The red rose and the white are on his face,
The fatal colours of our striving houses:
The one his purple blood right well resembles;
The other his pale cheeks, methinks, presenteth:
Wither one rose, and let the other flourish;
If you contend, a thousand lives must wither.

SON

How will my mother for a father's death
Take on with me and ne'er be satisfied!

FATHER

How will my wife for slaughter of my son
Shed seas of tears and ne'er be satisfied!

KING HENRY VI

How will the country for these woful chances
Misthink the king and not be satisfied!

SON

Was ever son so rued a father's death?

FATHER

Was ever father so bemoan'd his son?

KING HENRY VI

Was ever king so grieved for subjects' woe?
Much is your sorrow; mine ten times so much.

SON

I'll bear thee hence, where I may weep my fill.
Exit with the body

FATHER

These arms of mine shall be thy winding-sheet;
My heart, sweet boy, shall be thy sepulchre,
For from my heart thine image ne'er shall go;
My sighing breast shall be thy funeral bell;
And so obsequious will thy father be,
Even for the loss of thee, having no more,
As Priam was for all his valiant sons.
I'll bear thee hence; and let them fight that will,
For I have murdered where I should not kill.
Exit with the body

KING HENRY VI

Sad-hearted men, much overgone with care,
Here sits a king more woful than you are.

Henry VI, II. v. 55–113

This is perhaps the most upsetting scene that has ever been written about warfare. It employs a high degree of formality. This formality in construction, on the one hand, heightens the horror and, on the other hand, contains and gives shape to emotions that are otherwise almost unbearable. The arrival of the son bearing the corpse of his father is echoed by the arrival of a father bearing his son's dead body. There is a balance and counterpoint in their speeches; they match each other in the weight of their grief. Shakespeare reflects this in similar speech length and rhythm. Henry VI acts as a chorus and the scene develops a music that has terrible beauty. There is an inevitability about the situation; the moment it is revealed that the son has killed his own father, we know what will happen next. This unavoidability is the tragic mirror to a civil war that still created seismic shock waves in Shakespeare's lifetime. It is a scene that remains a paradigm for similar conflicts, whether they be in the United States in the 1860s or the Balkans in the 1990s.

I would now like to look at the dialogue in a couple of opening scenes. These are often difficult to pull off because the audience is probably still settling down and the ear needs to adjust to the language. We examined the opening Chorus of *Henry V* and noticed the techniques used to grab the audience's attention. This is a slightly shortened version of the opening movement of *Hamlet*. Here we are straight into narrative, situation and character. Story is paramount. (The cuts are those I used in the 2008 production in Stratford, Ontario.)

Elsinore. A platform before the castle.

FRANCISCO at his post. Enter to him BARNARDO

BARNARDO

Who's there?

FRANCISCO

Nay, answer me: stand, and unfold yourself.

BARNARDO

Long live the king!

FRANCISCO

                Barnardo?

BARNARDO

                       He.

FRANCISCO

You come most carefully upon your hour.

BARNARDO

'Tis now struck twelve; get thee to bed, Francisco.

FRANCISCO

For this relief much thanks: 'tis bitter cold,
And I am sick at heart.

BARNARDO

Have you had quiet guard?

FRANCISCO

                  Not a mouse stirring.

BARNARDO

Well, good night.

FRANCISCO

                Stand, ho! Who's there?
Enter HORATIO and MARCELLUS

HORATIO

Friends to this ground.

MARCELLUS

                  And liegemen to the Dane.

FRANCISCO

Give you good night.

MARCELLUS

                 O, farewell, honest soldier:
Who hath relieved you?

FRANCISCO

                   Barnardo has my place.
Give you good night.
Exit

MARCELLUS

              Holla! Barnardo!

BARNARDO

                         Say,
What, is Horatio there?

HORATIO

               A piece of him.

BARNARDO

Welcome, Horatio: welcome, good Marcellus.

MARCELLUS

What, has this thing appear'd again to-night?

BARNARDO

I have seen nothing.

MARCELLUS

Horatio says 'tis but our fantasy.

HORATIO

Tush, tush, 'twill not appear.

BARNARDO

                      Sit down awhile;
And let us once again assail your ears,
That are so fortified against our story
What we have two nights seen.

HORATIO

                        Well, sit we down,
And let us hear Barnardo speak of this.

BARNARDO

Last night of all,
When yond same star that's westward from the pole
Had made his course to illume that part of heaven
Where now it burns, Marcellus and myself,
The bell then beating one,–
Enter Ghost . . .

                                  Hamlet, I. i. 1–37

First of all, imagine you are at the very first performance in London over four hundred years ago. You may have heard that it was a revenge play and perhaps that there was a ghost, but not much else. I think there would be huge excitement – a new play by Shakespeare! The whole crowd would be straining to listen. So how does he tell the story and what are the implications for me as a performer?

What strikes me every time I read this scene is how fast it goes. I know that in performance it is sometimes delivered at a solemn pace. If you look at the text, this seems to me to be all wrong. I have laid out the lines above in the way that I believe it was intended to be acted. Time after time, one actor completes another's line, indicating no pauses. Just look at the opening lines:

BARNARDO

Who's there?

FRANCISCO

Nay, answer me: stand, and unfold yourself.

BARNARDO

Long live the king!

FRANCISCO

               Barnardo?

BARNARDO

                         He.

This suggests to me that there is only one silence in this passage, after 'Who's there?'. There is a question, a pause, then the rest is bang bang, word on word! Try this for yourself with a partner. Played like this, you first get an act of listening, which is vital in the theatre, and then you get a series of staccato phrases tight on each other. It communicates a jittery nervousness. Why? The audience doesn't know at this point. There is respite:

FRANCISCO

For this relief much thanks: 'tis bitter cold,
And I am sick at heart.

And another pause after 'sick at heart'. Very telling, especially when you consider that they are professional soldiers. The rhythm continues tight after this right up to Barnardo's line 'I have seen nothing'. Significantly, another silence is suggested. The final pause is after 'Last night of all' when, in an inspired detailed moment, Barnardo sees the very same star that he saw when the ghost last appeared. The effect of this idea is like suddenly introducing a huge close up of Barnardo's face in a movie. It's a human detail that draws the listener in just at the moment when . . . the ghost appears. Great dramaturgy. Try this whole scene, honouring the line structure, and I promise you that the story will instantly become much more vivid. The nervous, fearful state of these men is communicated through the verse structure.

Now let's look at the shape of the scene, remembering that the audience don't know at the beginning what is about to happen. Shakespeare gives us a mighty headline: 'Who's there?' (Interestingly, when Peter Brook created his version of *Hamlet* at the Bouffes du Nord in 1996, he entitled it *Qui est là?*.) The question is repeated in a slightly different form a few lines later.

When you watch this scene or start to rehearse it, you realize that there is a fair amount of coming and going, and it might be a good idea to divide the scene into three using the two entrances/exits as our beginning, middle and end. If you look at editions of classical French drama, you will notice that they begin a new scene every time a character enters or exits. I find this a very useful exercise that I employ to this day. I would advise young directors to try it; it instantly gives a shape to the scene or act. And this is the real point of dividing a scene or speech into three. It gives you a narrative structure to work with in rehearsals and it provides a framework within which you can debate with yourself about interpretation. For example, in this case, I would take my first beat on the entrance of Horatio, but I would ponder where to put my second. The line 'What, has this thing appear'd again to-night?' is the first time that the ghost has been referred to in the play and is therefore a key moment in the story. I would take this as my second beat and ensure that the silence that follows Barnardo's line 'I have seen nothing' resounds. If you wish, you could take the pause before the line; you would still retain the iambic structure, but it would be Barnardo who showed the hesitation or, perhaps, fear.

Of course none of the above matters if, as performers, you do not bring onto the stage with you the remarkable situation Shakespeare has provided, if you do not enter into a world in which heaven and hell and sin and redemption are realities of your existence. This is an exercise of the imagination that requires an ability to step into someone else's shoes. All the work we have been doing will help you and guide you, but it must be in support of a transitive action in a fully realized situation.

Finally, I want to look at the opening scene of *Julius Caesar* to begin our examination of how to deal with prose. Read the following and notice the way that Shakespeare moves between verse and prose. Marullus and Flavius are representatives of the people, known as Tribunes. Shakespeare has them speaking in verse. The others are commoners and they speak in prose.

Rome. A street.

Enter FLAVIUS, MARULLUS, and certain Commoners

FLAVIUS

Hence! home, you idle creatures get you home:
Is this a holiday? what! know you not,
Being mechanical, you ought not walk
Upon a labouring day without the sign
Of your profession? Speak, what trade art thou?

CARPENTER

Why, sir, a carpenter.

MARULLUS

Where is thy leather apron and thy rule?
What dost thou with thy best apparel on?
You, sir, what trade are you?

COBBLER

Truly, sir, in respect of a fine workman, I am but,
as you would say, a cobbler.

MARULLUS

But what trade art thou? answer me directly.

COBBLER

A trade, sir, that, I hope, I may use with a safe
conscience; which is, indeed, sir, a mender of bad soles.

MARULLUS

What trade, thou knave? thou naughty knave, what trade?

COBBLER

Nay, I beseech you, sir, be not out with me: yet,
if you be out, sir, I can mend you.

MARULLUS

What meanest thou by that? mend me, thou saucy fellow!

COBBLER

Why, sir, cobble you.

FLAVIUS

Thou art a cobbler, art thou?

COBBLER

Truly, sir, all that I live by is with the awl: I
meddle with no tradesman's matters, nor women's
matters, but with awl. I am, indeed, sir, a surgeon
to old shoes; when they are in great danger, I
recover them. As proper men as ever trod upon
neat's leather have gone upon my handiwork.

FLAVIUS

But wherefore art not in thy shop today?
Why dost thou lead these men about the streets?

COBBLER

Truly, sir, to wear out their shoes, to get myself
into more work. But, indeed, sir, we make holiday,
to see Caesar and to rejoice in his triumph.

MARULLUS

Wherefore rejoice? What conquest brings he home?
What tributaries follow him to Rome,
To grace in captive bonds his chariot-wheels?
You blocks, you stones, you worse than senseless things!
O you hard hearts, you cruel men of Rome,
Knew you not Pompey? Many a time and oft
Have you climb'd up to walls and battlements,
To towers and windows, yea, to chimney-tops,
Your infants in your arms, and there have sat
The livelong day, with patient expectation,
To see great Pompey pass the streets of Rome:
And when you saw his chariot but appear,
Have you not made an universal shout,
That Tiber trembled underneath her banks,
To hear the replication of your sounds
Made in her concave shores?
And do you now put on your best attire?
And do you now cull out a holiday?
And do you now strew flowers in his way
That comes in triumph over Pompey's blood? Be gone!
Run to your houses, fall upon your knees,
Pray to the gods to intermit the plague
That needs must light on this ingratitude.

Julius Caesar, I. i. 1–55

Julius Caesar was almost certainly first performed in 1599 in the Globe Theatre, which had only recently been opened on the South Bank. The 'yard', or the standing space that surrounds the stage, would have been packed with working men and tradespeople very similar to the Carpenter and Cobbler featured in the opening moments of this play, so we can assume they had sympathetic hearing from the crowd. Furthermore, the Cobbler gets all the jokes, which would endear him. I believe that by a very clever piece of writing, the two Tribunes find themselves not only trying to control the tradesmen in the play, but also to cope with an audience that is biased against them. Shakespeare was exploiting the adversarial positions that are taken up from the opening lines to create a volatile atmosphere that is appropriate to the situation and theme of the play.

I've often said that a verse line equips the actor well to control a situation and here is no exception. The Tribunes are formidable opponents and display considerable powers of oratory. Read the whole scene aloud, preferably with a partner reading the Carpenter and Cobbler lines, and pay particular attention to the shape of the verse, to the line endings, to the questions that need to be asked transitively, to the alliterations and to all the rhetorical devices we have worked on through these chapters. Try this a couple of times to get a strong sense of using the language to deal with the crowd. The better you deal with the verse, the more distinct the prose will sound and the characters will become more differentiated. And, crucially, two rhythms will emerge: a heightened, more patrician rhythm and a more naturalistic rhythm of the streets. (You may have heard that in Shakespeare's plays, the aristocrats and the gentry use verse and common folk use prose. Although in the majority of cases this is correct, there are important and frequent exceptions to the rule. In the *Henry IV* plays, Falstaff, a knight, largely speaks in prose and Hal, the Prince of Wales, follows suit in his scenes with the fat man. In *Richard II*, the Gardener speaks in verse.)

Not only the Tribunes, but also the Cobbler is playing to the crowd, both in the play and within the auditorium. He is in a holiday humour and uses his unstoppable gift for punning to avoid the Tribunes' questions and to entertain his mates. Flavius's first question 'Is this a holiday?' is not answered for twenty-eight lines! We will look at how to do prose in the next chapter; for the time being, here are one or two pointers. As in verse, play through to the full stops and avoid chopping up the lines too much. Look out for appositions and antitheses, and play these clearly. Relish the puns and word play. It may be more naturalistic, but it has shape and structure.

9

PROSE

Some years back, I was approached to organise and direct a gala evening of music, drama and dance in the ballroom at Buckingham Palace to raise money in support of young people hoping to make a career in the arts. The performers would be drawn from the major training establishments. I chose a programme of quartets selected from chamber music, opera, musical theatre, dance and drama for them to present. It was a joyous evening in which brilliant young artists gave stunning performances in Barber's *Adagio*, *Fidelio*, *West Side Story*, *As You Like It* and a new contemporary dance piece. The audience consisted of the 'great and the good' and a contingent of the eye-wateringly wealthy. In addition to raising money, we wanted to raise awareness of the importance of the arts for young people, to which end I asked Stephen Fry to make an address on this subject. Well, the technical rehearsals and dress rehearsals ran frighteningly late, so we ended up with a very short supper break. As we were chatting over sandwiches, it became clear that Stephen had not yet written a single word of what he was going to say in his speech. Occasionally he would jot down the odd phrase on a scrap of paper. Only his nonchalance reassured me.

Fast-forward to the performance and the moment arrived for Stephen to persuade these ladies and gents to shell out large quantities of cash. He stands up, still no script, and proceeds to deliver the finest argument in support of the arts that I have ever heard, an astonishing, virtuoso piece of oratory, which was recorded and subsequently published.

I find that truly amazing. Not just the ability virtually to improvise at an important event, albeit on a theme close to his heart, but to create great prose. Looking back, I have always been in awe of great speeches. When my family finally acquired a record player in the late 1950s, the first three records that entered the house were some Debbie Reynolds numbers, some songs from *Oklahoma* and the war speeches of Winston Churchill. So quite early on, I formed a passion for beautifully constructed sentences and a strong feeling for the hypnotic power that they can exercise. (I also got a liking for post-war popular American music that I have only latterly been able to indulge in my work.) I have remained fascinated by persuasive, intellectually-invigorating oratory and elegant, precise prose.

Shakespeare's prose can strike the same spine-tingling chords that his verse can. But his prose also does something very special and very important: it gives us the sound of England. He gives us the vocabulary, the rhythm, the cadence of everyday English speech in a way that communicates across the centuries far better than any recording. Why? How? Because it is distilled. It offers to you an open doorway into a different world and it is the purpose of this chapter to help you and to encourage you to walk through. I want you to read this excerpt from *Henry IV Part I*.

Rochester. An inn yard.

Enter a Carrier with a lantern in his hand

FIRST CARRIER

Heigh-ho! an it be not four by the day, I'll be
hanged: Charles' wain is over the new chimney, and
yet our horse not packed. What, ostler!

OSTLER

[Within] Anon, anon.

FIRST CARRIER

I prithee, Tom, beat Cut's saddle, put a few flocks
in the point; poor jade, is wrung in the withers out
of all cess.
Enter another Carrier

SECOND CARRIER

Peas and beans are as dank here as a dog, and that is the next
way to give poor jades the bots: this house is turned upside
down since Robin Ostler died.

FIRST CARRIER

Poor fellow, never joyed since the price of oats rose; it was the
death of him.

SECOND CARRIER

I think this be the most villanous house in all London road for
fleas: I am stung like a tench.

FIRST CARRIER

Like a tench! by the mass, there is ne'er a king christen could be
better bit than I have been since the first cock.

SECOND CARRIER

Why, they will allow us ne'er a jordan, and then we leak in your
chimney; and your chamber-lie breeds fleas like a loach.

FIRST CARRIER

What, ostler! come away and be hanged!

SECOND CARRIER

I have a gammon of bacon and two razors of ginger, to be
delivered as far as Charing-cross.

FIRST CARRIER

God's body! the turkeys in my pannier are quite starved. What,
ostler! A plague on thee! hast thou never an eye in thy head?
canst not hear? An 'twere not as good deed as drink, to break the
pate on thee, I am a very villain. Come, and be hanged! hast
thou no faith in thee?

Henry IV Part I, II. i. 1–31

The two parts of *Henry IV* present a magnificent portrait of English life in the
late sixteenth century. Together they chart the political aftermath of Henry's
seizure of the throne from Richard II. Parallel to the struggle to secure the
throne runs Hal's progress to maturity and responsibility, aided and often
impeded by his friend, mentor, fellow reveler, ersatz father, companion on
the wild side and general collaborator in all things dubious, the fat knight
Falstaff. The canvas upon which Shakespeare paints in these two plays is
immense. From the corridors of power to the highways of England, from
the king's bedchamber to the pubs of Eastcheap, from town to country, the
pageant of characters teeming through the plays is breathtaking: monarchs,
nobles, prelates, rebels, tradesmen and tradeswomen, criminals, prostitutes,
country landowners and, as in the above passage, ordinary, working men.
Each character or group of characters has a distinctive voice, and taken
together they form a vast portrait of an emerging nation.

The two characters above are carriers, what we would call lorry drivers.
They have stopped overnight at an inn in Rochester on the road from Dover

to London, have risen early and are in a hurry to get on the road. Say their speeches aloud again. Can't you hear them? Can't you see them? You could probably overhear a similar exchange in any motorway service station in the land or between a couple of cab drivers at a breakfast stop. There is a lot of grumbling going on, plenty of complaints about the service and copious gossip. They have their own rhythms, vocabulary and idiosyncratic turn of phrase. What Shakespeare has achieved is a pretty accurate slice of life, in other words, fairly naturalistic speech. His purpose is to conduct his audience right into the heart of this working world. I think the best way of starting with such a passage (after you've looked up the words you don't understand) is to repeat phrases and sentences out loud, over and over again. What you are seeking is what the French call 'la musique de la langue'. Don't worry about accent at this stage; the music will probably tell you what accent you might try. Be aware that they mostly talk in monosyllabic words, so take care not to rush. The language of the first carrier seems to be quite percussive: tat, tat, tat tat. 'Heigh-ho! an it be not four by the day, I'll be hanged'. Try this. Try and catch the flavour of it. It contrasts with the long, lazy vowels of the offstage Ostler, 'Anon, anon', clearly late out of bed and not in a hurry. Try the language of the second carrier: 'Peas and beans are as dank here as a dog'. Can you discern a difference? Perhaps his vowels are a little longer; certainly his phrasing has more flow. Look for the detail. Play with their speeches; they will teach you about the characters. The aim is to create an accurate portrait of two totally realistic working men. At the close of this scene they will disappear from the play, but you can make the memory of them indelible.

There are many reasons why Shakespeare chose to have his characters speak prose. We have looked at one and will now proceed to examine several other circumstances. The thing to remember is that his choice of form (what kind of verse, what kind of prose) is directly related to his intention with the speech or scene. So, with our carriers above, he wanted to create a realistic world, so he has them speak naturalistic prose. Thus the how is directly related to the why. So when you encounter someone who speaks entirely in prose or when you move from verse to prose, first ask yourself why. It will point you in the right direction as to how to do it.

Basically, the same techniques apply with prose as with verse. It's just that some of them are not quite so easy to spot. Prose will invariably have a clear rhythm, although it is not accented as in verse. Characters will use apposition, metaphor and word play. A character in a specific situation will have his own vocabulary and will often be quite idiomatic, a trait which is not easily expressed within the verse line. A prose speech will have a clear structure that you should learn to recognize. Not all prose is naturalistic; prose can be heightened, as we will see, and it is capable of a wide variety of expression. Prose is frequently trickier to deal with than verse. This is partly because the structure is less obvious but partly because you may be seduced into thinking 'Well, it's just like normal speech, so I don't have to do anything with it.' To this I would reply, 'The golden rule is to make the audience listen'.

Let us stay in the same play, *Henry IV Part I*, and take a speech of Falstaff. Here he is, just before the battle of Shrewsbury:

FALSTAFF

Hal, if thou see me down in the battle and bestride me, so; 'tis a point of friendship.

PRINCE HENRY

Nothing but a colossus can do thee that friendship. Say thy prayers, and farewell.

FALSTAFF

I would 'twere bed-time, Hal, and all well.

PRINCE HENRY

Why, thou owest God a death.
Exit PRINCE HENRY

FALSTAFF

'Tis not due yet; I would be loath to pay him before his day. What need I be so forward with him that calls not on me? Well, 'tis no matter; honour pricks me on. Yea, but how if honour prick me off when I come on? how then? Can honour set to a leg? no: or
an arm? no: or take away the grief of a wound? no. Honour hath no skill in surgery, then? no. What is honour? a word. What is in that word honour? what is that honour? air. A trim reckoning! Who hath it? he that died o' Wednesday. Doth he feel it? no. Doth he hear it? no. 'Tis insensible, then. Yea, to the dead. But will it not live with the living? no. Why? detraction will not suffer it. Therefore I'll none of it. Honour is a mere scutcheon: and so
ends my catechism.

Henry IV, V. i. 121–145

Now Falstaff is of the gentry, but speaks entirely in prose, with the possible exception of a line to Hal, who has just been crowned King Henry V at the end of Part II. So it is obviously not a rule that posh people speak verse and ordinary folk speak prose. So why does Shakespeare have Falstaff speak prose? First, it's worth noting that all of Shakespeare's clowns and most of his characters celebrated for their great wit speak largely in prose: Rosalind and Celia in *As You Like It*, Beatrice and Benedict in *Much Ado about Nothing*, the Fool in *King Lear*, to name but a few. Evidently there is something in how their minds work and the way they deliver their humour that is best served by the freedom (and disciplines) of prose. This is the case with Falstaff, who is a highly articulate man, trained as a lawyer and a close companion to the Prince of Wales, but whose natural demesne is the pub, the street or the brothel. He is one of those creatures who carry his world around with him, requiring all those he meets to partake of his subversive humour. He is, literally, larger than life. And a creator of great prose.

With the above speech, start with the situation and try to ascertain what he is doing. Picture the scene: a grossly fat man in full armour in the final seconds before a battle begins. He has spent his life living off his wits rather than his sword. He encounters his pal, the Prince of Wales, and a short, rather telling exchange ensues. I can't help but feel that Falstaff is very vulnerable here, which is all the more moving because he is such a life force. He asks for help, but in such a way that invites a humorous response. His self-assessment that has already been quoted in this book could not be more apposite: 'I am not only witty in myself, but the cause that wit is in other men'. (By the way, observe the perfect antithesis in that sentence from Part II. It's a great sentence to practice with.) Here, the simplest sentence with monosyllabic vocabulary touches our hearts: 'I would 'twere bed-time, Hal, and all well'. Now that's a plea that has been heard through the ages from Troy to Gettysburg, from the Somme to Iraq. I find it fascinating that often it is the funny men, the Chaplins or the Tony Hancocks, who move us most. You have to imagine the situation and play it simply, avoiding sentimentality, the antidote to true emotion.

So left alone he delivers this astonishing speech about honour, a speech that Verdi filleted out and used as the basis for a great aria in *Falstaff*, his opera of *The Merry Wives of Windsor*. Let's apply some of the techniques we have learnt. What's the headline? 'Honour' would fit the bill well, or perhaps you could take a clue from his conclusion: 'Catechism'. That would be a useful pointer to how to do the speech. A catechism is a series of questions and answers. A perfect way in. Remember when you see a question, ask it, don't state it. To help you do this, imagine you are addressing someone and pose the question in order to elicit a response, in other words, be transitive.

The speech starts with a reaction to Hal, which is perfect Falstaff because he reduces the act of dying to a pecuniary transaction: ' 'Tis not due yet; I would be loath to pay him before his day'. Even this detail may give you another small clue as to what's going on. Perhaps he is belittling death because like most of us he's frightened? I leave that up to you. This leads him on to his first question: 'What need I be so forward with him that calls not on me?' This in turn leads him onto the idea of 'honour', the badge that soldiers have worn since time immemorial. Through a series of questions and answers, he proceeds to demolish the intellectual foundation of the concept. Try the whole speech, asking the questions and answering them. You will find that one thought leads organically to the next. I would say that this is how the character's thought moves. To whom do you address the questions? I always advise my actors to really engage with the audience. Look at them. Ask them. Even risk eliciting a reaction. Now look again at the speech and see if there are any other techniques you can adapt. I believe that the whole speech is based on apposition. First, he juxtaposes the mighty concept of honour with the human cost of war. Second, he reevaluates 'honour' as merely a word, as air, of no use to the dead and corruptible by slander during life. Remember, Falstaff is a lawyer and he argues his case. These appositions need to be worked through; there is muscularity about them. Although there are no lines endings to guide you, play the energy right through the sentences. He concludes with the only metaphor of the speech: 'Honour is a mere scutcheon'. Invent it; it adds a final dash of colour. If you pursue the questions, you will get a good sense of the rhythm, but let us examine a short section in detail.

> Can honour set to a leg? no: or an arm? no: or take away the grief of a
> wound? no. Honour hath no skill in surgery, then? no. What is honour?
> a word. What is in that word honour? what is that honour? air.

Think back to our early work on the weight of words or phrases. Try balancing the question 'Can honour set to a leg?' with the little word 'No.' You have got the rhythm straight away. Do the next phrase: 'or an arm?' and balance that with 'no'. There is a subtle shift of rhythm; it's short with short. Read on. There are two longer questions, each balanced with 'no'. So he concludes that honour is just a word, which probably takes us to the middle section of the speech. He follows with two questions, which flow the one into the other and lead us to 'air', which is a breath and could be almost soundless, or if it sounds like anything, it would be the last breath of a dying man. You will get all this by balancing point with counterpoint.

Let's now take a character from the other end of the social spectrum, who, nevertheless, strikes me as a first cousin to Falstaff. Here is Bottom, released from the asses head, trying to recall the extraordinary events that took place with the Fairy Queen while he was enchanted.

BOTTOM

[Awaking] When my cue comes, call me, and I will answer: my
next is, 'Most fair Pyramus.' Heigh-ho! Peter Quince! Flute, the
bellows-mender! Snout, the tinker! Starveling! God's my life,

stolen hence, and left me asleep! I have had a most rare vision. I
have had a dream, past the wit of man to say what dream it was:
man is but an ass, if he go about to expound this dream.
Methought I was – there is no man can tell what. Methought I
was, – and methought I had, – but man is but a patched fool, if
he will offer to say what methought I had. The eye of man hath
not heard, the ear of man hath not seen, man's hand is not able to
taste, his tongue to conceive, nor his heart to report, what my
dream was. I will get Peter Quince to write a ballad of this
dream: it shall be called Bottom's Dream, because it hath no
bottom; and I will sing it in the latter end of a play, before the
duke: peradventure, to make it the more gracious, I shall sing it at her
death.

A Midsummer Night's Dream, IV. i. 198–213

Bottom's situation is as unusual and particular as Falstaff's. So start with
your imagination. What would I do if . . .? Always try to define a character's
situation as precisely as possible. Furthermore, attempt to make that situation
special. For example, when Bottom, Peter Quince and their friends meet
in Act I to consider putting on a play for the duke, make it the first time
they have ever acted. I once saw a production in which the mechanicals
were played as a seasoned, rather pretentious experimental drama group. It
was dead in the water. No charm, no discoveries and not many laughs. Make
it special.

Again, start with a headline. 'Bottom's Dream' would serve you well and,
unsurprisingly, it's found in the conclusion. In this speech, it's useful to
divide it into three: in the first section Bottom seeks his friends; in the second
section he endeavours to remember and explain his dream; in the third
section he gets the brainwave of using his dream in the play that they are
preparing. In fact, in this speech, Shakespeare offers us a neat paradigm of the
method acting process. Recall through memory; explore; utilize in action.
The simple division into three will help you tell the story and also see clearly
which bits need to be addressed directly to the audience. Although there is
no line ending, you will certainly want to pause before you embark on the
second section, beginning 'I have had a most rare vision'. Here is a marvellous
moment of recollection for Bottom and recognition for the audience. We
know what's happened! With this line, I think it's best to play through to the
end of the line, 'vision'. The word 'rare' is often stressed but this doesn't
make sense to me. There is no verse line to guide you, but if in doubt, play
through to the end of the sentence. Interestingly, the word 'vision' connects
Bottom's speech to the many themes and references to sight and perception
throughout the play; 'rare' communicates little beyond its own sense. In

the next passage, your headline word, 'dream', will guide you through like stepping stones across a stream. Try it.

> I have had a dream, past the wit of man to say what dream it was: man is but an ass, if he go about to expound this dream.

It's monosyllabic, so it can't be rushed, but there is a clear rhythm that leads you through to the third 'dream'. In this context, 'ass' is a metaphor and can be coined, but I wouldn't dwell too heavily on it. Play the rhythm through to the third 'dream'. A choice then would be to pause as a big bell rings in your skull. Ass? The next section is quite naturalistic broken speech as Bottom grapples with the enormity of what has taken place. The only way he can find to describe it is in a bit of heightened language:

> The eye of man hath not heard, the ear of man hath not seen, man's hand is not able to taste, his tongue to conceive, nor his heart to report, what my dream was.

Which of course makes him feel much better but, being Bottom, he gets it wrong. And then he has his brainwave, which is topped by a second brainwave: he'll sing it! The speech therefore grows in stature as it progresses and gives the actor a superb exit. Crescendo, not diminuendo.

Let's stick with the longer, more formal speeches for now because they present great challenges and opportunities for the actor. Here is Benedick in Much Ado about Nothing. A confirmed bachelor, he is appalled by his friend Claudio's intention to marry.

BENEDICK

I do much wonder that one man, seeing how much another man is a fool when he dedicates his behaviors to love, will, after he hath laughed at such shallow follies in others, become the argument of his own scorn by falling in love: and such a man is Claudio. I have known when there was no music with him but the drum and the fife; and now had he rather hear the tabour and the pipe: I have known when he would have walked ten mile a-foot to see a good armour; and now will he lie ten nights awake, carving the fashion of a new doublet. He was wont to speak plain and to the purpose, like an honest man and a soldier; and now is he turned orthography; his words are a very fantastical banquet, just so many strange dishes. May I be so converted and see with these eyes? I cannot tell; I think not: I will not be sworn, but love may transform me to an oyster; but I'll take my oath on it, till he have made an oyster of me, he shall never make me such a fool. One woman is fair, yet I am well; another is wise, yet I am well; another virtuous, yet I am well; but till all

graces be in one woman, one woman shall not come in my grace. Rich she shall be, that's certain; wise, or I'll none; virtuous, or I'll never cheapen her; fair, or I'll never look on her; mild, or come not near me; noble, or not I for an angel; of good discourse, an excellent musician, and her hair shall be of what colour it please God. Ha! the prince and Monsieur Love! I will hide me in the arbour.
Withdraws

Much Ado about Nothing, II. iii. 5–33

The first half of Much Ado is written almost entirely in prose, which is well suited to the house party atmosphere that Shakespeare creates. In this relaxed post-war environment, affairs of the heart can flourish and great conversationalists like Beatrice and Benedick are in their element. As the themes of the play darken, more verse is introduced. If you are ever in any doubt as to whether a speech is written in verse or prose, just look at the beginnings of lines. In verse, they will start with capital letters and in prose, lower case letters (with the obvious exception of the first word in a sentence). We will look at the impact of moving from verse to prose and vice versa, later in the chapter.

First of all, read the above speech aloud, seeking out the appositions and antitheses. This is the main feature to address. If you can get a grip of this, you will be in control of the speech. Benedick sets out his stall in the first four lines, concluding with 'and such a man is Claudio'. This is the beginning and the audience needs to understand it in order to follow the rest of the speech. Work the antitheses in these lines and, crucially, don't break it up too much; it is a single sentence. Hold the whole thought in your mind. Another tip: when you get a complex sentence like this, assume your audience is highly intelligent and mentally alert. Paradoxically, the danger of such a line is to overexplain it, which invariably loses the listener.

The next section is pretty straightforward, a before and after contrast of Claudio's behavior which he concludes with a rich banquet metaphor. Practice the counterpoints, ensuring you don't break it up too much. Now look at the transition:

May I be so converted and see with these eyes? I cannot tell; I think not: I will not be sworn, but love may transform me to an oyster; but I'll take my oath on it, till he have made an oyster of me, he shall never make me such a fool.

The key here is to precisely pose the question and then to work through your thoughts one by one, using the plumbing of the religious vocabulary: 'converted', 'sworn' and 'oath'. This will lead you to the inventory of women's assets and attributes that comprise the final section. Bear in mind that Benedick's description of the ideal woman must be invented in the moment, at each performance. I remember standing next to Michael Gambon in the queue for a cup of tea in the canteen at Stratford. The television monitor was on, showing the matinee of *Much Ado* that was playing a few feet away in the theatre. Derek Jacobi was playing Benedick and he was delivering this speech and the audience was yelping with laughter. Mike, who had just played the part rather well at the National, turned to me, shook his head, and asked, rather wanly, 'How does he do that?'

I can't answer that question. I only know that Derek had created a very special relationship with the audience; it was intimate, yet conversational.

Prose can contain the heightened as well as the conversational, and sometimes both within the same speech. Let's look at some heightened prose and consider how to play it. Here's a speech from *Hamlet*. The prince has just encountered his old school friends, Rosencrantz and Guildenstern, and in a scene full of friendly banter, written in prose, he realizes that they have been sent to spy on him by the king. At this point, they have just confessed to being sent for.

HAMLET

I will tell you why; so shall my anticipation prevent your discovery, and your secrecy to the king and queen moult no feather. I have of late – but wherefore I know not – lost all my mirth, forgone all custom of exercises; and indeed it goes so heavily with my disposition that this goodly frame, the earth, seems to me a sterile promontory, this most excellent canopy, the air, look you, this brave o'erhanging firmament, this majestical roof fretted with golden fire, why, it appears no other thing to me than a foul and pestilent congregation of vapours.

What a piece of work is a man! how noble in reason! how infinite in faculty! in form and moving how express and admirable! in action how like an angel! in apprehension how like a god! the beauty of the world! the paragon of animals! And yet, to me, what is this quintessence of dust? man delights not me: no, nor woman neither, though by your smiling you seem to say so.

Hamlet, II. ii. 294–308

The first feature to notice is the way Hamlet moves from naturalistic speech to heightened, poetic speech, and then back again. You will remember from the third chapter that an image is made more vivid by preceding or following it with quite plain language. The same applies to this whole speech.

The story of the speech is announced in the first line: 'I will tell you why'. And that's what he proceeds to do after giving a short explanation as to why they are the fortunate ones. These early lines must not be overcoloured as there is extraordinary imagery to come. Simply play the apposition: 'anticipation'/'discovery' and 'secrecy'/'moult no feather'. Look at these next lines:

> I have of late – but wherefore I know not – lost all my mirth, forgone all custom of exercises; and indeed it goes so heavily with my disposition that this goodly frame, the earth, seems to me a sterile promontory, this most excellent canopy, the air, look you, this brave o'erhanging firmament, this majestical roof fretted with golden fire, why, it appears no other thing to me than a foul and pestilent congregation of vapours.

It is one long sentence that starts naturalistically and moves into heart-stoppingly beautiful phrases. You can deduce how he is thinking. He clearly doesn't know exactly what he is going to say, but the single sentence indicates that he is in possession of the rough shape. And that shape resides in the big antithesis (beautiful world . . . pestilent vapours). So how do you achieve it? Ask yourself what he is doing. I think he is searching for an explanation; he is seeking an understanding. It is probably as much for his own benefit as that of Rosencrantz and Guildenstern. The act of searching will give you a forward drive to the lines, important in a five- or six-line sentence. Then when you get to the images ('sterile promontory', etc.), invent them as you would any metaphor. Try this section a couple of times. Endeavour to find the balance between the overall shape and the brilliant details, which need to be coined. With heightened language like this, the thorny issue of where to breathe reappears. With prose, I would advise you to breathe when you are inventing a phrase. Opera singers will often mark in their scores where they need to breathe in complex passages and it's not a bad idea to do the same with difficult texts, at least until you feel sufficiently confident to let go. As with verse, try to avoid taking too many breaths as this will make it more difficult for the listener to follow. So be bold. Perhaps the first breath is not until 'sterile promontory'. Experiment for yourself, always trying to discover how Hamlet thinks.

Look at the last section beginning with what may well be the headline:

> What a piece of work is a man! how noble in reason! how infinite in faculty! in form and moving how express and admirable! in action how like an angel! in apprehension how like a god! the beauty of the world! the paragon of animals! And yet, to me, what is this quintessence of dust? man delights not me; no, nor woman neither, though by your smiling you seem to say so.

Here I want you to notice the rhythm. The qualifying phrases are all contrapuntal. I'll list them:

how noble in reason!
how infinite in faculty!
in form and moving how express and admirable!
in action how like an angel!
in apprehension how like a god!
the beauty of the world!
the paragon of animals!

Look at the first words: 'how', 'how'; 'in', 'in', 'in'; 'the', 'the'. This gives you a shape. Group them into three. The first pair has the same rhythm, so play these together, allowing the word 'infinite' to resonate, as it will create imaginative space. The third, fourth and fifth lines are a little longer, so perhaps approach them with greater fluency. This will create more impact when you coin the two metaphors, which amplify from 'angel' to 'god'. The last pair is the most percussive. After asking a profound question, 'what is this quintessence of dust?', he ends the speech with a totally naturalistic exchange. This analysis will give you a framework with which to approach the speech. But there is no single way of interpreting this material. I want to arm you with a methodology that is based on careful reading of the text. In the heat of performance, you will have to trust your own instincts. You can, however, prepare!

You will remember that I said earlier that Shakespeare's choice of form directly relates to his dramatic intentions. If you notice a change, ask yourself why and it will point you in the right direction. Read this scene from *Antony and Cleopatra*. Enobarbus, Mark Antony's second in command, meets up with some old friends following a hastily agreed peace treaty between Antony and Caesar.

MAECENAS

Welcome from Egypt, sir.

ENOBARBUS

Half the heart of Caesar, worthy Maecenas! My honourable
friend, Agrippa!

AGRIPPA

Good Enobarbus!

MAECENAS

We have cause to be glad that matters are so well digested. You
stayed well by 't in Egypt.

ENOBARBUS

Ay, sir; we did sleep day out of countenance, and made the night light with drinking.

MAECENAS

Eight wild-boars roasted whole at a breakfast, and but twelve persons there; is this true?

ENOBARBUS

This was but as a fly by an eagle: we had much more monstrous matter of feast, which worthily deserved noting.

MAECENAS

She's a most triumphant lady, if report be square to her.

ENOBARBUS

When she first met Mark Antony, she pursed up his heart, upon the river of Cydnus.

AGRIPPA

There she appeared indeed; or my reporter devised well for her.

ENOBARBUS

I will tell you.
The barge she sat in, like a burnish'd throne,
Burn'd on the water: the poop was beaten gold;
Purple the sails, and so perfumed that
The winds were love-sick with them; the oars were silver,
Which to the tune of flutes kept stroke, and made
The water which they beat to follow faster,
As amorous of their strokes. For her own person,
It beggar'd all description: she did lie
In her pavilion – cloth-of-gold of tissue –
O'er-picturing that Venus where we see
The fancy outwork nature: on each side her
Stood pretty dimpled boys, like smiling Cupids,
With divers-colour'd fans, whose wind did seem
To glow the delicate cheeks which they did cool,
And what they undid did.

Antony and Cleopatra, II. ii. 179–211

Notice how the conversation moves from friendly greetings to general enquiries about life in Egypt, to the real centre of interest: Cleopatra! This is wonderful writing! We learn volumes about the characters and the situation. Enobarbus is evidently excellent company and is more than happy to entertain his friends with juicy tales of life by the Nile. Maecenas and Agrippa, followers of the more ascetic Octavius, are clearly gagging for good gossip. Enobarbus in no way disappoints them. He blithely embellishes the hyperbole and exaggerates the tall tale like a good tabloid journalist. But when it comes to a description of Cleopatra herself, he delivers an account that is almost beyond beauty and reveals great sensitivity in the speaker. It is quite unexpected and does great credit to both Cleopatra and Enobarbus. There is undoubtedly a mighty appetite for any report of Cleopatra; she appears to enjoy the status of a Jackie Kennedy, a Princess Diana and a Britney Spears all rolled into one. But at the same time she commands real respect. Furthermore, the contrast between the austere life of Octavian Rome and the sybaritic lifestyle of Egypt is highlighted.

The switch from prose to heightened verse is the key element in achieving all this. First of all, the rhythm changes to a more accented pulse and to the pentametric form. The tone changes from the conversational to the more formal. The language in the verse is distinctive, distilled and potent. It is almost like an act of worship and sits in sharp contrast to the matey atmosphere of the earlier prose section. It elevates Cleopatra and enables us to understand how a living legend is created.

Enobarbus' language is, of course, quite highly flavoured right from the start. He adds the epithet 'Half the heart of Caesar' to Maecenas, and presses the envy button with his contrapuntal description 'we did sleep day out of countenance, and made the night light with drinking'. The colourful language continues with the 'fly by an eagle' metaphor and the word 'pursed'. Then the simplest words in the passage before he embarks on the verse: 'I will tell you'. And he is straight in with a fabulous metaphor that elevates the situation: 'The barge she sat in, like a burnish'd throne'. The prose dialogue preceding this is good to work on for characterisation and phrasing – play to the ends of the sentences! The verse speech is a great and rewarding challenge. Look out for appositions, metaphor, line endings, word play and all the elements we have discussed.

Finally, we should take a quick look at some prose from a mad scene. Shakespeare's mad characters invariably speak in prose, although Ophelia also uses snatches from several songs. This is Lady Macbeth, observed by her Gentlewoman and a Doctor.

Enter LADY MACBETH, with a taper

GENTLEWOMAN

Lo you, here she comes! This is her very guise; and, upon my
life, fast asleep. Observe her; stand close.

DOCTOR

How came she by that light?

GENTLEWOMAN

Why, it stood by her: she has light by her continually; 'tis her command.

DOCTOR

You see, her eyes are open.

GENTLEWOMAN

Ay, but their sense is shut.

DOCTOR

What is it she does now? Look, how she rubs her hands.

GENTLEWOMAN

It is an accustomed action with her, to seem thus washing her hands: I have known her continue in this a quarter of an hour.

LADY MACBETH

Yet here's a spot.

DOCTOR

Hark! she speaks: I will set down what comes from her, to satisfy my remembrance the more strongly.

LADY MACBETH

Out, damned spot! out, I say! – One: two: why, then, 'tis time to do't. – Hell is murky! – Fie, my lord, fie! a soldier, and afeard? What need we fear who knows it, when none can call our power to account? – Yet who would have thought the old man to have had so much blood in him.

DOCTOR

Do you mark that?

LADY MACBETH

The thane of Fife had a wife: where is she now? – What, will these hands ne'er be clean? – No more o' that, my lord, no more o' that: you mar all with this starting.

DOCTOR

Go to, go to; you have known what you should not.

GENTLEWOMAN

She has spoke what she should not, I am sure of that: heaven
knows what she has known.

Macbeth, V. i. 18–46

The key to Lady Macbeth's speeches is to find precise connections between
her words and real or reported events in the play. If you look carefully, you
will discover that every single phrase refers to a specific event and, taken
separately, are quite sane. It is the context and the sequence that betray her
insanity. It's as if she has collected photographs of pivotal events from her
life, ripped them into tiny pieces and thrown them up into the air. She then
picks them up in a seemingly random order. So having identified the memories, you have to create an inner logic, a sequence for their delivery. These
memories, these scraps of old photographs, must have a highly potent emotional significance. They are selected emotional memories – triggers, if you
like. Such a scene calls for a creative meeting of the two traditions we talked
of earlier, the Stanislavskian, almost Freudian, and the Shakespearean.

Such scenes require acting of the highest order and it is no wonder that
they are often regarded as great opportunities for virtuosity. I would counsel
a methodical approach. First, get the memories accurate. Second, ask yourself

Sinéad Cusack as Lady Macbeth at the Royal Shakespeare Theatre, 1986. Photo:
Reg Wilson © Royal Shakespeare Company

what she is doing, moment by moment. (For example, is she making Macbeth aware of the great danger by warning him?) Third, pay attention to the rhythm as you would in any other prose speech. Take a look at these lines:

> Out, damned spot! out, I say! – One: two: why, then, 'tis time to do't. – Hell is
> murky! – Fie, my lord, fie! a soldier, and afeard? What need we fear who
> knows it, when none can call our power to account? – Yet who would have
> thought the old man to have had so much blood in him.

The first words are presumably connected to the action of hand washing and could be wrung out or spat out. The 'one: two' is listening to a bell so will have a sustained rhythm. This is followed by four short phrases, including the terrifying 'Hell is murky!' At this moment, she is actually there. Then we get a longer question, really posed, and finally, in a totally different direction, another longer sentence. So there is a whole variety of rhythms in this short speech. Your job is to match them to her complex psychology.

In conclusion, my advice is to tackle prose speeches with the same degree of scrutiny as you would a passage of verse. Try to be methodical. Identify what kind of prose it is: naturalistic or heightened. Then seek out all the features of Shakespeare's craft that you have learnt about in these pages. The same maxim applies as to verse: make the audience listen.

10

SOLILOQUY

Talking to the audience

In order to understand how to do a soliloquy, we must start with the audience.

The front row of the Dress Circle in the Royal Shakespeare Theatre (RST), now demolished, was known as 'Death Row' among the creative teams of directors, designers and choreographers. After weeks in a studio, the whole company would move into the theatre for technical rehearsals and dress run-throughs. The 'creatives' would camp out in the stalls ('orchestra' in the US), in close proximity to the lighting desk. For the first preview in front of an audience we would move upstairs to the Dress Circle, in order to get a better perspective on the show. It's like switching to long shot after working almost exclusively in close and medium shot. It allows you to observe the whole event with more clarity: you can tell when the storytelling is imprecise or confused; where the staging is clumsy or dull; and where the lighting, costuming or decor can be improved. But crucially, the first preview brings in the first paying audience and, without fail, this acts like a gigantic searchlight playing on every aspect of the proceedings. Especially the acting.

I love this stage in the process. It's when you notice everything that's wrong. Every fault, weakness or incompetence just jumps out and emphatically smacks you around the face. It can be a *nightmare* – which is why row A of the Dress Circle was known as 'Death Row'. I am not, however, a masochist. As well as revealing all the blemishes and wrinkles, the presence of an audience will teach you the way forward and it will set the agenda for the remainder of the rehearsals. One of the signs of a true director is his ability to read the previews. To a large extent, this is a skill that can be learnt. There are, however, directors who appear to be of the view that audiences are a bit of a nuisance and that the actors should do everything in their power to ignore them. I find this not only patronising and insulting, but also antipathetical to what I believe the act of theatre to be. For me, there is no theatre without the audience; actors' playing for themselves is sterile and self-indulgent. At best, it is therapy. There is a circle of creativity that connects the text with the actor and with the public. Our work in rehearsal is incomplete until we get an audience. The individual in the darkened theatre is not just a consumer; he is a contributor. In a large space like the RST, the Olivier or Shakespeare's own Globe Theatre, the audience is a mighty presence that has the power to shape an event. A good actor will be open to the audience and will have the skill to take them on a journey that will be enhanced by their contribution.

Whatever preparation is undertaken, the move from studio to auditorium can be highly traumatic for the acting company. That which seems to be the quintessence of truthfulness in the rehearsal room can often, quite simply, not communicate. An example is burned in my memory. One autumn evening I sat in Death Row with my team for the first preview of my production of *Macbeth* in unusually optimistic mood. Jonathan Pryce, the eponymous hero, had built a spellbinding character in rehearsal: dangerous, vulnerable, sexy, full of spontaneity and brilliant insights into the text. Actors and staff unconnected with our production had slid into the studio to watch him. That night, the house was packed and the audience was evidently jumping out of their skin with excitement. Then slowly, inexorably and painfully, we lost them. First of all, the odd cough, then a shuffle, then even a giggle. They were restless. We earned a generous but unenthusiastic response. Major gloom! I couldn't work it out. Jonathan was doing exactly what he did in the Ashcroft room, but it wasn't getting across in the theatre. Driving home that night, the penny dropped. Part of the genius of his interpretation was the creation of a vortex of concentration that fuelled and drove his actions. This was especially true of his many soliloquies, which he played entirely to himself, looking at the ground most of the time. The following evening saw a transformation. He looked at the audience, he engaged with us, confided in us, scared the life out of us. He took us on a journey. Standing ovation!

So with soliloquies, it's not just a case of delivering the lines looking out front (although this can help.) You have to engage with us. How? What does this mean?

Well, start off by asking what is a soliloquy (or 'monologue', as I usually refer to them)? Try this: A character is left alone and expresses his thoughts out loud. He is overheard by a group of people (the audience) who we pretend are not there. This is what we attempted in *Macbeth*. On that occasion it didn't work, although it may have been more successful in a small theatre. In more intimate circumstances we may have felt that we were inside

Jonathan Pryce as Macbeth at the Royal Shakespeare Theatre, 1986. Photo: Reg Wilson © Royal Shakespeare Company

Macbeth's head or were witnessing something terrible, like voyeurs. I think this is a valid approach, but it limits the scope of audience engagement. A fundamental differentiation between Shakespeare and the school of play-wrighting that emerged at the end of the nineteenth century is the way he exposed the inner self in public. The work of Ibsen and Strindberg lead directly to film, which is basically a private medium; you have no need of any other human being to engage with it. Shakespeare's work is essentially a public theatre; a person's private thoughts, even their inner torment are public events. (This is why, for me, Shakespeare is a political playwright.) He juxtaposes the public man with the private man, which is hugely exciting for an audience. When the character is left alone he doesn't just express his thoughts, he must *share* them. Such exposure requires great courage and skill from the actor, but I believe it is enormously satisfying.

The confidence required to open yourself in this way to an anonymous crowd cannot be taught. However, you can prepare yourself to a large extent by defining the purpose of a soliloquy and empower yourself by embracing the skills we have worked on earlier chapters.

I think there are probably four different categories of soliloquy:

1   The soliloquy in which you attempt to solve a particular problem.
2   The soliloquy in which you attempt to persuade the audience of some-thing or other.

3   The soliloquy in which you undertake an existential exploration.
4   The comic monologue.

We will examine each of these categories separately. You will discover that some soliloquies span two or more of the above, but there is an acid test that you should apply to all cases: What is the difference in my character or in the situation between the beginning and the end of the speech? This is a discipline I learnt in the musical theatre. I would ask myself: How does this song advance the story? What's the difference between the beginning and the end? It's instantly adaptable to straight theatre: How does this monologue advance the story? What would be missing if I cut it out completely? As always, we are looking for clear storytelling and dynamic action.

Let's start with a speech from the first category. This is Isabella from *Measure for Measure*. She has twice visited Angelo, the duke's deputy, who is now in sole charge of the state, to plead for her brother's life. He faces the death sentence for fornication. Angelo presents her with a terrible ultimatum:

> Redeem thy brother
> By yielding up thy body to my will;
> Or else he must not only die the death,
> But thy unkindness shall his death draw out
> To lingering sufferance.
>
> *Measure for Measure*, II. iv. 163–168

She is left alone.

ISABELLA

To whom should I complain? Did I tell this,
Who would believe me? O perilous mouths,
That bear in them one and the self-same tongue,
Either of condemnation or approof;
Bidding the law make court'sy to their will:
Hooking both right and wrong to the appetite,
To follow as it draws! I'll to my brother:
Though he hath fallen by prompture of the blood,
Yet hath he in him such a mind of honour.
That, had he twenty heads to tender down
On twenty bloody blocks, he'ld yield them up,
Before his sister should her body stoop
To such abhorr'd pollution.
Then, Isabel, live chaste, and, brother, die:
More than our brother is our chastity.

I'll tell him yet of Angelo's request,
And fit his mind to death, for his soul's rest.
Measure for Measure, II. iv. 171–187

This is a magnificently dramatic speech. Angelo has put her in an impossible position! I have stood at the back of the auditorium during the interval and heard kids violently arguing about what she should do. It raises vital questions about public and private morality.

This is a necessary, urgent soliloquy. Isabella is attempting to solve a life or death problem and she uses the monologue to work out what she should do. There is a stunning difference between the beginning and the end of the speech, which is why it is so dramatic. It is active, it is dynamic and the way it is written allows the audience immediate access to her dilemma. She starts with two questions:

To whom should I complain? Did I tell this,
Who would believe me?

The secret here is to really pose the question. Don't assume you know the answer. Think it through. The brain engages in a very particular way when the question is not rhetorical. If you search for the answer then the audience will search for the answer. They are engaged. You can look them straight in the eye if you wish or you can share the question with them – it doesn't matter which, as long as it's not closed off and private. I believe there is special significance in making the audience think about this one. If you live in a society governed by an absolute ruler or, worse, a tyrant, there is no recourse to justice and no one to hold the executive to account. This was, of course, to become the central political issue of the seventeenth century and Shakespeare could not but be aware of the emerging debate. It remains a fundamental issue to this day in many parts of the world. So Isabella's question is political.

Now apply what you have already learnt to this speech. It clearly has a beginning, a middle and an end. I would say that part one takes you through to her resolve to visit her brother; part two tells us what she is going to do when she gets there; part three, begins 'Then, Isabel'.

Look at the first section:

To whom should I complain? Did I tell this,
Who would believe me? O perilous mouths,
That bear in them one and the self-same tongue,
Either of condemnation or approof;
Bidding the law make court'sy to their will:

> Hooking both right and wrong to the appetite,
> To follow as it draws! I'll to my brother:

You might say quite reasonably: 'If I'm going to really consider these questions at the beginning, then I'll need to take my time. I'll need to take pauses.' To which I'll answer, 'Learn to think on the line. Think and speak at the same time.' And as I've said before, you can always pause at the line endings. It might be interesting here to take a moment after 'Did I tell this'. Certainly avoid pausing after 'believe me' not just because the rhythm runs on, but the indication is that her thought runs on, indeed it probably runs away with her. She must be near panic. There's a breathlessness about the verse. Don't slow Isabella down to suit yourself, rather raise your own game to match her. During the next lines, she is grappling with Angelo's despicable behaviour. The sequence of appositions gives her argument muscularity. I've always felt that she would make a brilliant lawyer! She arrives at a plan of action, almost with relief. 'I'll to my brother' finishes the line. Read on:

> Though he hath fallen by prompture of the blood,
> Yet hath he in him such a mind of honour.
> That, had he twenty heads to tender down
> On twenty bloody blocks, he'ld yield them up,
> Before his sister should her body stoop
> To such abhorr'd pollution.

This is one sentence, one developing thought. Keep sharing with the audience. We don't know him as well as you so you must make us understand. As an exercise, try and do this whole sentence on a single breath. Don't worry if you can't do it. What I want you to sense is the forward motion of the language. The line 'To such abhorr'd pollution' is a short line. This indicates a pause. You can either take this pause after the line or, perhaps more exciting, you could take a full moment after 'stoop' before you deliver these words, full of disgust, 'abhorr'd pollution'. This is the visceral gut response of the abused, of the rape victim; this choice would make sense to me of her decision.

In the final section she has arrived at her decision, her action is complete and she feels so much calmer:

> Then, Isabel, live chaste, and, brother, die:
> More than our brother is our chastity.
> I'll tell him yet of Angelo's request,
> And fit his mind to death, for his soul's rest.

Nothing runs over; each thought occupies a single line. Two simple appositions tell the story and the conclusion is wrapped up by a neat rhyme. (Some pedants might even tell you that 'die' rhymes with 'chastity', which would truly package the ending, but I think in the twenty-first century this is unacceptable and unnecessary.) Isabella has arrived at a safe haven. She has argued through her hideous problem in public with no great colour, no metaphors, just good strong argument.

Now let's tackle the second category: the soliloquy in which you attempt to persuade the audience of something. A good example of this is in *Richard* III where Richard of Gloucester encounters Lady Anne en route to the funeral of her father-in-law, Henry VI. Despite having murdered both King Henry and his son Edward, Anne's husband, Gloucester sets about persuading her to become his mistress. Eventually she accepts his ring and abandons the funeral. Gloucester is left alone.

GLOUCESTER

Was ever woman in this humour woo'd?
Was ever woman in this humour won?
I'll have her; but I will not keep her long.
What! I, that kill'd her husband and his father,
To take her in her heart's extremest hate,
With curses in her mouth, tears in her eyes,
The bleeding witness of her hatred by;
Having God, her conscience, and these bars against me,
And I nothing to back my suit withal,
But the plain devil and dissembling looks,
And yet to win her, all the world to nothing!
Ha!
Hath she forgot already that brave prince,
Edward, her lord, whom I, some three months since,
Stabb'd in my angry mood at Tewksbury?
A sweeter and a lovelier gentleman,
Framed in the prodigality of nature,
Young, valiant, wise, and, no doubt, right royal,
The spacious world cannot again afford
And will she yet debase her eyes on me,
That cropp'd the golden prime of this sweet prince,
And made her widow to a woeful bed?
On me, whose all not equals Edward's moiety?
On me, that halt and am unshapen thus?
My dukedom to a beggarly denier,
I do mistake my person all this while:

Upon my life, she finds, although I cannot,
Myself to be a marvelous proper man.
I'll be at charges for a looking-glass,
And entertain some score or two of tailors,
To study fashions to adorn my body:
Since I am crept in favour with myself,
Will maintain it with some little cost.
But first I'll turn yon fellow in his grave;
And then return lamenting to my love.
Shine out, fair sun, till I have bought a glass,
That I may see my shadow as I pass.

Richard III, I. ii. 215–250

It's evident from this speech that Richard is a true force of nature. He can barely contain his glee at his conquest and his exuberance is quite infectious. It's this irrepressibility coupled with a dazzling wit that makes the role so attractive to actors. Furthermore, you don't need matinee-idol looks to qualify; Richards come in all shapes and sizes.

From the very first line of the play, 'Now is the winter of our discontent', Richard creates a special relationship with the audience. He confides in us, he shocks us, he makes us laugh, he gloats about his exploits and he boasts about the dreadful deeds he is planning. He has an unusual number of monologues and they are all fairly lengthy. He conceals nothing from us and over the course of the play he builds up a bond, almost a mutual dependency with the audience. As the death toll rises, we find ourselves uncomfortably intimate with this mass murderer. We are skin to skin with a killer.

All this is, of course, totally deliberate on Shakespeare's part. The audience is not just a consumer of events but a player in the complex morality of the dynastic struggle that is taking place. The needful relationship that the writer builds up implicates us.

Now this is a monologue that unquestionably needs an audience. We have just witnessed an outrageous episode: a woman, recently widowed, being seduced at her father-in-law's funeral. Richard turns to us and makes us party to his delight. He refuses to countenance any disapproval. He puts his arm round us, takes us into a bar, buys us a drink and makes us his pal. Look at the mechanics of what he does.

He kicks off with a pair of questions, a device with which we are familiar. An identical rhythm leads us directly to the progression of 'woo'd' and 'won'. Even Richard can hardly believe his luck! Then a short phrase 'I'll have her'. It's hard not to get a laugh there. But in the very moment of laughter, he finishes the line with the shocking 'but I will not keep her long'. So in the first three lines you will have appalled and delighted the audience in equal measure. Clearly this speech cannot be done looking at the floorboards. You must have a totally open and frank relationship with the house. Build the rapport. Read the next section.

> What! I, that kill'd her husband and his father,
> To take her in her heart's extremest hate,
> With curses in her mouth, tears in her eyes,
> The bleeding witness of her hatred by;
> Having God, her conscience, and these bars against me,
> And I nothing to back my suit withal,
> But the plain devil and dissembling looks,
> And yet to win her, all the world to nothing.
> Ha!

What do you notice? What is the most important feature? I think it's the length of the sentence, which is eight lines. It means that you must play the thought through to 'nothing'. On the way, you can throw colour at the alliterations and muster as much savagery and glee as you wish, but keep your eye on the goal. This leads directly to the triumphant cry, 'Ha!' It stands alone on the line, a moment of naked power.

He embarks on the next section with more questions, of which the second is a seven-liner.

> Hath she forgot already that brave prince,
> Edward, her lord, whom I, some three months since,
> Stabb'd in my angry mood at Tewksbury?
> A sweeter and a lovelier gentleman,
> Framed in the prodigality of nature,
> Young, valiant, wise, and, no doubt, right royal,
> The spacious world cannot again afford
> And will she yet debase her eyes on me,
> That cropp'd the golden prime of this sweet prince,
> And made her widow to a woeful bed?
> On me, whose all not equals Edward's moiety?
> On me, that halt and am unshapen thus?

Questions engage the audience. This time he uses them as a giant form of antithesis between the 'brave prince' who was 'Young, valiant, wise, and, no doubt, right royal' and himself. Try this section for yourself. Play the thoughts through to the question mark but allow yourself enough time, space and colour to fully sing the praises of young Edward. The second question takes you to the heavily accented, alliterated line: 'And made her widow to a woeful bed?' The last two lines of this section deliver a mighty punch; each begins with the same words, which, to my ears, sound like two heavy blows: 'On me' 'On me'. They have the same energy as the earlier 'Ha!'. This staccato rhythm only works if you have played through the last seven lines without breaking it up too much. There is a music here. The first 'On me' is followed by a contrasting, rather elegant apposition: 'whose all not equals Edward's moiety'. The second 'On me' is followed by a highly provocative question: 'that halt and am unshapen thus?' This confronts the audience with his physical disability and leads us on to the final section.

His deformity engenders some fascinating issues. An Elizabethan audience would come face to face with serious disability on a daily basis. It's likely that many of them would see it as a cause for mockery or aggression, rather than pity or understanding. Richard demands that we look at him, that we stare at him. There is an underlying challenge in the way he talks about it that would have been even more confrontational with his original audience. I have witnessed productions in which Richard is played with no deformity at all. His deformity is in his mind, we are told. Rubbish, of course! Richard's disability is part of his identity and he uses it as a weapon. In this case, having drawn attention to his 'unshapen' body and his halting walk, he proceeds to tease the audience by making fun of himself. He leads us to expect a harangue and we get wit. It's a clever reversal that further charms us.

It's worth considering which characters are given soliloquies and which are not. There is an old saying that the devil has the best tunes; this is certainly the case in many of Shakespeare's plays. Apart from Richard, there is Edmund from *King Lear*, whose 'Thou nature' monologue we have already studied. There's Iago, a very dangerous creature, in *Othello*. The first line of one of his speeches goes: 'And what's he then that says I play the villain?' Again, a question, daring the audience to pass judgment when they have been fascinated by his trickery and lies. And then there's Macbeth. All of these characters are given superior access to the audience to make their case. This is partly because we all love a story about a baddie, but also to sharpen and focus the moral issues.

In *Henry V*, the king unsurprisingly has a number of monologues. But consider who else has. The Boy who follows the camp and Pistol, the braggart soldier, each have one. Why would Shakespeare do this? I think it is because he is exploring the idea of soldiership and the Boy and Pistol give us diametrically opposed perspectives on the subject. The Boy offers us a clear-eyed critique of Pistol's cowardly behaviour and is then killed in a massacre. Pistol, having been humiliated by Fluellen for his arrogance, confides in the audience that his wife has just died. Our sympathies undergo a switch back. He then proceeds to tell us that he plans to return to England, cover some old scars with patches and claim he received them in the French wars. He's incorrigible and, like most comic characters, irrepressible. All this is only made possible by this simple, highly sophisticated device of the soliloquy.

Let's now move on to our third category: the soliloquy in which the character undertakes an existential exploration. And let us return to *Macbeth*. In the final minutes of the play, Macbeth learns of his wife's death. We have witnessed her descent into insanity and her estrangement from her husband. Shakespeare does not tell us how she died. Here is Macbeth's response to the news.

MACBETH

Wherefore was that cry?

SEYTON

The queen, my lord, is dead.

MACBETH

                           She should have died hereafter;
There would have been a time for such a word.
To-morrow, and to-morrow, and to-morrow,
Creeps in this petty pace from day to day
To the last syllable of recorded time,
And all our yesterdays have lighted fools
The way to dusty death. Out, out, brief candle!
Life's but a walking shadow, a poor player
That struts and frets his hour upon the stage
And then is heard no more: it is a tale
Told by an idiot, full of sound and fury,
Signifying nothing.

                       Macbeth, V. v. 15–27

I suppose that, strictly speaking, this is not a soliloquy as there is a servant on the stage. To all intents and purposes, however, this is a monologue in which the character explores the very meaning of his existence. By this point in the story, Macbeth is isolated and emotionally exhausted by the bloodshed and the horrific visions that haunt him. Apart from the odd servant, he has no one left but the audience, and it is the audience that, through soliloquy, has been his constant companion. So it is no wonder that he shares these, his bleakest thoughts, with us. Again he needs us, but not in a neurotic way to solve some particular problem, but in a condition of lucid reflection. For me, this is his most private statement and we, the audience, are privileged to share it, however ghastly his deeds.

As you read through this monologue, observe how one thought leads logically to the next. It is like a chain of pearls. 'hereafter' leads you to 'To-morrow', which leads you through 'day to day' to 'To the last syllable of recorded time'. Our 'yesterdays' are 'lighted' to 'dusty death', which leads the thought to the 'candle'. 'Candles' create 'shadows', and a 'player' is a shadow 'That struts and frets his hour upon the stage'. Players tell stories, or tales, only this time,

> It is a tale
> Told by an idiot, full of sound and fury,
> Signifying nothing.

This is what I mean by an exploration. It is a private moment, shared by the audience, in which he assesses his life. Notice also that the passage is full of metaphor, which, on the one hand, gives us vivid insights into his spiritual state and, on the other hand, gives the performer useful forward energy at two key moments. Although they are based on metaphor, the first few lines have a stunning simplicity:

> To-morrow, and to-morrow, and to-morrow,
> Creeps in this petty pace from day to day
> To the last syllable of recorded time,
> And all our yesterdays have lighted fools
> The way to dusty death.

The thought and the line are one. But at this crucial juncture ('dusty death') he has an idea, a metaphor that gives him a burst of forward energy to the end of the line: 'Out, out, brief candle'. The next line is completed by another image, the 'poor player', which takes his thoughts through to the end of the speech. For Macbeth, this is journey's end; it signifies nothing.

Stay with Macbeth for now and look at a speech that is both an existential exploration and one that seeks a definite conclusion. Much earlier in the play, King Duncan has arrived at his castle for the night and is presently celebrating victory in battle at a lavish feast. The Witches have prophesied Macbeth's accession to the throne, but, despite his wife's powerful entreaties, he is unable to commit to the path of murder. At this point in the play, he walks away from the festivities in an agony of indecision.

MACBETH

> If it were done when 'tis done, then 'twere well
> It were done quickly: if the assassination
> Could trammel up the consequence, and catch

With his surcease success; that but this blow
Might be the be-all and the end-all here,
But here, upon this bank and shoal of time,
We'ld jump the life to come. But in these cases
We still have judgment here; that we but teach
Bloody instructions, which, being taught, return
To plague the inventor: this even-handed justice
Commends the ingredients of our poison'd chalice
To our own lips. He's here in double trust;
First, as I am his kinsman and his subject,
Strong both against the deed; then, as his host,
Who should against his murderer shut the door,
Not bear the knife myself. Besides, this Duncan
Hath borne his faculties so meek, hath been
So clear in his great office, that his virtues
Will plead like angels, trumpet-tongued, against
The deep damnation of his taking-off;
And pity, like a naked new-born babe,
Striding the blast, or heaven's cherubim, horsed
Upon the sightless couriers of the air,
Shall blow the horrid deed in every eye,
That tears shall drown the wind. I have no spur
To prick the sides of my intent, but only
Vaulting ambition, which o'erleaps itself
And falls on the other.

Macbeth, I. vii. 1–28

Society reserves a special place for child killers in its hierarchy of disgust. Macbeth orders the assassination of Banquo's son and murders all of Macduff's children ('What, all my pretty chickens and their dam at one fell swoop.') So it is a piece of daring dramaturgy on Shakespeare's part not only to forge a close relationship between him and the audience through a series of monologues, but also to give him some of the most beautiful poetry in the English language.

In the above speech, Macbeth wrestles with his indecision and uses the monologue to try to find a resolution. But in doing so, he must address fundamental issues of human responsibility and trust, and guilt and retribution.

When tackling this speech, or indeed any soliloquy, it is important to play the action and not the emotional state. He may well be in a frenzy of indecision and he may well have walked out of a royal feast to many a raised eyebrow, but ask yourself what he is doing, not what he is feeling. He is trying to resolve a crisis. Look at the language he uses. Much of

it is logical, well expressed and clearly thought out. Look at the opening
lines:

> If it were done when 'tis done, then 'twere well
> It were done quickly: if the assassination
> Could trammel up the consequence, and catch
> With his surcease success; that but this blow
> Might be the be-all and the end-all here,
> But here, upon this bank and shoal of time,
> We'ld jump the life to come.

It is not until the sixth and seventh lines that he uses metaphor. So don't
overcolour the early lines. Think them through carefully and the high
emotion will look after itself. Then coin the metaphor and it will sit proud in
the speech and communicate something particular about how Macbeth sees
himself in this moment. Notice the way the energy keeps moving forward as
the thought moves forward to the line endings on 'the assassination' and 'this
blow'. I'll repeat an important guideline from earlier in the book: the energy
will usually lie in the second half of a line, after the caesura. So don't dig in
too hard with the first few words of a line. Likewise, very often the centre of
gravity of a speech will sit in the latter part.

Read the next section:

> But in these cases
> We still have judgment here; that we but teach
> Bloody instructions, which, being taught, return
> To plague the inventor: this even-handed justice
> Commends the ingredients of our poison'd chalice
> To our own lips. He's here in double trust;
> First, as I am his kinsman and his subject,
> Strong both against the deed; then, as his host,
> Who should against his murderer shut the door,
> Not bear the knife myself.

This is an intelligent, rational debate and it should be played as such. There is
some metaphor, but the principal dynamic is antithesis, which is the main
conduit of debate in all Shakespeare's plays. So play out the argument with
the audience, lawyer-like. Now read the penultimate section:

> Besides, this Duncan
> Hath borne his faculties so meek, hath been
> So clear in his great office, that his virtues
> Will plead like angels, trumpet-tongued, against

The deep damnation of his taking-off;
And pity, like a naked new-born babe,
Striding the blast, or heaven's cherubim, horsed
Upon the sightless couriers of the air,
Shall blow the horrid deed in every eye,
That tears shall drown the wind.

Play through to the line ending at 'Duncan'; don't pause before 'Besides,', otherwise you miss the startling apposition of 'knife' and 'Duncan.' As Macbeth imagines the moment of murder, the language undergoes a massive transformation and is filled with metaphor and colour. The visions get larger and larger, more and more vivid until they almost run away with him. These need to be precisely conceived but forcefully played and the cooler and more rational you have played the earlier lines, the more power you can unleash here. He concludes the speech with another metaphor, which tells a rather prosaic tale, a downbeat:

> I have no spur
> To prick the sides of my intent, but only
> Vaulting ambition, which o'erleaps itself
> And falls on the other.

Finally, I want to take a look at the fourth category: the comic monologue. This is a form that preceded Shakespeare and survives to this day. Will Kempe, his first clown, was considered a master and was entrusted with the creation of many of the comic roles in the company until he was fired, partly as a result of the darkening of tone and the increased complexity of Shakespeare's comedies. The English music hall in the nineteenth and twentieth centuries was blessed by the genius of such performers as Robb Wilton and Stanley Holloway. The tradition continues in contemporary theatre and television in the work of the so-called 'alternative' comedians and their founding father, Lenny Bruce. Here is Launce, accompanied by his dog Crab, from *The Two Gentlemen of Verona*. Launce is a servant. The speech is self-explanatory:

Enter LAUNCE, with his Dog
LAUNCE

When a man's servant shall play the cur with him, look you, it goes hard: one that I brought up of a puppy; one that I saved from drowning, when three or four of his blind brothers and sisters went to it. I have taught him, even as one would say precisely, 'thus I would teach a dog.' I was sent to deliver him as a present to Mistress Silvia from my master; and I came no sooner into the dining-chamber but he steps me to her trencher and steals her capon's leg: O, 'tis a foul thing when a cur cannot keep himself in all companies! I would have, as one should say, one that takes upon him to be a dog indeed, to be, as it were, a dog at all things. If I had not had more wit than he, to take a fault upon me that he did, I think verily he had been hanged for't; sure as I live, he had suffered for't; you shall judge. He thrusts me himself into the company of three or four gentlemanlike dogs under the duke's table: he had not been there – bless the mark! – a pissing while, but all the chamber smelt him. 'Out with the dog!' says one: 'What cur is that?' says another: 'Whip him out' says the third: 'Hang him up' says the duke. I, having been acquainted with the smell before, knew it was Crab, and goes me to the fellow that whips the dogs: 'Friend,' quoth I, 'you mean to whip the dog?' 'Ay, marry, do I,' quoth he. 'You do him the more wrong,' quoth I; ' 'twas I did the thing you wot of.' He makes me no more ado, but whips me out of the chamber. How many masters would do this for his servant? Nay, I'll be sworn, I have sat in the stocks for puddings he hath stolen, otherwise he had been executed; I have stood on the pillory for geese he hath killed, otherwise he had suffered for't. Thou thinkest not of this now. Nay, I remember the trick you served me when I took my leave of Madam Silvia: did not I bid thee still mark me and do as I do? when didst thou see me heave up my leg and make water against a gentlewoman's farthingale? didst thou ever see me do such a trick?

The Two Gentlemen of Verona, IV. iv. 1–32

Part of the charm of this scene is that, by this point in the play, we know Launce well and his dog, Crab, better. And that's really the first lesson: create a credible character who has a place in the society of the play and a function in the story. In other words, if you approach Launce as you would any other character then this monologue will have a natural place in his narrative. At the moment of Launce's entrance, an event has happened offstage and he needs to share it with the audience – this is what we would call the previous circumstances. His entrance is a gift to an actor; the moment you walk onstage with a dog, it's highly likely that the audience will laugh. Then the work begins.

Launce is telling a story with a beginning, a middle and an end. Given the likely warm reception that the dog, if not the actor, will receive, the actor can confide in the audience in the first section, which I think takes us down to 'thus I would teach a dog'. In the middle section he tells the story of what has just happened, which contains the bulk of the speech and takes us down to 'whips me out of the chamber'. In the last section he admonishes Crab for his disgraceful behaviour. Crab says nothing and maintains a haughty distance throughout. And here lies the key to the speech. The speech and indeed the whole story are predicated upon a reversal of roles. The dumb animal has assumed the status of master and Launce has taken the role of servant. Shakespeare announces this in the very first line, your headline: 'When a man's servant shall play the cur with him, look you, it goes hard'. The humour of the situation is based upon this droll hypothesis. Of course the dog won't answer back; of course the dog will occasionally look up at you with a disdainful glance and will then probably stare balefully at the audience when they laugh. And the more that Launce projects self-importance on Crab, the more this trait will appear in the animal.

The humour of the story is based upon the same hypothesis. The dog hobnobs with the posh dogs and Launce takes the punishment on his part. It's a great piece of comic writing and really does not need to be dressed up with any overacting, coarse mime or dodgy regional accents. Hold onto your basics. The prose is conversational but this does not mean that you should break up the sentences into lots of small gobbets like a modern film script. Play through the lines to the full stops and remember that the centre of gravity of a line will very often be in the second half. Visualise every detail of the story accurately and hear the different voices clearly.

Perhaps the best advice I can give you if you attempt a character like Launce is to get hold of some recordings of great comic storytellers and listen to how they do it. It doesn't matter that they are not doing Shakespeare. Get hold of a copy of Ronnie Corbett doing one of his to-camera monologues or an old sound archive of Robb Wilton. It's the phrasing that's brilliant; they often run whole sections together to get a big laugh. For instance look at this passage:

> Out with the dog!' says one: 'What cur is that?' says another: 'Whip him
> out' says the third: 'Hang him up' says the duke.

I can imagine that being delivered quite quickly on one breath, as one energy production, in a monotone, with a pause after 'duke'. You build up tension and anticipation, ready for the next line: 'I, having been acquainted with the smell before'. Take another pause there; big laugh. Try it!

The soliloquy is, of course, a paradox. On the one hand, a character expresses his private thoughts. On the other hand, these thoughts must be made public to achieve any real dramatic currency. In many ways, the soliloquy is the defining feature of Shakespeare's drama because that public/private dynamic pervades his work. A Shakespeare play is a public event that requires a lively and continuous engagement with an audience. I once heard an experienced RSC actor describing this as 'bouncing dialogue off the audience back to your fellow actor'. It's a thought-provoking concept.

11

DIALOGUE

Actions and reactions

In this chapter I want to arm you with a practical, dynamic approach to dialogue. Furthermore, I want to encourage you to view it not just as a conversation between two or more characters on the stage, but as a craft, an entertainment, an art form in its own right. I want to offer you an intelligent, methodical way of approaching dialogue, which requires skills that you can learn.

Perhaps the best working definition of dialogue is shared storytelling. If every monologue tells a story then so does every dialogue. A dialogue will have a beginning, a middle and an end, it will have a structure and the story will advance measurably from the start of a section to its close. Many of the techniques we have grappled with will be present, but they will be shared between two or more characters. The ball will be passed between you to a common end. We have to appreciate the importance of teamwork in this context; you rely upon one another for the delivery of the story and the quality of the exchange. We will learn to notice all these things.

The ancient Greeks had a different but quite useful definition of dialogue. They saw it as a formal exchange that offered both entertainment and instruction. I find it exciting to regard a conversation as entertainment; it is a challenge and an opportunity. By this I don't mean just witty banter that one might hear in a Noel Coward play, but well constructed, well delivered exchanges that bear some scrutiny. Listen out for good dialogue on television or on film. There was a golden era of cinema writing in the early 1970s with

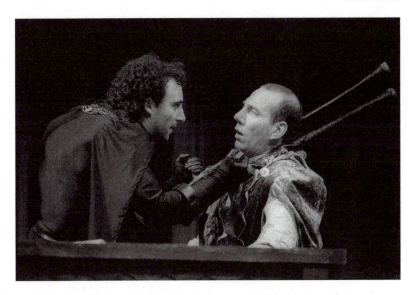

Tony Sher as Richard and Pete Postlethwaite in *Richard III* at the Royal
Shakespeare Theatre, 1984. Photo: Reg Wilson © Royal Shakespeare Company

movies such as *The Conversation, Serpico* and *All the President's Men* which boast
wonderful nuggets of dialogue.

And 'instruction' is an interesting word in this context. Ask yourself
whether a particular piece of dialogue is about something. What is its subject? I would suggest that in a great piece of writing – in theatre, film or the
novel – all dialogue somehow feeds and throws light upon the central ideas
of the work. Perhaps this is another definition for classical. We will look out
for this as we examine different passages.

Before we embark, here are some basic rules of dialogue. First, learn to
listen. Sounds absurdly simple but really try to hear the other person's lines
for the first time each time you hear them. In the Romeo and Juliet "sonnet"
dialogue you are entirely dependent on the particular words used by the
other character for your responses. Furthermore, if you listen, then you have
a fair chance that the audience will listen. Second, learn to be sensitive to
nuance and variations in performance. Dialogue is shared storytelling, so if
your colleague changes the way he delivers a line or creates a thought, then
you must adapt what you are doing in response. This is one of the great joys
of acting, especially in the context of a run or series of performances. Third,
learn to speak aloud your thoughts (avoid the dreaded think/pause/speak
syndrome). Fourth, avoid soggy cues. By this I mean don't drop the last word
of your speech because it becomes extremely hard for your partner to

respond positively. Pass the baton! Fifth, be responsible; if your partner has a metaphor or an idea that is dependent on something you say, tee it up for him.

A good place to start is function. What is the function of a piece of dialogue or a scene? How does it advance the story and what does it tell us about the characters? Let us take a situation in which two characters meet for the first time in a play. This is the first meeting between Romeo and his best friend, Benvolio. The fight between the Montagues and the Capulets has just taken place and Romeo's parents have expressed to Benvolio their concern about their son's melancholy mood.

BENVOLIO

Good-morrow, cousin.

ROMEO

        Is the day so young?

BENVOLIO

But new struck nine.

ROMEO

        Ay me! sad hours seem long.
Was that my father that went hence so fast?

BENVOLIO

It was. What sadness lengthens Romeo's hours?

ROMEO

Not having that, which, having, makes them short.

BENVOLIO

In love?

ROMEO

Out –

BENVOLIO

Of love?

ROMEO

Out of her favour, where I am in love.

BENVOLIO

Alas, that love, so gentle in his view,
Should be so tyrannous and rough in proof!

ROMEO

Alas, that love, whose view is muffled still,
Should, without eyes, see pathways to his will!
Where shall we dine?

Romeo and Juliet, I. i. 157–170

So what happens, what's the story? See if you can put it into your own words. That's often difficult to do, so try this: What's the key line, the uncuttable line, in this exchange? I would suggest it is 'Out of her favour, where I am in love'. Romeo tells his friend Benvolio why he is so sad. Simple. That's the story! Ask yourself another question: What is the subject of this short scene? Again, here's a tip if you are unsure: What word is repeated most? No prizes, it's the word 'love', used five times in a dozen lines. This plugs the scene directly into the theme of the play: love.

Let's quickly analyse how it's written. In the first exchanges, the two best friends share the pentameters:

BENVOLIO

Good-morrow, cousin.

ROMEO

　　　　　　　Is the day so young?

BENVOLIO

But new struck nine.

ROMEO

　　　　　　　Ay me! sad hours seem long.

So when playing this, you must deliver clear cues and be tight on each other's rhythms. This will get the scene off to a good brisk start and also, subliminally, communicate to the audience closeness between the pair. They are immediately on the same page. Notice that Benvolio's lines are conversational but Romeo's contain a hidden agenda from the outset. This creates a useful tension. Because they are written on the half-line, we know they are spontaneous. We can probably deduce that Romeo is open to talking to his buddy. Read on:

ROMEO

Was that my father that went hence so fast?

BENVOLIO

It was. What sadness lengthens Romeo's hours?

ROMEO

Not having that, which, having, makes them short.

Romeo diverts the conversation, naturalistically, to his father; Benvolio gets it back on track by his question that picks up the word 'sad' from Romeo's earlier line. Now, every line relates in some way or other to time. This is the hard-wiring of this passage; this is what you need to hear and follow through, from one actor to the other. Try the opening section, keeping the rhythm tight while taking us through the 'time' stepping stones. You won't need to emphasize every 'time' word; just be conscious of the thoughts. And remember not to bash us too hard!

There's a little example of mutual dependency in these first few lines. If the actor playing Benvolio drops the word 'lengthen' in his line, the guy playing Romeo will have no proper impulse to play his line through to the word 'short'. And the exchange depends on the apposition between these two words.

Shakespeare asks for a good regular rhythm in these lines because he is about to go right off rhythm when he introduces the main theme:

BENVOLIO

In love?

ROMEO

Out –

BENVOLIO

Of love?

This is what it's all about, so Shakespeare uses a totally different beat for emphasis. The melody returns in the next line: 'Out of her favour, where I am in love'. As I pointed out earlier, this is the centre of gravity of the scene. This section is concluded with two appositions and a rhyme that help to rule off, allowing the conversation to move onto its next phase, the brawl:

BENVOLIO

Alas, that love, so gentle in his view,
Should be so tyrannous and rough in proof!

ROMEO

Alas, that love, whose view is muffled still,
Should, without eyes, see pathways to his will!

Again, notice how the two actors are dependent upon each other for a clear reading of these few lines. Romeo picks up Benvolio's word 'view' for his reply. Benvolio, of course, should not be dropping this word as Shakespeare puts it on the end of the line.

Now look at the opening lines of *Measure for Measure*. This is the duke, addressing Escalus an old, loyal Lord:

DUKE VINCENTIO

Escalus.

ESCALUS

My lord.

DUKE VINCENTIO

Of government the properties to unfold,
Would seem in me to affect speech and discourse,
Since I am put to know that your own science
Exceeds, in that, the lists of all advice
My strength can give you.

Measure for Measure, I. i. 1–7

This is a very economical piece of storytelling that sets up the play superbly. The first thing I notice is the rhythm. It goes 'Escalus' . . . silence . . . 'My lord' . . . silence . . . It's like two bangs of a stick, which is the traditional way of starting French classical drama. Then he's into 'Of government'. This simple piece of dialogue instantly gets the audience listening as something of great import is about to happen. Straightaway, we learn who is superior in the relationship. And the rhythm sets up the word 'government', which is the subject of the speech and turns out to be the subject of the play.

Let's take another example of an opening dialogue. These are the opening few lines from the first scene between Portia and Nerissa, her waiting woman, in *The Merchant of Venice*. A character's opening scene is of especial importance. As with the *Measure* extract, look out for information and clues in the dialogue about the characters and their relationship.

PORTIA

By my troth, Nerissa, my little body is aweary of this great world.

NERISSA

You would be, sweet madam, if your miseries were in the same abundance as your good fortunes are; and yet, for aught I see, they are as sick that surfeit with too much as they that starve with nothing. It is no mean happiness, therefore, to be seated in the mean. Superfluity comes sooner by white hairs, but competency lives longer.

PORTIA

Good sentences, and well pronounced.

NERISSA

They would be better if well followed.

The Merchant of Venice, I. ii. 1–11

When approaching a character for the first time, it's a good exercise to imagine that it is a brand new play and that you are the very first person to have laid eyes on the part. This is especially important with a well-known text like *The Merchant*. Think of it as a script and not a work of literature.

Start off by looking at how it's laid out on the page: Portia has a single line of prose; Nerissa replies with a much longer speech, again in prose; then they each have a line of identical length. That itself tells us something. It's as if they come together at that point. Now read it through, out loud. Portia opens with a weary statement of how she feels, expressed through apposition ('little body' and 'great world'). It's a wonderful expression of her ennui. Nerissa's reply is well argued, elegant and, again, constructed in appositions. She employs a good vocabulary. Portia acknowledges her wisdom in a line with an iambic pulse (de dum, de dum) and Nerissa replies with the same pulse.

PORTIA

Good sentences, and well pronounced.

NERISSA

They would be better if well followed.

It's witty writing. 'Good' becomes 'better' and 'well pronounced' becomes 'well followed'. The simple adjustments and rhythmic variations communicate worlds to the audience and should be accurately delivered. They help to define their relationship and help to set up Nerissa as a substantial character worthy of the audience's attention. She's smart, well educated, a wise counsellor and a witty girl. I also find it revealing that in these early speeches, the characters talk of dimension ('little', 'great', 'abundance', etc.). This becomes a vital issue later in the play when exact measurements become a matter of life or death for Antonio when faced with Shylock and his knife. Obviously, you must address the matter of what they are doing in the scene, what their actions are, but a quick analysis of the text at face value, will reveal much.

In this scene, Portia and Nerissa create something together. It is a conversation that is entertaining and instructive. It introduces to the audience a team that makes a formidable impact in the play.

In *As You Like It*, the second meeting of Orlando and Rosalind takes place in the Forest of Arden. In the opening section of this scene, they construct a gorgeous verbal creation that forms the foundation to a relationship that blossoms into marriage. Orlando, smitten with love for Rosalind, has to flee the wrath of the duke; Rosalind, in turn, has to seek refuge in the Forest of Arden, disguised as a boy. Here they meet, Orlando passionate about Rosalind, and Rosalind no less in love than him, but determined to maintain her disguise.

ROSALIND

[Aside to CELIA] I will speak to him, like a saucy lackey and under that habit play the knave with him. Do you hear, forester?

ORLANDO

Very well: what would you?

ROSALIND

I pray you, what is't o'clock?

ORLANDO

You should ask me what time o' day: there's no clock in the forest.

ROSALIND

Then there is no true lover in the forest; else sighing every minute and groaning every hour would detect the lazy foot of Time as well as a clock.

ORLANDO

And why not the swift foot of Time? had not that been as proper?

ROSALIND

By no means, sir: Time travels in divers paces with divers persons. I'll tell you who Time ambles withal, who Time trots withal, who Time gallops withal and who he stands still withal.

ORLANDO

I prithee, who doth he trot withal?

ROSALIND

Marry, he trots hard with a young maid between the contract of her marriage and the day it is solemnized: if the interim be but a se'nnight, Time's pace is so hard that it seems the length of seven year.

ORLANDO

Who ambles Time withal?

ROSALIND

With a priest that lacks Latin and a rich man that hath not the gout, for the one sleeps easily because he cannot study, and the other lives merrily because he feels no pain, the one lacking the burden of lean and wasteful learning, the other knowing no burden of heavy tedious penury; these Time ambles withal.

ORLANDO

Who doth he gallop withal?

ROSALIND

With a thief to the gallows, for though he go as softly as foot can fall, he thinks himself too soon there.

ORLANDO

Who stays it still withal?

ROSALIND

With lawyers in the vacation, for they sleep between term and term and then they perceive not how Time moves.

ORLANDO

Where dwell you, pretty youth?
                    As You Like It, III. ii. 289–325

This really is a scene in which the actress playing Rosalind has to jump out of the aeroplane and hope that the parachute opens. She is truly living off her wits! I have been very lucky with this play and had the good fortune to witness two great actresses in rehearsal. My first job at the RSC was as an assistant and the first production I worked on was directed by Terry Hands with the late Susan Fleetwood as Rosalind. A few years later, I directed my own version with Juliet Stephenson. Juliet adored the role but called her character 'the mouth' as she never seemed to stop talking. Both actresses created passionate, intelligent women, willful yet vulnerable; both had the ability to handle long speeches in often-complex prose and sound as if they were making it up in the moment.

And that's the real key to this passage. It is a brilliant improvisation. Rosalind, having observed that Orlando does not particularly want company, cannot resist the opportunity to engage with him and jumps in, feet first, without a clue as to what she might say or do. All she knows is that she 'will speak to him, like a saucy lackey and under that habit play the knave with him'. She has a clear action, but not much of a plan. Celia, her friend, almost certainly disapproves. It's a risky strategy that, at first, does not go especially well. Try the opening few lines, preferably with a partner:

ROSALIND

Do you hear, forester?

ORLANDO

Very well: what would you?

ROSALIND

I pray you, what is't o'clock?

ORLANDO

You should ask me what time o' day: there's no clock in the forest.

ROSALIND

Then there is no true lover in the forest; else sighing every minute and groaning every hour would detect the lazy foot of Time as well as a clock.

Now if she genuinely has no plan, the improvisation starts almost immediately. Having hailed him, she comes up with the weediest of opening lines. She asks him the time! She may, of course, be thrown off balance by the fact that she is now in close contact with the boy she is crazy about. Sometimes it's worth varying the situation to find a way into the scene. Here, for example, you could try the scene pretending you are in a bar; he's on a stool and Rosalind slides onto the one next to him. You'll soon discover what a lame pick-up line she comes out with! Improvisations like that are not an end in themselves and can be quickly discarded as soon as you have a key into the scene.

Orlando is playing a separate action from Rosalind; he wants to be alone and has no interest in chatting to this youth. He may even go to leave after 'there's no clock in the forest'. Rosalind has to recover as quick as a flash and plays the card that is certain to hook him: 'Then there is no true lover in the forest'. We know from the fact that Orlando has written a hundred and one love poems that he has taken on the mantle of 'lover' in a mighty way. You can send up those overworked lover's clichés of 'sighing' and 'groaning' in the hope they will prick his vanity. We get a glimpse at this early stage of what her purpose turns out to be. She wants to test the mettle of his love. Is it the real thing? I doubt this is a conscious decision on her part. Instinctively, she is suspicious of the traditional lover's behaviour.

The strategy is successful; Orlando replies with the antithesis and lays the way open for Rosalind:

ORLANDO

And why not the swift foot of Time? had not that been as proper?

ROSALIND

By no means, sir: Time travels in divers paces with divers persons. I'll tell you who Time ambles withal, who Time trots withal, who Time gallops withal and who he stands still withal.

Orlando's line is printed here with two question marks, but play through to the end, with just a caesura after 'Time', just as you would on a verse line. It keeps the energy moving forward and the pressure on Rosalind. And if you are playing Rosalind, you must think as you speak. Don't pause, work out your reply and then speak – anyone can do that. Rosalind is special, brave and not frightened of making a fool of herself. Crucially, the pressure and the situation make her articulate. She finds her voice in the moment.

At this juncture, she sets herself a task, like in an improvisation game, hoping that Orlando will take her up on the challenge. Even at this point, I believe that she is unsure of exactly what she's going to say. It's a game and Orlando sets her to it. Try the 'By no means' speech a couple of times. The first line is rather bossy and expansive. Then, when she gets the idea, she changes her rhythm; she is looking to the future, so she quickens. The operative words are the verbs 'trots', 'ambles', 'gallops' and 'stands'. Think of each verb as you get to it. Use the slight variation on the last clause; there is no 'Time' used, so perhaps it flows more.

Notice that Orlando does not start in the order that Rosalind has laid out. This suggests to me that, at this point, Orlando fully embraces the game. He commences with 'trot' to throw her off balance and thereafter she never knows which circumstance she will have to address next. This allows both actors to fully participate, with Orlando trying to catch her out. The important thing is that they create a dialogue together. Rosalind needs to listen carefully and play her responses nimbly. She's fast, mercurial and clever. Seek out the appositions because, at speed, you'll need to hang on to them for dear life, otherwise Orlando and the audience will get lost. Look at this short section:

ORLANDO

Who ambles Time withal?

ROSALIND

With a priest that lacks Latin and a rich man that hath not the gout, for the one sleeps easily because he cannot study, and the other lives merrily because he feels no pain, the one lacking the burden of lean and wasteful learning, the other knowing no burden of heavy tedious penury; these Time ambles withal.

This requires quick, accurate thought and great technique. Orlando is like a bowler or pitcher who varies the speed of his delivery with every ball. Try and false foot her. Rosalind, don't allow yourself a second's hesitation. Start talking and find the ideas (the mouth!). Perhaps you alight on the word 'priest' at first, which is then immediately qualified, without hesitation, by 'that lacks Latin'. Rosalind's answer is improved by the 'rich man' idea. She has hereby set herself a double challenge, which she works through by apposition after apposition. Consider the rhythm. There is no full stop in Rosalind's speech. You will need to play the whole speech through as one developing thought, ideally in one single breath as far as 'penury'. Then you have earned a contrast: the final four words can be slowed right up.

Look at the last few speeches in the passage:

ORLANDO

Who doth he gallop withal?

ROSALIND

With a thief to the gallows, for though he go as softly as foot can fall, he thinks himself too soon there.

ORLANDO

Who stays it still withal?

ROSALIND

With lawyers in the vacation, for they sleep between term and term and then they perceive not how Time moves.

ORLANDO

Where dwell you, pretty youth?

They are shorter, which suggests to me that the pace hots up again leading to the high five moment of 'Where dwell you, pretty youth?' You can certainly vary the pace within each speech to colour it as necessary, but, overall, keep it moving. This way there will be more to celebrate when you have successfully completed the challenge. Orlando and Rosalind have built something together. They have taken a few more steps on the road to matrimony. The dialogue has most certainly been entertaining. It has been instructive as well because, while we have enjoyed her wit, she has enlightened us about that strangest of phenomena: the elasticity of time.

Let us remain with the dialogue of lovers and return to *The Merchant of Venice*. Lorenzo and Jessica have found refuge at Portia's home at Belmont. Here they create a beautiful confection that is both a celebration of their love and a musical invocation of a very special atmosphere. Like Rosalind and Orlando, the dialogue that they compose together augments their love:

LORENZO

The moon shines bright: in such a night as this,
When the sweet wind did gently kiss the trees
And they did make no noise, in such a night
Troilus methinks mounted the Troyan walls
And sigh'd his soul toward the Grecian tents,
Where Cressid lay that night.

JESSICA

                    In such a night
Did Thisbe fearfully o'ertrip the dew
And saw the lion's shadow ere himself
And ran dismay'd away.

LORENZO

                    In such a night
Stood Dido with a willow in her hand
Upon the wild sea banks and waft her love
To come again to Carthage.

JESSICA

                    In such a night
Medea gather'd the enchanted herbs
That did renew old Aeson.

LORENZO

                    In such a night
Did Jessica steal from the wealthy Jew
And with an unthrift love did run from Venice
As far as Belmont.

JESSICA

                    In such a night
Did young Lorenzo swear he loved her well,
Stealing her soul with many vows of faith
And ne'er a true one.

LORENZO

                    In such a night
Did pretty Jessica, like a little shrew,
Slander her love, and he forgave it her.

JESSICA

I would out-night you, did no body come;
But, hark, I hear the footing of a man.
                    The Merchant of Venice, V. i. 1–24

As a member of the audience, I always arrive back in Belmont in this scene with a sense of relief after the bustle of the Venetian streets and the disturbing events of the courtroom. Shakespeare can't use a long, slow, establishing shot to ease us into this magical location. He does it with words. So here, through language, he conjures the spirit of the place. There is a function in this Jessica and Lorenzo scene that is above and beyond the particular necessities of character and narrative. You could describe it as a choral function. If you are required to perform such a passage, then you must approach the text exactly as any other piece, but be aware that the play requires something particular of you at this time. With a writer of such genius, there is rarely any contradiction between the two requirements; they are consonant.

Never be afraid of stating the obvious; therein often lies the secret of a passage. Start by observing what it looks like on the page. In this scene, the characters contribute almost equal amounts: the speeches are of the same length; each character completes the half-line of the other; and there is considerable repetition. To extend the musical analogy, one could say that they are in harmony and that they hand the melody over to each other. They repeat and develop each other's motifs. Their minds are interlocked like the shared pentameters and their imaginations stimulate one another as they build classical allusion upon classical allusion.

It strikes me as a glorious illusion of young love: no other lovers have ever felt as you do, your experience is unique – which I suppose it is! Paradoxically, the exceptional nature of your love is defined by placing it in a tradition of great lovers of the past, especially from the classical tradition. So here, Lorenzo and Jessica summon the tragic lovers of the ancient world and, through particular episodes from well-known narratives, invoke the bittersweet transience of first love.

This dialogue requires a confident grasp of rhythm from both participants. Let's take the opening lines:

> The moon shines bright: in such a night as this,
> When the sweet wind did gently kiss the trees
> And they did make no noise, in such a night
> Troilus methinks mounted the Troyan walls . . .

Lorenzo's verse is quite regular to start off and it is not until he introduces Troilus that we get a trochee: dum de. Try these lines and find the change of rhythm at the beginning of line four. Inhabit Lorenzo's skin. The night is evidently overwhelmingly beautiful, but he doesn't linger or get sentimental. 'The moon shines bright' does not sit at the end of the line. The implication is that his thought moves forward to the line ending with 'in such a night as this'. This makes sense because Shakespeare wants to make those words special. Lorenzo continues in regular verse and repeats, with a slight variation, 'in such a night', which provides the perfect launch for his first classical allusion, 'Troilus'. This line also has more muscularity with its alliterated 't's and 'm's.

It's best to treat allusions or literary references as you would any metaphor. You need to coin them, think of them in the moment. Once Lorenzo has established the pattern, Jessica joins in and together they create a pageant of mythical lovers. There is both fun and romance in this game. Technically, it is all achieved on a perfectly regular pulse and you need to come in precisely on the beat in the half-line. The two actors need to be at one here. It's a challenging piece to work on because, while passing the baton at the exact moment, you also have to invent the thoughts and be absolutely real.

In a very witty and teasing way, Shakespeare turns the lovers into actors in their own play. They become both the subject of the story and the storytellers. In a quintessential piece of Shakespearean writing, their romantic idyll is interrupted by a very prosaic sound:

> I would out-night you, did no body come;
> But, hark, I hear the footing of a man.

Let us now turn our attention from dialogues that create concord to dialogues that explore contention, disagreement or even violence. In his paradigm of tragedy, Aristotle identified action as a prerequisite of tragedy, and this will usually take the form of conflict. It is important, therefore, as we examine some examples, that we identify the action of the characters. A common mistake is to pursue objectives of contention. In other words, you rarely set out to quarrel; you set out to achieve your objectives, which, if they contradict another person's objectives, will lead to conflict. Of course there are occasions when the characters are quite simply looking for a fight – for example, the opening of *Romeo and Juliet* – but these are the exception rather than the rule.

Shakespeare, a professional writer, well understood the value of conflict to the success of his plays. Let's start with the scene in *Julius Caesar* in which the co-conspirators Brutus and Cassius meet with their respective armies prior to the decisive battle with Mark Antony. We'll take the first section of the scene:

CASSIUS

Stand, ho!

BRUTUS

Stand, ho! Speak the word along.

FIRST SOLDIER

Stand!

SECOND SOLDIER

Stand!

THIRD SOLDIER

Stand!

CASSIUS

Most noble brother, you have done me wrong.

BRUTUS

Judge me, you gods! wrong I mine enemies?
And, if not so, how should I wrong a brother?

CASSIUS

Brutus, this sober form of yours hides wrongs;
And when you do them –

BRUTUS

                              Cassius, be content.
Speak your griefs softly: I do know you well.
Before the eyes of both our armies here,
Which should perceive nothing but love from us,

Let us not wrangle: bid them move away;
Then in my tent, Cassius, enlarge your griefs,
And I will give you audience.

CASSIUS

                              Pindarus,
Bid our commanders lead their charges off
A little from this ground.

BRUTUS

Lucilius, do you the like; and let no man
Come to our tent till we have done our conference.
Let Lucius and Titinius guard our door.
Exeunt the armies
BRUTUS and CASSIUS remain

CASSIUS

That you have wrong'd me doth appear in this:
You have condemn'd and noted Lucius Pella
For taking bribes here of the Sardians;
Wherein my letters, praying on his side,
Because I knew the man, were slighted off.

BRUTUS

You wronged yourself to write in such a case.

CASSIUS

In such a time as this it is not meet
That every nice offence should bear his comment.

BRUTUS

Let me tell you, Cassius, you yourself
Are much condemn'd to have an itching palm;
To sell and mart your offices for gold
To undeservers.

CASSIUS

                    I an itching palm!
You know that you are Brutus that speak this,
Or, by the gods, this speech were else your last.

BRUTUS

The name of Cassius honours this corruption,
And chastisement doth therefore hide his head.

CASSIUS

Chastisement!

Julius Caesar, IV. ii. 32–69

This is thrilling theatre. Shakespeare heightens the drama by staging their first encounter in full view of both armies and begins with much military kerfuffle. A row very nearly breaks out so they must contain the emotions and move inside the tent. So within thirty seconds we shift from wide shot to close-up – a technique that Alfred Hitchcock frequently employed in his suspense movies, by the way. Now let us consider the actions of the protagonists. It would be a mistake to think that they were both merely looking for a showdown. Brutus and Cassius are both soldiers, both willful, both independent-minded and have both risked all in the assassination of Julius Caesar. But they are different creatures. Brutus is very much the Stoic hero and believes that passionate emotions cause errors of judgment; Cassius strikes me as a character very much defined by his emotional responses to events. So Shakespeare is planning a particular kind of quarrel. Cassius will push Brutus to the very limit of his self-control; Brutus, as seen in this short extract from a lengthy scene, will confront Cassius with a harsh audit of his inadequacies and poor judgements. So, attempt to define their objectives, not through contention, but using transitive actions. Always use the word 'make'. For example, 'I want to *make* Cassius acknowledge his errors.' Given Cassius's character, a quarrel is almost certain to materialize.

With clear, transitive actions, you will find that you can closely argue the dialogue. If you want to increase the temperature of the scene, raise the stakes: make it more of a life or death encounter. Don't just throw emotion at it!

Cassius immediately announces the subject of the meeting with the last word of his first line: 'wrong'. This word is repeated on several occasions and infects the whole scene. To follow the story of the first public encounter, do the e.e. cummings-style exercise. Read out the last word of each line. Cassius's two lines end with 'wrong' and 'wrongs'. Brutus's read 'enemies', 'brother', 'content', 'well', 'here', 'us', 'away' and 'griefs'. You can read their respective actions through these words.

Inside the tent, their actions are more fully fleshed out. But what stops the row from just flaring up? Well, I believe that every action has an inner resistance. What does this mean? Well, Cassius may want a full apology and redress from Brutus, but this is tempered by the fact that he has enormous respect for Brutus, more than for any other human being. Brutus has a different philosophy but his actions are partly defined by a private grief – his wife Portia has committed suicide by swallowing fire – that he withholds for the greater part of the scene. To recap, in a dialogue, we have an action (to effect change in another person) and a resistance (something that alters or tempers that action).

Let us take this further in another scene, this time from *Measure for Measure*. Isabella, a novitiate nun, visits Angelo to plead for the life of her brother, who has been sentenced to death for fornication. The duke has given Angelo absolute power in the state. In this scene, we can also examine the impact of other characters on the main action, for her brother's friend, Lucio, accompanies her and the Provost witnesses the suit. It's a fairly long extract (the scene continues for some time), but read it carefully.

ANGELO

You're welcome: what's your will?

ISABELLA

I am a woeful suitor to your honour,
Please but your honour hear me.

ANGELO

Well; what's your suit?

ISABELLA

There is a vice that most I do abhor,
And most desire should meet the blow of justice;
For which I would not plead, but that I must;
For which I must not plead, but that I am
At war 'twixt will and will not.

ANGELO

Well; the matter?

ISABELLA

I have a brother is condemn'd to die:
I do beseech you, let it be his fault,
And not my brother.

PROVOST

[Aside] Heaven give thee moving graces!

ANGELO

Condemn the fault and not the actor of it?
Why, every fault's condemn'd ere it be done:
Mine were the very cipher of a function,
To fine the faults whose fine stands in record,
And let go by the actor.

ISABELLA

                              O just but severe law!
I had a brother, then. Heaven keep your honour!

LUCIO

[Aside to ISABELLA] Give't not o'er so: to him again,
     entreat him;
Kneel down before him, hang upon his gown:
You are too cold; if you should need a pin,
You could not with more tame a tongue desire it:
To him, I say!

ISABELLA

                    Must he needs die?

ANGELO

Maiden, no remedy.

ISABELLA

Yes; I do think that you might pardon him,
And neither heaven nor man grieve at the mercy.

ANGELO

I will not do't.

ISABELLA

                    But can you, if you would?

ANGELO

Look, what I will not, that I cannot do.

ISABELLA

But might you do't, and do the world no wrong,
If so your heart were touch'd with that remorse
As mine is to him?

ANGELO

He's sentenced; 'tis too late.

LUCIO

[Aside to ISABELLA]   You are too cold.

ISABELLA

Too late? why, no; I, that do speak a word.
May call it back again. Well, believe this,
No ceremony that to great ones 'longs,
Not the king's crown, nor the deputed sword,
The marshal's truncheon, nor the judge's robe,
Become them with one half so good a grace
As mercy does.
If he had been as you and you as he,
You would have slipt like him; but he, like you,
Would not have been so stern.

ANGELO

                    Pray you, be gone.

ISABELLA

I would to heaven I had your potency,
And you were Isabel! should it then be thus?
No; I would tell what 'twere to be a judge,
And what a prisoner.

LUCIO

[Aside to ISABELLA]
                    Ay, touch him; there's the vein.

ANGELO

Your brother is a forfeit of the law,
And you but waste your words.

ISABELLA

                    Alas, alas!
Why, all the souls that were were forfeit once;
And He that might the vantage best have took
Found out the remedy. How would you be,
If He, which is the top of judgment, should
But judge you as you are? O, think on that;

And mercy then will breathe within your lips,
Like man new made.

ANGELO

> Be you content, fair maid;
> It is the law, not I condemn your brother:
> Were he my kinsman, brother, or my son,
> It should be thus with him: he must die tomorrow.

Measure for Measure, II. ii. 26–84

This is a scene in which Isabella's action is clear and Angelo's resistance to her is fairly constant, but it is also a scene in which her inner resistance changes as the dialogue progresses. This is partly due to the timely pressure put upon her by Lucio, partly due to Angelo's immutability and partly due to a subtle shift in her moral standpoint as the scene progresses. In other words, she undergoes a moral journey as the scene develops. Isabella becomes a subtly different person through the scene. This is a human characteristic that clearly fascinated Shakespeare as it occurs throughout his plays.

Juliet Stevenson as Isabella and David Schofield as Angelo in *Measure for Measure* at the Royal Shakespeare Theatre, 1983. Photo: Joe Cocks Studio Collection © Shakespeare Birthplace Trust

Here's the opening exchange:

ANGELO

You're welcome: what's your will?

ISABELLA

I am a woeful suitor to your honour,
Please but your honour hear me.

ANGELO

                        Well; what's your suit?

ISABELLA

There is a vice that most I do abhor,
And most desire should meet the blow of justice;
For which I would not plead, but that I must;
For which I must not plead, but that I am
At war 'twixt will and will not.

ANGELO

                        Well; the matter?

ISABELLA

I have a brother is condemn'd to die:
I do beseech you, let it be his fault,
And not my brother.

PROVOST

[Aside]   Heaven give thee moving graces!

Observe how it is laid out on the page. It takes Isabella seven lines to get to the point. Twice Angelo completes her line, posing his question. When she finally puts her request, Angelo does not speak straightaway; he has a small pause during which we hear the Provost's thought. He then replies and Isabella gives up the fight:

ANGELO

Condemn the fault and not the actor of it?
Why, every fault's condemn'd ere it be done:
Mine were the very cipher of a function,
To fine the faults whose fine stands in record,
And let go by the actor.

ISABELLA

O just but severe law!
I had a brother, then. Heaven keep your honour!

What do we learn from all this? We learn that Isabella has a strong moral resistance to fornication. She is reluctant and attempts to draw a distinction between the vice and the perpetrator. Inadvertently, she gives Angelo the perfect argument with which to dismiss the case. Angelo is focused and alert, ready to come in bang on cue. Likewise, the Provost is concentrated and hangs on her every word. Isabella's last speech in this section also completes Angelo's line. There is no hesitation; she is ready to speak. She agrees with him: her brother must die.

Notice the language they use. Both speak contrapuntally and fluently, with Isabella using a very regular rhythm in her speech 'There is a vice . . .'. They both work ideas in a manner that becomes increasingly muscular as the scene progresses. I always feel that in many ways they are the perfect match!

It is Lucio who spurs her on, and all his words have a down-to-earth quality. There's nothing cerebral about it; it's urgent and life or death:

LUCIO

[Aside to ISABELLA] Give't not o'er so: to him again, entreat him;
Kneel down before him, hang upon his gown:
You are too cold; if you should need a pin,
You could not with more tame a tongue desire it:
To him, I say!

ISABELLA

Must he needs die?

ANGELO

Maiden, no remedy.

ISABELLA

Yes; I do think that you might pardon him,
And neither heaven nor man grieve at the mercy.

ANGELO

I will not do't.

ISABELLA

But can you, if you would?

ANGELO

Look, what I will not, that I cannot do.

ISABELLA

But might you do't, and do the world no wrong,
If so your heart were touch'd with that remorse
As mine is to him?

ANGELO

He's sentenced; 'tis too late.

LUCIO

[Aside to ISABELLA]   You are too cold.

Again, look at the evidence on the page: Isabella pitches back in to the argument on the half-line. There is a pause either before or after Angelo's speech that suggests he has been taken by surprise. Perhaps he has already returned to his work. The rest of this section consists of short speeches, tightly argued, often picking up the half-line. It's therefore faster. It remains contrapuntal and muscular; the temperature is clearly rising. Read through the next section once more:

ISABELLA

Too late? why, no; I, that do speak a word.
May call it back again. Well, believe this,
No ceremony that to great ones 'longs,
Not the king's crown, nor the deputed sword,
The marshal's truncheon, nor the judge's robe,
Become them with one half so good a grace
As mercy does.
If he had been as you and you as he,
You would have slipt like him; but he, like you,
Would not have been so stern.

ANGELO

Pray you, be gone.

ISABELLA

I would to heaven I had your potency,
And you were Isabel! should it then be thus?
No; I would tell what 'twere to be a judge,
And what a prisoner.

LUCIO

[Aside to ISABELLA]
                    Ay, touch him; there's the vein.

ANGELO

Your brother is a forfeit of the law,
And you but waste your words.

ISABELLA

                    Alas, alas!
Why, all the souls that were were forfeit once;
And He that might the vantage best have took
Found out the remedy. How would you be,
If He, which is the top of judgment, should
But judge you as you are? O, think on that;
And mercy then will breathe within your lips,
Like man new made.

ANGELO

                    Be you content, fair maid;
It is the law, not I condemn your brother:
Were he my kinsman, brother, or my son,
It should be thus with him: he must die tomorrow.

What's the evidence on the page? Obviously, Isabella has found her tongue and is now able to construct persuasive argument. She has two substantial speeches. Notice also that all the characters are completing half-lines; this passage needs to play as tight as a drum.

Isabella's first speech in this section contains a long sentence that displays all the weight and force of a seasoned advocate. It builds to a silence after 'as mercy does'. It could be Portia speaking! Her second speech revolves around the invocation of divine justice. She is by now dealing with large concepts and she impresses her ideas upon him by running on the thoughts over the full stops. So don't pause after the word 'remedy', press on to the line ending; don't pause after 'you are', but continue your thought on through 'O, think on that'.

After this passage, the scene takes on a whole new urgency, after Isabella has learnt that the death sentence is to be executed 'tomorrow'.

Something extraordinary has happened. We are witnessing a metamorphosis. The necessity to act, the gravity of the situation and the exposure to different company have all contributed to what can only be described as a transformation. She enters the room as a diffident nun and leaves as a confident advocate, having mightily impressed all who witnessed her. Action causes character development. Unfortunately, the same is true of Angelo, who, by the close of the scene, has changed from a man of virtue to a man of vice.

We will return to this phenomenon, which is central to Shakespeare's work.

As we move on, recap the main points: listen; hear the dialogue for the first time, every time; speak as you think; pass the baton positively; and take responsibility for your fellow performer. Finally, think of dialogue as a story told by two people.

12

COMEDY

'The course of true love never did run smooth'
A Midsummer Night's Dream, I. i. 134

I have always approached comedy as a serious art and regarded masters of the craft with awe. The masters possess meticulous technique, cunningly disguised in a relaxed spontaneity. The results of their efforts are immediately and cruelly manifest: the audience either laugh or they don't. Small wonder then that the lunchtime hubbub in the green room of the Bristol Old Vic when I started out as a director in the late 1970s was always sharply divided: unrestrained hysteria and mirth from the actors rehearsing the tragedy and intense, urgent negotiations amongst those working on the comedy.

Before you give up and turn to the next chapter, let me say this: comedy is a craft, a craft that to a considerable extent can be learnt. Of course, there are some human beings who are naturally very funny people, but that does not necessarily equip them to handle Shakespeare. Shakespeare, as we know, is a language-based artist. His humour emanates largely from words – words spoken by characters, recognisable human beings. So our approach to Shakespeare's comedy will follow our usual method: we will examine the text; we will deduce character from the text and from the function the character performs in the play; and we will look at ways of performing it.

Let's start with a few definitions. For Shakespeare, the comedy genre was inextricably bound up with marriage. The large majority of the plays that we would define as comedies feature multiple weddings or betrothals in the last act. *As You Like It*, *A Midsummer Night's Dream*, *Twelfth Night*, *Much Ado about Nothing*, *The Taming of the Shrew*, *The Merry Wives of Windsor* and *The Merchant of Venice* all contain multiple marriages in Act V, onstage or off. *Love's Labour's Lost* holds the promise of a multiple marriage in a year's time. *The Comedy of Errors*, one of Shakespeare's earliest triumphs, features at least one betrothal at the end as well as the reuniting of two more couples that have been estranged, either through ill fortune or emotional differences. Indeed the title of the play may contain a pun on 'Errors'. The pronunciation of the word 'Eros', the Greek god of love, may well have been very similar. So the meaning of the title could have been 'The Comedy of Love'.

I think that pun is quite revealing. Lysander says in *A Midsummer Night's Dream*, 'The course of true love never did run smooth'. That is a fairly accurate summary of the plot line of most of Shakespeare's comedies. So let's try a definition of Shakespearean comedy: a play that describes the journey of a couple or couples to marriage. It is the nature of that journey that is of interest to us here: along the road, the lovers encounter opposition, heartache, ecstatic moments, trials, torments and separations, all of which prepare them for a solemn promise of a life together. That journey also provides the writer and actor with boundless comic opportunities. A lover is a highly attractive character and the euphoria of love inspired much of the greatest poetry in the canon; we identify, we share, we relive our own romances. A lover, however, can also be an absurd figure. For me, one of the pleasures of Shakespeare's portrayal of love is his keen sense of the irrational, the illogical and the ridiculous, as well as the euphoric, the tender and the vulnerable.

It is not my opinion, however, that Shakespeare's portrayal of the lover somehow represents an eccentric or biased view of the world. On the contrary, the sexual instinct and its social manifestation, marriage, is the great life force; it offers the possibility of children and thus secures the future. It's the obsession of lovers that is absurd. There's an old Marx Brothers movie in which there's a shot where Groucho is striding, head down, across a busy square; we see a shapely pair of ankles in high heels cross his path at right angles. On a sixpence, Groucho makes a ninety-degree turn and follows the girl (whose face we never see) out of shot. For me, that sums up something essential about comedy: Groucho is blinkered and single-minded, but he represents a life force. He is indestructible.

The Elizabethan practice of boys playing girls parts, of course, offers Shakespeare considerable opportunity for comedy and certainly contributed to the alacrity with which so many of Shakespeare's heroines leapt into breeches. Think only of Viola and Rosalind. The fact that they were played by boys dressed as girls disguised as boys gives occasion for ambiguity and word play in their sexual encounters and a certain plangency in their love scenes. The emotions displayed by his women, however, appear to be totally authentic in quality and catholic in range – innumerable actresses have attested this over the centuries. So while the squeaking Cleopatras can add a further layer to the comic situations and have provided a starting point for some brilliant productions in recent years, the fundamental comic energy of the plays does not appear to be inextricably bound up with the acting conventions of the day. Therefore, the work we undertake in this chapter applies equally whether you are a girl playing a girl or a boy playing a girl. In either case you have to be real.

So in this chapter we must start with our lovers and examine their text, their character traits and the situations in which they find themselves. We have already explored some of this territory, but it is important to review it through the particular lens of comedy. We will not look at his clowns as a separate entity. (We have already analysed a considerable number of their scenes and monologues in previous chapters.) We will consider them as any other character, as individuals, as real people. Suffice it to say at this juncture that, as a group, they possess a powerful sexual drive and are driven by a strong life force. And we will open a window on the glorious pageant of ordinary men and women who parade through the plays, whose humanity, frailties and eccentricities are celebrated in comic form.

We have already encountered Celia in *As You Like It*. She is a marvellous example of a character that is knocked sideways, suddenly and unexpectedly, by love. She is Rosalind's best friend and has had to endure all her sighing, groaning and pining. Then out of the blue she meets Oliver. This is Rosalind's description of what happened:

ROSALIND

There was never any thing so sudden but the fight of two rams and Caesar's thrasonical brag of 'I came, saw, and overcame:' for your brother and my sister no sooner met but they looked, no sooner looked but they loved, no sooner loved but they sighed, no sooner sighed but they asked one another the reason, no sooner knew the reason but they sought the remedy; and in these degrees have they made a pair of stairs to marriage which they will climb incontinent, or else be incontinent before marriage: they are in the very wrath of love and they will together; clubs cannot part them.

As You Like It, V. ii. 28–39

This is a very useful point of departure if you are setting out to play one of Shakespeare's lovers. There's nothing modest, polite or restrained about the act of falling in love. It is obsessive. Your character is possessed. Normal patterns of behaviour disappear and you become single-minded. This leads to wonderful comic opportunities.

Consider *A Midsummer Night's Dream* as an example. Shakespeare takes four young people (two boys and two girls). He starts with a situation instantly recognisable from any school bus stop in the country: two boys are in love with one pretty girl and a second girl, her best friend, is in love with one of the boys. This is excruciatingly painful for the second girl, Helena, and for one of the boys, Demetrius, whose love is spurned. The escape and subsequent chase to the woods near Athens at night-time is complicated by Puck's incompetent interference. The love juice that he uses has exactly the same effect on them as love at first sight. Like Romeo and Juliet, there's no slow build up – love comes instantaneously, like a thunderbolt. And this is how it needs to be acted. Shakespeare sets up a scenario, witnessed by Oberon, King of the Fairies, in which the mortals, high on love, pursue their sexual and romantic desires in a totally obsessive way. It's a fascinating Freudian experiment that has huge comic potential. It also fulfills a broader instructive brief to prepare these youngsters for marriage. They learn through their wild adventures.

We pick up the text when both Lysander and Demetrius have been zapped with the juice. Lysander pursues Helena through the wood close to where Demetrius lies sleeping:

Enter LYSANDER and HELENA

LYSANDER

Why should you think that I should woo in scorn?
Scorn and derision never come in tears:
Look, when I vow, I weep; and vows so born,
In their nativity all truth appears.
How can these things in me seem scorn to you,
Bearing the badge of faith, to prove them true?

HELENA

You do advance your cunning more and more.
When truth kills truth, O devilish-holy fray!
These vows are Hermia's: will you give her o'er?
Weigh oath with oath, and you will nothing weigh:
Your vows to her and me, put in two scales,
Will even weigh, and both as light as tales.

LYSANDER

I had no judgment when to her I swore.

HELENA

Nor none, in my mind, now you give her o'er.

LYSANDER

Demetrius loves her, and he loves not you.

DEMETRIUS

[Awaking] O Helena, goddess, nymph, perfect, divine!
To what, my love, shall I compare thine eyne?
Crystal is muddy. O, how ripe in show
Thy lips, those kissing cherries, tempting grow!
That pure congealed white, high Taurus snow,
Fann'd with the eastern wind, turns to a crow
When thou hold'st up thy hand: O, let me kiss
This princess of pure white, this seal of bliss!

HELENA

O spite! O hell! I see you all are bent
To set against me for your merriment:
If you were civil and knew courtesy,
You would not do me thus much injury.
Can you not hate me, as I know you do,
But you must join in souls to mock me too?
If you were men, as men you are in show,
You would not use a gentle lady so;
To vow, and swear, and superpraise my parts,
When I am sure you hate me with your hearts.
You both are rivals, and love Hermia;
And now both rivals, to mock Helena:
A trim exploit, a manly enterprise,
To conjure tears up in a poor maid's eyes
With your derision! none of noble sort
Would so offend a virgin, and extort
A poor soul's patience, all to make you sport.

LYSANDER

You are unkind, Demetrius; be not so;
For you love Hermia; this you know I know:
And here, with all good will, with all my heart,
In Hermia's love I yield you up my part;
And yours of Helena to me bequeath,
Whom I do love and will do till my death.

HELENA

Never did mockers waste more idle breath.

DEMETRIUS

Lysander, keep thy Hermia; I will none:
If e'er I loved her, all that love is gone.
My heart to her but as guest-wise sojourn'd,
And now to Helen is it home return'd,
There to remain.

LYSANDER

    Helen, it is not so.

DEMETRIUS

Disparage not the faith thou dost not know,
Lest, to thy peril, thou aby it dear.
Look, where thy love comes; yonder is thy dear.
    A Midsummer Night's Dream, III. ii. 121–177

This scene is like a great Mozartian finale. It starts with a couple, a
duet; it's then pepped up by the sudden awakening of the third lover
and becomes a trio; at the point above where Hermia enters the scene,
it becomes a quartet, which develops in a madder and madder progression. The subject of the scene is blinkered love, the single-minded pursuit
of the loved one to the exclusion of all else. It follows that the chase
requires a complete loss of inhibition. It is a scene that calls for great
physical dexterity as well as command of the language. (You may find it of
great benefit to explore the lovers' situation through simple games and
improvisations.)

As usual, begin by looking out for the obvious. Lysander and Helena's
first speeches are exactly the same length and have exactly the same rhyme
scheme. After this, they begin to rhyme in couplets, and at this point,
Demetrius awakes, thereby interrupting a rhyme:

LYSANDER

Why should you think that I should woo in scorn?
Scorn and derision never come in tears:
Look, when I vow, I weep; and vows so born,
In their nativity all truth appears.
How can these things in me seem scorn to you,
Bearing the badge of faith, to prove them true?

HELENA

You do advance your cunning more and more.
When truth kills truth, O devilish-holy fray!

These vows are Hermia's: will you give her o'er?
Weigh oath with oath, and you will nothing weigh:
Your vows to her and me, put in two scales,
Will even weigh, and both as light as tales.

LYSANDER

I had no judgment when to her I swore.

HELENA

Nor none, in my mind, now you give her o'er.

LYSANDER

Demetrius loves her, and he loves not you.

DEMETRIUS

[Awaking] O Helena, goddess, nymph, perfect, divine!

Begin by working the rhyme. The first couple of times through you should consciously seek to invent the rhyme. Never pretend the rhyme is not there; it is your ally, pointing up the sense and revealing how the character is thinking. You will need to establish in the audience's mind the word that will eventually be rhymed (for example, 'scorn') and then proceed to coin the word that pairs with it (in this case 'born'). The need for constant invention that this method requires will give your character a wonderfully alive quality, which is exactly what Shakespeare is seeking: a lover in the first flush of his passion. The rhyme scheme is a, b, a, b, c, c. The c-c rhyme sums up your case and ends the speech on a positive note. And remember to always give your partner in a dialogue a firm cue. This will happen for free if you are coining the rhyme.

The rhyme also gives to the dialogue a heightened quality; it's not exactly artificial, but it renders their arguments a little larger than life, reinforcing the humour. Bear in mind that the word 'comedy' does not mean a laugh a line. There are laughs in this passage but they flow naturally from the extraordinary situation, from the characters' obsessive response to that situation and from a vivid delivery of this quite particular, heightened text. We've looked at the situation; we've begun to examine the text; now what about the characters' behavior? Look at the evidence. Lysander says, 'When I vow, I weep'. You must take that literally. He loves her so much; he is so frustrated that he is weeping. When you find that level of emotion, you are getting there. Helena, who, presumably, is reeling from the sudden, overwhelming attention that she is receiving, responds forcefully with exactly the same structure as Lysander, employing apposition to support her argument and rhyme to nail it.

She has no time to respond to Lysander's 'Demetrius loves her, and he loves not you.' Perfectly on cue, Demetrius awakes. His speech demonstrates precisely the extremity of his love:

DEMETRIUS

[Awaking] O Helena, goddess, nymph, perfect, divine!
To what, my love, shall I compare thine eyne?
Crystal is muddy. O, how ripe in show
Thy lips, those kissing cherries, tempting grow!
That pure congealed white, high Taurus snow,
Fann'd with the eastern wind, turns to a crow
When thou hold'st up thy hand: O, let me kiss
This princess of pure white, this seal of bliss!

No half measures! Shakespeare introduces a different rhyme scheme for the new character, but my note to you is the same: invent. His speech is overflowing with metaphor. You will remember what I said in an earlier chapter: metaphor is the highway to the imagination and needs to be coined on the spot. His imagination is teeming with quite extreme imagery. The result of all this inventiveness is to give the character a humorous, over-the-top quality, which, of course, is very funny.

Now imagine you are Helena, hearing this for the first time. You have longed for him to say a fraction of these beautiful, loving things. And then the penny drops:

HELENA

O spite! O hell! I see you all are bent
To set against me for your merriment:
If you were civil and knew courtesy,
You would not do me thus much injury.
Can you not hate me, as I know you do,
But you must join in souls to mock me too?
If you were men, as men you are in show,
You would not use a gentle lady so;
To vow, and swear, and superpraise my parts,
When I am sure you hate me with your hearts.
You both are rivals, and love Hermia;
And now both rivals, to mock Helena:
A trim exploit, a manly enterprise,
To conjure tears up in a poor maid's eyes

With your derision! none of noble sort
Would so offend a virgin, and extort
A poor soul's patience, all to make you sport.

All of their feelings are absolutely real. The extremity of their passion finds expression in their tears, their violent quarrelling and their moving expressions of love. You must not send up any of this. It is their need to rhyme that, somehow, gives the scene a playful side.

Sometimes, when you encounter a long response from a character (like this one from Helena), it is worth the silent characters articulating their thoughts out loud, as an exercise. So for the purposes of rehearsal, the scene involves three voices: two of them commenting on, responding to, the first. Try it. It may sound crazy, but it can often help to animate the scene and it certainly helps the tacit characters – those listening but not speaking – to find their line of thought. As a response to her speech, the boys begin to turn on each other; as the play progresses, this becomes outright hostility. Again, the key here is to take them at face value. Their love for Helena is a matter of life or death and, in the moment, they would die for her. The comedy all emanates from this fundamental tenet.

Shakespeare's lovers come in all shapes and sizes and we have met a whole host of them in the pages of this book: Petruchio and Kate, Antipholus and Luciana, Rosalind and Orlando and, of course, Beatrice and Benedick. Beatrice and Benedick are often portrayed as more mature than some of Shakespeare's other lovers and for good reason: there is a world-weariness about them, a diffidence about commitment and a fear of getting emotionally burnt. But with this couple, Shakespeare is only exploring another aspect of the dance of courtship. For our studies, they serve a particular purpose. From their first moment together on stage, they display this vital Shakespearean ingredient: wit. The Elizabethans put a high price on wit – that ability to stimulate our intelligence while making us laugh, or at the least, smile – and regarded it as the natural accompaniment to all aspects of a civilized adult life. The prerequisites of wit are dexterity with words, flexibility of mind and a love of conversation. As we examine how to do Shakespeare's comedy, it is critical to embrace the concept of wit.

Here is an after-supper scene between Beatrice and her two uncles, Leonato and Antonio; her cousin, Hero, is also present. The subject of the conversation soon finds its way towards husbands and marriage:

LEONATO

Was not Count John here at supper?

ANTONIO

I saw him not.

BEATRICE

How tartly that gentleman looks! I never can see him but I am heart-burned an hour after.

HERO

He is of a very melancholy disposition.

BEATRICE

He were an excellent man that were made just in the midway between him and Benedick: the one is too like an image and says nothing, and the other too like my lady's eldest son, evermore tattling.

LEONATO

Then half Signior Benedick's tongue in Count John's mouth, and half Count John's melancholy in Signior Benedick's face, –

BEATRICE

With a good leg and a good foot, uncle, and money enough in his purse, such a man would win any woman in the world, if a' could get her good-will.

LEONATO

By my troth, niece, thou wilt never get thee a husband, if thou be so shrewd of thy tongue.

ANTONIO

In faith, she's too curst.

BEATRICE

Too curst is more than curst: I shall lessen God's sending that way; for it is said, 'God sends a curst cow short horns;' but to a cow too curst he sends none.

LEONATO

So, by being too curst, God will send you no horns.

BEATRICE

Just, if he send me no husband; for the which blessing I am at him upon my knees every morning and evening. Lord, I could not endure a husband with a beard on his face: I had rather lie in the woollen.

LEONATO

You may light on a husband that hath no beard.

BEATRICE

What should I do with him? dress him in my apparel and make him my waiting-gentlewoman? He that hath a beard is more than a youth, and he that hath no beard is less than a man: and he that is more than a youth is not for me, and he that is less than a man, I am not for him: therefore, I will even take sixpence in earnest of the bear-ward, and lead his apes into hell.

LEONATO

Well, then, go you into hell?

BEATRICE

No, but to the gate; and there will the devil meet me, like an old cuckold, with horns on his head, and say 'Get you to heaven, Beatrice, get you to heaven; here's no place for you maids:' so deliver I up my apes, and away to Saint Peter for the heavens; he shows me where the bachelors sit, and there live we as merry as the day is long.

Much Ado about Nothing, II. i. 1–44

What can we learn about Beatrice from this passage? I think the most important thing is her ability to improvise. A thought enters her head or she is thrown an idea and, whoosh, she's away. This gift for running with the ball is matched by a superb mastery of language; she displays all of the techniques that we have worked on in this book – above all a love of word play. Yet there is something more, something that makes her special and makes her a great comic as well as a great human being. She can see the absurd in our everyday life and the unusual in the commonplace; crucially, she has the instinct to connect the two.

Let's observe how she works and practice her speeches. First, try to identify the connections. What is it that triggers a particular train of thought? Her imagination may sometimes be quite wild but there is logic to it. And this logic you need to trace diligently in order for the audience to follow every step and appreciate all the humour.

Her first contribution to the conversation relates to Count John and is clearly sparked by Leonato's reference to the supper they have just enjoyed. It's a post prandial quip par excellence and encapsulates her reaction to Count John with crystalline accuracy. It gets the scene off to a terrific start: 'How tartly that gentleman looks! I never can see him but I am heart-burned an hour after'. This line is the very definition of wit. It plays nimbly on our intelligence. We enjoy the pun on 'tartly' and are ambushed by the brilliant leap to heartburn! It is logical but daring. Does she have the sequence of thought in her head at the beginning of the speech? Probably yes. In comedy, beware of taking too many pauses. The dialogue is naturalistic but, as we observed in the chapter on prose, you need to play the thoughts through. The thought does not end on 'looks' but moves on through to 'after'.

That's where the laugh is. The line needs a confidence in delivery that comes from the strength of her opinions.

Interestingly, it is Beatrice who introduces Benedick into the conversation; like all lovers, the loved one is never far from her thoughts. The notion of creating the perfect man is a lovely conceit that engages everyone's imagination:

BEATRICE

He were an excellent man that were made just in the midway between him and Benedick: the one is too like an image and says nothing, and the other too like my lady's eldest son, evermore tattling.

LEONATO

Then half Signior Benedick's tongue in Count John's mouth, and half Count John's melancholy in Signior Benedick's face, –

BEATRICE

With a good leg and a good foot, uncle, and money enough in his purse, such a man would win any woman in the world, if a' could get her good-will.

The mention of Benedick's name would almost certainly get some sort of reaction from her family as a possible match has been mooted earlier in the play, so you are well set up for the elegant apposition that follows. Again, the thought moves through to the final word 'tattling'.

Let's take a minute here to talk about phrasing and timing. Phrasing and timing reveal how your character thinks and how she creates anticipation in the audience. As I said, the thought finishes with 'tattling', but you have a choice as to how you phrase it. You can play straight through or you can take a moment after 'my lady's eldest son', build the anticipation as if it were a line ending in verse and then deliver the last phrase 'evermore tattling'. This way you score a good point at Benedick's expense and probably make your family laugh. Try different ways of phrasing this speech. You could try the same technique on her next speech, taking a pause after 'any woman in the world', making your friends wait for the final 'if a' could get her good-will'. This would be even more effective if you played the earlier list of 'leg', 'foot' and so on extravagantly and rapidly. As with all of Shakespeare's language, you must keep varying the pace – Beatrice is nothing if not sharp as a knife. Such questions of phrasing and timing need practice and good judgment. They are why, in the professional theatre, actors need previews in a comedy to test the reactions of the audience. It's no good playing a laugh that simply isn't there!

Beatrice, without question, is an entertainer, and like many entertainers she is very lonely; her wit is a form of defence. She is great company. She is an excellent conversationalist, which, in this context, means that she actively progresses the dialogue. She makes connections. She picks up the ball and runs with it. Even when the conversation touches upon her unmarried state, she does not retreat from engagement with her uncle. On the contrary, it seems to make her more articulate to the extent that the thoughts almost run away with her. Read this passage:

LEONATO

You may light on a husband that hath no beard.

BEATRICE

What should I do with him? dress him in my apparel and make him my waiting-gentlewoman? He that hath a beard is more than a youth, and he that hath no beard is less than a man: and he that is more than a youth is not for me, and he that is less than a man, I am not for him: therefore, I will even take sixpence in earnest of the bear-ward, and lead his apes into hell.

It's extraordinary! She's like the trumpet player in a jazz band. Her uncle cues her in and off she goes. You need to get your brain and your mouth in gear when you deliver that speech. Practice it by playing the progression of appositions in a fairly sober way then, as you gain control over her thoughts, up the tempo and find the extravagance and the panache implied in the speech. The speech leads her into quite surreal territory in the next speech when she imagines an encounter with the devil. Beatrice has to be on your desert island dinner party list!

In this book, we have already looked at one or two of Shakespeare's celebrated comic characters – Launce, Dromio and Bottom, for example. There is an indestructibility about them. Like Groucho, you believe they will never die. They are also, almost without exception, of relatively lowly status within the play. The important word here is 'relatively'. Status is not an absolute concept or a fixed position. Take Bottom as an example: he is a mechanical, a workingman who performs before the duke and courtiers. Much of the comedy of the final 'play within a play' springs from the social divide between the two groups. But amongst his peers, Bottom is a monarch. Take Malvolio: his comedy and tragedy emanates from his discomfort at being a mere steward. Sir Toby and his crew, who are looked down upon by Malvolio, exploit his ambition and vanity mercilessly. Launce, a servant in *The Two Gentlemen of Verona*, by rights ought to be the master of his dog Crab, but we soon learn that the dog is really in charge.

Status is a subject that needs careful consideration in a Shakespeare play. This is partly because the society in which he was writing was considerably more hierarchical than contemporary Western society and partly because the dramatic tradition of which he was part stretched back to the ancient Greeks and master/servant situations are a staple part of that cultural diet.

In our more egalitarian world, the complex social stratifications of Elizabethan society can appear remote and difficult to grasp. However, a sound appreciation of how your character fits in and functions in his world is fundamental. This understanding needs to be visceral and imaginative, rather than academic. I would recommend some practical work, especially if you are tackling Shakespearean comedy. There are plenty of exercises to help a group to explore status and relative hierarchies.

Reading the situation is a crucial step in the playing of Shakespeare's comedy. You need to know who you are, where you are, what you are doing and what your relationship with the other characters is. Let's examine the first scene of the mechanicals in *A Midsummer Night's Dream*:

Enter QUINCE the Carpenter, SNUG the Joiner, BOTTOM the Weaver, FLUTE the Bellows-mender, SNOUT the Tinker, and STARVELING the Tailor

QUINCE

Is all our company here?

BOTTOM

You were best to call them generally, man by man, according to the scrip.

QUINCE

Here is the scroll of every man's name, which is thought fit, through all Athens, to play in our interlude before the duke and the duchess, on his wedding-day at night.

BOTTOM

First, good Peter Quince, say what the play treats on, then read the names of the actors, and so grow to a point.

QUINCE

Marry, our play is, the most lamentable comedy, and most cruel death of Pyramus and Thisbe.

BOTTOM

A very good piece of work, I assure you, and a merry. Now, good Peter Quince, call forth your actors by the scroll. Masters, spread yourselves.

QUINCE

Answer as I call you. Nick Bottom, the weaver.

BOTTOM

Ready. Name what part I am for, and proceed.

QUINCE

You, Nick Bottom, are set down for Pyramus.

BOTTOM

What is Pyramus? a lover, or a tyrant?

QUINCE

A lover, that kills himself most gallant for love.

BOTTOM

That will ask some tears in the true performing of it: if I do it, let the audience look to their eyes; I will move storms, I will condole in some measure. To the rest: yet my chief humour is for a tyrant: I could play Ercles rarely, or a part to tear a cat in, to make all split:

> The raging rocks
> And shivering shocks
> Shall break the locks
> Of prison gates;
> And Phibbus' car
> Shall shine from far
> And make and mar
> The foolish Fates.

This was lofty! Now name the rest of the players. This is Ercles' vein, a tyrant's vein; a lover is more condoling.

QUINCE

Francis Flute, the bellows-mender.

FLUTE

Here, Peter Quince.

QUINCE

Flute, you must take Thisbe on you.

FLUTE

What is Thisbe? a wandering knight?

QUINCE

It is the lady that Pyramus must love.

FLUTE

Nay, faith, let me not play a woman; I have a beard coming.

QUINCE

That's all one: you shall play it in a mask, and you may speak as small as you will.

BOTTOM

An I may hide my face, let me play Thisbe too, I'll speak in a monstrous little voice. 'Thisne, Thisne;' 'Ah, Pyramus, lover dear! thy Thisbe dear, and lady dear!'

QUINCE

No, no; you must play Pyramus: and, Flute, you Thisbe.

BOTTOM

Well, proceed.

QUINCE

Robin Starveling, the tailor.

STARVELING

Here, Peter Quince.

QUINCE

Robin Starveling, you must play Thisbe's mother. Tom Snout, the tinker.

SNOUT

Here, Peter Quince.

QUINCE

You, Pyramus' father: myself, Thisbe's father: Snug, the joiner; you, the lion's part: and, I hope, here is a play fitted.

SNUG

Have you the lion's part written? pray you, if it be, give it me, for I am slow of study.

QUINCE

You may do it extempore, for it is nothing but roaring.

BOTTOM

Let me play the lion too: I will roar, that I will do any man's heart good to hear me; I will roar, that I will make the duke say 'Let him roar again, let him roar again.'

A Midsummer Night's Dream, I. ii. 1–59

This is a remarkably economical piece of writing. Although Bottom and Quince have most of the lines, every character is properly introduced and we can learn volumes about them from their reactions to the parts they are allocated, as well as whatever reaction they may have off the text. When approaching a scene like this, my advice is not to try to create a funny character. Shakespeare has written real working people with jobs and skills. We meet them at a precise moment in time when they have come together to plan an entertainment for the duke. They have precise relationships with each other and a precise attitude towards the prospect of the entertainment. It is the situation in which they find themselves that makes them funny, although, of course, they have particular characteristics that lend themselves to comedy.

So what is the situation? When and where does it take place? They are working people, so it's likely to take place straight after work or perhaps after they have had supper. Which of these two options will feed most into the scene? I would think that hurrying straight from work would give a sense of urgency and anticipation that would help launch the scene. Where? It could be at Peter Quince's house, but that assumes he has a room large enough to accommodate six of them. Perhaps that means that the space is quite small; this could be useful. When I made a film of the play, I decided that they had hired the local scout hut for the occasion. Whatever you decide, ensure that it feeds into the scene, that it adds something. My motto is: make it special.

I think the evidence suggests that the occasion is very special. Perhaps Quince has acquired some sort of document that licenses them to perform:

'Here is the scroll of every man's name, which is thought fit, through all Athens, to play in our interlude before the duke and the duchess, on his wedding-day at night.'

Seeing their names written on an official paper would indeed be thrilling. They are no longer workingmen but actors! They have scripts and parts and rehearsals. The play, as described by Quince, gets the best of all possible worlds: 'Marry, our play is, the most lamentable comedy, and most cruel death of Pyramus and Thisbe'.

Import your own experience into the characters as well. This is, in my view, the first time this group has got together to put on a play. Remember the first time that you became enamoured of the theatre; it was almost certainly a very magical time. You couldn't wait to get to rehearsals, you loved the parts (however small) and you relished using the terminology of the theatre. I think it is exactly the same for these six mechanicals. For example, there is no spoken reaction from either Starveling or Snout to the parts they have been assigned. Perhaps they are thrilled to get these roles and immediately set about dreaming of how they will play them and what costumes they might wear.

We have all met someone like Quince; he is not a natural leader but is a born organizer. This leads to the friction between Quince and Bottom, who is a natural leader and very bossy to boot. If you can bring someone to mind, someone you have met or just observed, this can give you a toehold into the character. You need to work hard to get the precise relationship between the two of them and between this pair and the rest of the group. There is a pecking order in most groups, however close their friendship, and it is fruitful to get a clear sense of where you fit in.

Bottom is a great life force. It is this irresistible energy that Oberon unleashes on his errant wife. He acquires an insatiable sexual appetite. And given the first flush of passion for the theatre that I described earlier, he is magnificent in this opening scene. Look at his vocabulary. It is studded with words appertaining to the theatre; use all of these with relish. He simply cannot stop himself from acting. Crucially, he displays the actor's ability to imagine himself in a part. He dreams of playing Pyramus:

BOTTOM

That will ask some tears in the true performing of it: if I do it, let the audience look to their eyes; I will move storms, I will condole in some measure. To the rest: yet my chief humour is for a tyrant: I could play Ercles rarely, or a part to tear a cat in, to make all split:

> The raging rocks
> And shivering shocks
> Shall break the locks
> Of prison gates;
> And Phibbus' car
> Shall shine from far
> And make and mar
> The foolish Fates.
> This was lofty!

Bottom is deadly serious. He can clearly see the performance, he can hear the storm of applause and his fellows think he is a marvel! He is obsessive, like our lovers. The more I look at this scene, the more I am convinced that the quality I most want to hear is wonder. It is this sense that plugs the mechanicals into the central themes of the play: love, the imagination and wonder.

You can apply this technique of analysis to other scenes in which ordinary people find themselves in extraordinary situations. Look at the recruiting scene in *Henry IV Part II*. Look at the Jack Cade rebellion in *Henry VI Part II*. Look at the first Dogberry scene in *Much Ado about Nothing*. In all of these cases you will find a larger-than-life character who is the driving force, someone who provides the irresistible energy that is a prerequisite for all comedy. But all of these scenes require a precise reading of situation and character and a good grasp of the underlying status of the participants.

Finally, remember that comedy is not farce. You will often find that, during the performance of a comedy, the laughter builds slowly during the course of the evening. Don't try to force the audience to laugh by adding extraneous or crude business. Audiences want to enjoy themselves. It is usually enough to invite them in, and they will accept with alacrity.

13

TRAGEDY

'. . . lighted fools the way to dusty death . . .'

Macbeth, V. v. 21

In Athens in the fifth century BC, thousands upon thousands of citizens gathered in the open-air Theatre of Dionysus for the festival of drama that took place in the late winter or early spring. The timing of the festival was certainly linked to the religious calendar as well as the exigencies of the Greek climate. It is not certain whether or not women attended the performances. The audience was probably as rowdy, certainly as active, as the Elizabethans, and enjoyed a bill of fare that included song, dance, comedy and, of course, tragedy. The comedies were frequently full of topical reference, but the tragedies, performed in full masks and in broad daylight, almost invariably told tales drawn from myth or former enemies of the state. The action was fairly high-octane stuff and featured patricide, matricide, fratricide, infanticide and even deicide.

In London in the sixteenth and early seventeenth centuries, thousands upon thousands of men and women packed the theatres to hear the plays that have been marked down in history as the great tragedies of our language. Playgoing was no longer regarded as the duty of citizenship that it was in ancient Athens, and the religious connection had all but severed. However, an urgent human need was addressed in both cities, centuries apart. It was something visceral, a hunger perhaps. I was still able to witness it in Stratford in my time as Artistic Director of the RSC, standing at the back of a darkened theatre, watching a packed auditorium, hearing them as they partook of the final breaths of a Hamlet, a King Lear or an Othello.

So what is going on here? Can we define the essence of tragedy and, if so, what are the implications for performing the genre?

In the theatre, a deal is made between the actors and the audience – a contract if you like – whereby one party agrees to tell a story to another party, usually in exchange for money. In the case of tragedy, that deal involves taking the audience on a journey that explores the very frontiers of human experience. The violent encounters, the fights, the often melodramatic story-lines and the bloodshed all contribute to the popularity of the genre. But in the final analysis, it is this close encounter with our mortality that gives tragedy its hypnotic impact. If comedy charts the path of love towards marriage then tragedy lights 'the way to dusty death', as Macbeth so eloquently puts it. At the root of comedy, there is an inextinguishable life force. At the very core of tragedy lies a contemplation of our mortality. The clichéd image for the genre of tragedy is Hamlet face to face with the skull of the jester, Yorick; in this case, it's bang on the nail!

In the chapter on comedy, we had to concern ourselves with how the journey to marriage unfolds itself and how to read the developing situations, as well as looking at the individuals and the manner in which they express themselves. With tragedy we must examine the imagination and the inner life of the protagonists, as well as considering the situations that occur and the way they deal with them. Are they responsible for what happens? To what degree does fate, coincidence or destiny play a part? Crucially, we must address the fundamental characteristics of the tragic hero. Despite the fact that death is his close companion, I believe that there is a volcanic – some would say demonic – energy that drives him. Death, murder and madness are all by-products of this energy. For Shakespeare, this energy often caused danger and destruction to the state that spread, collaterally, like a disease. This enabled him to chart the public and political consequences of a private event.

It is important to recognise that the English tradition of tragedy is fairly full-blooded. My own experience of watching tragedy is to be shocked and exhilarated in equal measure. In the Greek theatre, bloodshed and murder took place offstage and were reported through the function of a messenger. In Shakespeare, we tend to see it all. There are occasions when he chooses to use the reported method, often to devastating effect. One example involves Richard III's Tyrell, who describes the death of the child princes in the Tower in a chilling and magnificent speech. But the Elizabethan audiences clearly had a taste for blood and violence that is evident throughout the dozens of tragedies that have survived from different authors.

The singularity of the English tradition was brought home to me dramatic-ally when I was a young director starting out. I had a big success with

Webster's *The Duchess of Malfi*, starring Helen Mirren. It was seen in London by Peter Brook, one of my heroes, who was then instrumental in securing a production in Paris with French actors. I secured a top cast and the play was produced in a spectacular circus tent near the old abattoirs. Well, the difference of reaction between London and Paris could not have been greater. In London, the audience devoured the play and the wonderful performances with rapt attention and greeted the performers with storms of applause. In Paris, as the onstage body count rose, the house became more restless, started to giggle and was yelping with laughter by the end! I was mortified. They regarded this genre, which they called *Tragédie de sang* (Tragedy of Blood), as primitive and far inferior to their Racinian form in which the violence is reported, allowing the audience to focus on the psychology of the protagonists. Peter consoled me afterwards: 'Yes,' he said, 'the same thing happened when I brought *Titus Andronicus* to Paris with Laurence Olivier'. At least I was in good company.

When first approaching a leading tragic role, I think it's best to avoid completely any description of your character that smacks of judgement or morality. The world may well think that Macbeth is a bad man, but it's no use whatsoever to the playing of him. If you judge a character, you will almost inevitably end up with caricature or cliché. Best to explore what he thinks, how he thinks, what his hopes are and what he dreams of achieving. Look at his actions and try to deduce his super objectives.

It is a good idea to start by asking yourself what the play revolves around. This will certainly open up a few doors you can pass through. Take *Othello* as an example. What is the central concern of that play? Is it race? I'm not sure it is. Race enters into it, but I feel it is symptomatic and catalytic to something deeper. Is it a man's pride or vanity? Possibly. I would probably take sexual jealousy as a point of departure. The racial difference between Othello and his wife and between him and his fellow soldiers could play a part in this. Othello's powerful sense of pride might also contribute to this most destructive of human passions. Like an onion, peel back the layers until you find something that is essential to the character or, to change metaphors, something that is consonant with the very heartbeat of the play. Try to find a line that sums up, or headlines, your take on the character. Remember, the great thing about rehearsal is that you can change your mind!

Consider Romeo. Love is central to his character and to the play, but try to go deeper. What kind of love? The love that Romeo falls into is doomed from the start. Perhaps what he is seeking is a love in which he can lose himself. Perhaps at the heart of his actions is that most powerful of instincts, the desire for immortality – not the immortality conferred by the golden statue that Old Capulet intends to erect, but immortality in the conjoining of his soul with that of Juliet. Lurking behind such an instinct is the figure of death.

Consider King Lear, a man terrified of losing power – power over his family, power over the state, power over his destiny and power over his own wits.

If you examine any of these characters from within, you immediately discover a territory in which there is vulnerability, conflicting passions and probably a desire for a superior state of existence. These are the qualities that humanise these figures and make them accessible to your audience. So seek out their private thoughts and embrace their contradictions.

And these are big figures. They are not necessarily strong or noble or heroic or courageous or wise. They are mighty figures because of the energy they possess, which either causes cataclysmic events, as in the case of Macbeth, or is itself created by those events, as with Hamlet. Their energy is often framed by their ambition and conditioned by their passion, and these are all passion-ate men and women. Therefore, identify what it is that they want, what is it that fuels their energy. Try and name their super objective.

Having made an assessment of what the critical issues might be, consider what the character's position is at the beginning of the play. It's an astute strategy to assemble the most positive portrait possible (and I am not talking morality here). This will allow the journey through the play, which may involve much pain and even madness, to be as long and spacious as possible. For example, when we first meet Hamlet, he's trapped in Claudius's court, grieves for his father and is repulsed by his mother's hasty marriage. All negatives. But consider Ophelia's assessment of him:

> O, what a noble mind is here o'erthrown!
> The courtier's, soldier's, scholar's, eye, tongue, sword;
> The expectancy and rose of the fair state,
> The glass of fashion and the mould of form,
> The observed of all observers, quite, quite down!
> And I, of ladies most deject and wretched,
> That suck'd the honey of his music vows,
> Now see that noble and most sovereign reason,
> Like sweet bells jangled, out of tune and harsh;
> That unmatch'd form and feature of blown youth
> Blasted with ecstasy: O, woe is me,
> To have seen what I have seen, see what I see!
>
> *Hamlet*, III. i. 153–164

Even taking into account the fact that she was in love with him, this is a remarkable portrait of a young Renaissance prince. It's an interesting and fruitful back story. At the very least, it will discourage you from thinking that this guy was always gloomy and depressive. At best, it will give your first scene in the court an edge for both you and the other actors because he's not usually like this. Something is wrong, something is out of joint. Hamlet is off centre, which of course renders him dangerous to the court and vulnerable to the extraordinary events about to unfold.

There is a wealth of information and opinion in the opening act of *Othello* that points to a man of great achievement held in high esteem by the state; he is the very saviour of the nation. His own description of the wooing of Desdemona suggests a man of great charm and physical attraction, but, fascinatingly, also a man of great vanity and self-regard.

The king and his fellow soldiers similarly hold Macbeth in the highest regard. He is a war hero and a fine leader of men and might, ironically, have made a great king in different circumstances. On each occasion that I have directed the play, I found that the logical consequence of the early descriptions of Macbeth's actions and character was to position him as King Duncan's natural heir. Indeed, I had the thanes and the army display marked shock when the old king named Malcolm as his successor. This gave a context, indeed a logic, to Macbeth and Lady Macbeth's plots.

Already, in this brief analysis of some of the opening scenes, we have uncovered a fruitful mismatch between the public face and the private man. This is a tension that is central to Shakespeare's tragedies and key to the performance of the roles. For the inner man, I always look to the soliloquies and, particularly, to the imagery which reveals his imagination.

Let us look at this dichotomy between the inner and the outer man in Hamlet's first scene. In a dramaturgical masterstroke, Shakespeare has Hamlet remain silent for the first sixty lines of the scene. Important issues of state are dispatched, jobs are dispensed and even young Laertes's further education is sorted out. In performance, Hamlet's silence and his mourning dress isolate him from the court and present an implied criticism of Claudius's regime. Finally Claudius addresses him:

KING CLAUDIUS

But now, my cousin Hamlet, and my son, –

HAMLET

[Aside] A little more than kin, and less than kind.

KING CLAUDIUS

How is it that the clouds still hang on you?

HAMLET

Not so, my lord; I am too much i' the sun.

QUEEN GERTRUDE

Good Hamlet, cast thy nighted colour off,
And let thine eye look like a friend on Denmark.
Do not for ever with thy vailed lids
Seek for thy noble father in the dust:
Thou know'st 'tis common; all that lives must die,
Passing through nature to eternity.

HAMLET

Ay, madam, it is common.

QUEEN GERTRUDE

                If it be,
Why seems it so particular with thee?

HAMLET

Seems, madam! nay it is; I know not 'seems.'
'Tis not alone my inky cloak, good mother,
Nor customary suits of solemn black,
Nor windy suspiration of forced breath,
No, nor the fruitful river in the eye,
Nor the dejected 'havior of the visage,
Together with all forms, moods, shapes of grief,
That can denote me truly: these indeed seem,
For they are actions that a man might play:
But I have that within which passeth show;
These but the trappings and the suits of woe.

Hamlet, I. ii. 64–86

Hamlet's first responses are uncommunicative, even plain sulky. Then a word that Gertrude uses, 'seems', spurs him into quite vituperative action. 'Seems' is a trigger that releases an inner fury. Ponder that idea as it's crucial. His response is well organized, bang on target and devastating. It betrays a volcanic inner energy that immediately establishes him as the primary moral force in the play. Take a few moments to observe how it's written. He starts with an involuntary opening statement, almost spat out, bookended by this offensive word 'seems': 'Seems, madam! nay it is; I know not "seems"'. The apposition is unequivocal: seems/is. Try it. Hamlet then embarks on a list of hypocritical behaviour, drawn, presumably, from Gertrude's own conduct. I don't think that he has the whole list in his head when he starts; but one thought leads to another then another. It is an improvisation that gains momentum as he proceeds. Look at the rhythm he employs. At first, single thoughts occupy single lines:

> 'Tis not alone my inky cloak, good mother,
> Nor customary suits of solemn black,
> Nor windy suspiration of forced breath,
> No, nor the fruitful river in the eye,
> Nor the dejected 'havior of the visage

Play each one through to the line ending. Invent the next idea, then the next. Then the pace doubles up and you can hear the one, two, three, four rhythm:

> Together with all forms, moods, shapes of grief,
> That can denote me truly: these indeed seem,

He returns to the offending word 'seem' on the line ending, and it would certainly be smart to let that hang in the air before you complete the speech:

> For they are actions that a man might play:
> But I have that within which passeth show;
> These but the trappings and the suits of woe.

With these last words he reveals that there is something within, something that 'passeth show'. I think his thoughts are just within his control, but his rhythms betray a more violent, anarchic inner self. That inner self is dramatically exposed in the soliloquy that follows the exit of the king and court. We will not reanalyse this speech that begins:

> O, that this too too solid flesh would melt
> Thaw and resolve itself into a dew!

You will remember that we examined it in some detail in the chapter on metaphor. I described this opening as an 'horrific image of self-annihilation'. It springs from deep in Hamlet's psyche and to me speaks of self-loathing and a rejection of the flesh. This is the landscape that you must inhabit if you are to penetrate the mysteries of this character.

It is always worthwhile examining the imagery that a character uses when he is under great stress. Let's stay with Hamlet and look at two scenes that involve the women in his life, his girlfriend and his mother. This is part of his response to Ophelia after he realizes that her father is eavesdropping:

> I have heard of your paintings too, well enough; God has given you one
> face, and you make yourselves another: you jig, you amble, and you lisp,

and nick-name God's creatures, and make your wantonness your
ignorance. Go to, I'll no more on't; it hath made me mad. I say, we will
have no more marriages: those that are married already, all but one, shall
live; the rest shall keep as they are. To a nunnery, go.

> *Hamlet*, III. i. 136–143

This is the climax of the scene with Gertrude, just before his father's
ghost appears:

> Nay, but to live
> In the rank sweat of an enseamed bed,
> Stew'd in corruption, honeying and making love
> Over the nasty sty . . .

> *Hamlet*, III. iv. 91–94

Try saying these two speeches out loud. One cannot help but be struck by
the similarity. There is a rather sickening sensuality in both, a prurient insist-
ence on sexual imagery and a violence towards the women that, to me,
exposes a self-loathing. Of course, you must interpret such imagery in your
own way. The important thing is to embrace it and make connections from
image to image through the play. Look for the moments of crisis and see
how he expresses himself.

Let's continue with these twin ideas: the tension between the inner and the
outer man and the revelation of the character's inner life at times of great stress.

Macbeth is a fascinating study and can be a life-changing part to play. We
have already noted the enormous respect in which he is held. Now read his
first monologue that occurs just after the witches' first prophesies appear to
have come true:

> [Aside] Two truths are told,
> As happy prologues to the swelling act
> Of the imperial theme. – I thank you, gentlemen.
> [Aside] This supernatural soliciting
> Cannot be ill, cannot be good: if ill,
> Why hath it given me earnest of success,
> Commencing in a truth? I am thane of Cawdor:
> If good, why do I yield to that suggestion
> Whose horrid image doth unfix my hair
> And make my seated heart knock at my ribs,
> Against the use of nature? Present fears
> Are less than horrible imaginings:
> My thought, whose murder yet is but fantastical,

> Shakes so my single state of man
> That function is smother'd in surmise,
> And nothing is but what is not.
> *Macbeth*, I. iii. 127–142

When approaching this part, you must not fall into the trap of playing the end at the beginning. Neither you nor the audience knows what is about to happen. Allow this monologue to develop organically, beat by beat. The opening image of the 'imperial theme' is uplifting, even inspirational. It leaves an intriguing impression on us: this man has a fine mind, a nobility of spirit. It's important to cling on to that as long as you are able through the course of the play. His thoughts continue contrapuntally and logically. He is courteous to his fellows. And then this appalling image enters his mind, the meaning of which takes some time to sink in, but which very nearly suffocates Macbeth in horror. This speech very clearly reveals the way his mind works. He tries to stay in control and remain rational, but his subconscious is, in the end, out of his control.

Think back to Macbeth's next soliloquy, which we examined in the chapter on soliloquy ('If it were done when 'tis done'). He is at a moment of crisis. He has been performing his public function as host at the royal banquet, but cannot sustain the pretence. He leaves the room and thinks through his dilemma. Again, he starts logically. He argues the different sides of the case well, expressing himself contrapuntally and eloquently. And then the horror begins to possess him and his mind is filled with fearsome hallucinatory imagery. Do you remember these lines?

> And pity, like a naked new-born babe,
> Striding the blast, or heaven's cherubim, horsed
> Upon the sightless couriers of the air,
> Shall blow the horrid deed in every eye,
> That tears shall drown the wind.

I repeat, it's a very specific thought process that, on the one hand, leads us meticulously to the soul of the man and, on the other hand, makes him accessible, even attractive to the audience.

Now let's look at the big man, King Lear. At the beginning, we meet a man of enormous power. In a scene of elaborate theatricality he divests himself of 'rule/Interest of territory, cares of state', divides his kingdom in three and then proceeds to invest power on his daughters in a hideous emotional auction. His actions are measured, deliberate and precisely calculated. It is a spectacular show and even has an international dimension with the attendance of the Duke of Burgundy and the King of France. Then things start to go wrong. First, his youngest daughter, Cordelia, refuses to play, then the Duke of Kent objects. Cordelia points out that she must love her husband first. Look at the exchange that follows:

KING LEAR

But goes thy heart with this?

CORDELIA

Ay, good my lord.

KING LEAR

So young, and so untender?

CORDELIA

So young, my lord, and true.

KING LEAR

Let it be so; thy truth, then, be thy dower:
For, by the sacred radiance of the sun,
The mysteries of Hecate, and the night;
By all the operation of the orbs
From whom we do exist, and cease to be;
Here I disclaim all my paternal care,
Propinquity and property of blood,
And as a stranger to my heart and me
Hold thee, from this, for ever. The barbarous Scythian,
Or he that makes his generation messes
To gorge his appetite, shall to my bosom
Be as well neighbour'd, pitied, and relieved,
As thou my sometime daughter.

KENT

Good my liege, –

KING LEAR

Peace, Kent!
Come not between the dragon and his wrath.

King Lear, I. i. 104–121

The revealing thing about this passage is what it tells us about his self-image. Almost everything he utters aggrandizes his position and his action. He commences with a simple monosyllabic line, necessitating a measured delivery. He then summons the supernatural powers to endorse his oath. He amplifies the insult to his person by the 'barbarous Scythian' allusion. To Kent, he designates himself 'the dragon'. The oath itself is framed in portentous terms, weighed down with gravity of purpose, polysyllabic words and alliteration, and then closes with a chilling monosyllabic line:

> Here I disclaim all my paternal care,
> Propinquity and property of blood,
> And as a stranger to my heart and me
> Hold thee, from this, for ever.

This is so far from the frail old man at the end of the play who cradles the broken body of the same daughter and asks

> Why should a dog, a horse, a rat, have life,
> And thou no breath at all? Thou'lt come no more,
> Never, never, never, never, never!

In the early speeches of Lear, the language he uses and the imagery he summons tell of a man who believes he possesses God-like powers on earth. You need to use all the technical resources that Shakespeare puts at your disposal to create this magnificent, dangerous self-image. When his eldest daughter, Goneril, defies him, he curses her. Again, look at the imagery:

> Hear, nature, hear; dear goddess, hear!
> Suspend thy purpose, if thou didst intend
> To make this creature fruitful!
> Into her womb convey sterility!
> Dry up in her the organs of increase;
> And from her derogate body never spring
> A babe to honour her! If she must teem,
> Create her child of spleen; that it may live,
> And be a thwart disnatured torment to her!
> Let it stamp wrinkles in her brow of youth;
> With cadent tears fret channels in her cheeks;
> Turn all her mother's pains and benefits
> To laughter and contempt; that she may feel
> How sharper than a serpent's tooth it is
> To have a thankless child! Away, away!
>
> *King Lear*, I. iv. 273–287

For me, this is one of the most shocking speeches in all drama. From where does such violence issue? The role requires all the skill and energy that you can muster, but the real challenge is to imaginatively involve yourself with him. No wonder, then, that both the Lears that I have directed, Michael Gambon and Robert Stephens, found the first two acts infinitely more difficult to play than the final two. For me, it's not enough to say that he is an isolated, absolute monarch who has come to believe in his own immortality. For me, there is a profound terror at the core of the man. I think he is frightened of his own mortality and frightened of losing his mind. For me, the key line would be: 'O, let me not be mad, not mad, sweet heaven!'

Let us now turn our attention to the question of responsibility. It strikes me that if a character is unaware of the consequences of his actions then his responsibility for those actions must be mitigated and, I would argue, he is not a tragic figure. A psychopath in a crazed fury kills ten people; is he a tragic figure? I think not, because he has diminished responsibility. The question I am posing is important for two reasons. First, it affects how you may play a part and second, it is fundamental to Shakespeare's purpose in his writing. Let's start with the second matter.

D.H. Lawrence, in an essay on Walt Whitman in *Studies in Classic American Literature*, wrote: 'The essential function of art is moral. Not aesthetic, not decorative, not pastime and recreation. But moral. The essential function of art is moral'. I think that is quite a useful definition. It takes us beyond the many important but, perhaps, superficial reasons why we enjoy art and focuses us on something deeper and critical to the very purpose of art in society. This takes me back to the opening paragraph of this chapter. Going to the theatre in ancient Greece was regarded as a civic duty and it would appear that attendance was more or less obligatory, as was going to church for the middle classes in Britain in the nineteenth century. Put bluntly, theatregoing helped you to exercise your vote wisely in the Athenian democracy. It's quite easy to understand why. Although the tragedies largely drew their plots from mythology or from the exploits of foreigners or enemies or both and frequently told of ghastly crimes and familial bloodletting, at the centre of the work of Aeschylus, Sophocles and Euripides lies situations at the very threshold of human endurance that pose the great moral questions that define our life on earth. And the same is true of Shakespeare. The experience of watching a great tragedy can have the effect of making the spectator more morally educated, more emotionally articulate. The issues at the heart of, say, Sophocles's *Antigone* are of timeless importance. They include responsibility to the one's family vis-à-vis loyalty to the state. No wonder the story held such power in occupied France during the Second World War. In the theatre, you have a visceral connection to the debate and not just an intellectual one, and so the performance of a great play can engage with an audience in a very special way. I'll never forget watching the audience leave The Other Place in

Stratford after they had watched Cheryl Campbell as Nora in my production of Ibsen's *A Doll's House*, in which the eponymous heroine not only walks out on her husband, but also on her young children. I would peek over the balcony and watch couples leaving the theatre, either in heated debate or, frequently, in the frosty silence of disagreement.

The question of responsibility is crucial to the moral debate at the heart of these great plays and critical to the choices you must make as you play these parts. Like Sophocles and Ibsen, Shakespeare told stories that hold a moral argument at their centre. So it's important to try to identify that for yourself. The more I have worked on Shakespeare, the more convinced I am that justice was one of his great preoccupations, and justice requires a mature discussion of matters of right and wrong. When you track through a major part, try to chart how his moral awareness develops because it is that moral dimension that will enable your character to grow into a significant human being and connect the essence of your story to the heart of the play. We have already looked at Macbeth's soliloquy 'If it were done when 'tis done'. Macbeth is totally aware of the moral implications of his actions from the very beginning and so immediately has a tragic dimension. Hamlet has an acute and developing moral awareness that can be measured from monologue to monologue. In the scene with the Fool in which Lear prays not to be mad, he lets slip a short sentence: 'I did her wrong'. This reference to his treatment of Cordelia is not picked up by the Fool nor referred to again, but we see a crack that will open up into a chasm of insanity and self-destruction. For Othello, the awareness happens all too late.

Here is the key point: as a character's self-awareness grows, the landscape which he inhabits grows at the same time, exponentially. The world gets bigger! This is one of the great rewards of playing these parts and is a thrilling revelation to an audience.

Let's develop this idea and attempt a new definition: A Shakespearean tragedy tells the story of a man's progress towards wisdom. Let's test this notion. In the final act of the play, Hamlet arrives at a spiritual resting place. He has accepted the challenge from Laertes and demonstrates strength and maturity that eluded him earlier. He seems to have found peace with himself. This is the short exchange with Horatio:

HORATIO

You will lose this wager, my lord.

HAMLET

I do not think so: since he went into France, I have been in continual practise: I shall win at the odds. But thou wouldst not think how ill all's here about my heart: but it is no matter.

HORATIO

Nay, good my lord, –

HAMLET

It is but foolery; but it is such a kind of gain-giving, as would perhaps trouble a woman.

HORATIO

If your mind dislike any thing, obey it: I will forestall their repair hither, and say you are not fit.

HAMLET

Not a whit, we defy augury: there's a special providence in the fall of a sparrow. If it be now, 'tis not to come; if it be not to come, it will be now; if it be not now, yet it will come: the readiness is all: since no man has aught of what he leaves, what is't to leave betimes?

Hamlet, V. ii. 155–170

Shakespeare deliberately writes the scene in prose to enable him to commence in a quite conversational manner with a brief practical discussion about the likelihood of winning the duel. But, as in the scene between Lear and the Fool, Hamlet unexpectedly reveals something intimate, private. It's simple and monosyllabic and can't be rushed. I always find it devastating: 'But thou wouldst not think how ill all's here about my heart'. Then the rhythm quickens. Hamlet shuns Horatio's concerns but soon finds words to describe how he now feels. (I think it is important to discover these ideas in the moment.) In one sense, the philosophy is pure Stoicism, expressed in perfectly balanced antitheses, but the warmth of the relationship and the emotion that underpins Hamlet's words communicate something quite rare: a shared moment of communion before death. Hamlet has found grace.

In the final act of *King Lear*, King Lear and his daughter, Cordelia, are reunited but have been captured by Edmund. Read the dialogue:

CORDELIA

Shall we not see these daughters and these sisters?

KING LEAR

No, no, no, no! Come, let's away to prison:
We two alone will sing like birds i' the cage:
When thou dost ask me blessing, I'll kneel down,
And ask of thee forgiveness: so we'll live,
And pray, and sing, and tell old tales, and laugh

At gilded butterflies, and hear poor rogues
Talk of court news; and we'll talk with them too,
Who loses and who wins; who's in, who's out;
And take upon's the mystery of things,
As if we were God's spies: and we'll wear out,
In a wall'd prison, packs and sects of great ones,
That ebb and flow by the moon.

King Lear, V. iii. 6–19

The most powerful man in the kingdom has found freedom in captivity. He too has arrived at a state of grace. The price, of course, has been steep and the journey has been marked by terrible physical and mental suffering, but Lear has arrived at a place where he can forgive and ask forgiveness. He has humility. He also has the ability to conjure magical images for his beloved daughter. The language has profound beauty. Compare it to the bile expressed earlier in the play in the speech to Goneril quoted above.

Here's another example from the same play. Shakespeare was a great humanist artist and so shone his torch on the central dilemmas from every angle. The story of the Duke of Gloucester counterpoints King Lear's. At the very moment that Gloucester becomes aware of his appalling treatment of his son, Edgar, and his foolish trust in Edmund, he is blinded in a scene of unparalleled savagery. From that moment, he begins his long journey to enlightenment. This is Edgar's description of his father's death:

I ask'd his blessing, and from first to last
Told him my pilgrimage: but his flaw'd heart,
Alack, too weak the conflict to support!
'Twixt two extremes of passion, joy and grief,
Burst smilingly.

King Lear, V. iii. 195–199

Redemption and enlightenment for Gloucester carry contradictory emotions. This brings me to another point. Frequently the tragic hero becomes increasingly isolated and more and more lonely: Gloucester in his blindness, Lear in his madness. Macbeth becomes estranged from his partner, Lady Macbeth, Othello from Desdemona. So an important thing to remember when approaching these characters is, paradoxically, to seek out the friendships and the companionships and cherish them. If you are playing Hamlet, invest heavily in your relationship with Horatio. Mercutio and, especially, Benvolio, are crucial for Romeo. The Fool and Kent are there for Lear.

Finally, I want to talk a little more about the relationship between other characters in the play and the central figure – by this I mean the emotional relationship. Try to define the relationship both at the beginning of the play and at the end. In rehearsal, I usually explore this with a simple, abstract exercise. I ask the actor playing, say, Hamlet to stand in the middle of the space. I next ask each of the other actors to approach him one by one and create some sort of physical connection that encapsulates their emotional relationship to him at the top of the play. I encourage them to be as bold and as abstract as possible. So you might lie prone at his feet if that's the way you feel. Gradually, actor by actor, a living sculpture builds up that invariably sheds much light on the play.

In this chapter, we have looked at the state of mind exhibited by our tragic hero at the beginning of the play and considered the state of wisdom at which he arrives at the end. I talked about the energy of these characters that fuels and is fuelled by a tension between the private man and his public persona. This energy seeks to achieve its super objective, but en route causes untold personal and collateral damage. The stronger you can make the super objective, the more active the character becomes in striving to achieve it. It's vital that you play these figures as dynamic, otherwise they will quickly become victims and, to my mind, the core of the play goes soft. Lastly, we talked of the wisdom of nurturing the positive relationships in the play. Alongside of this, actively seek out the witty side of your character. An example of this would be the opening dialogue between Hamlet and Rosencrantz and Guildenstern (Hamlet, II. ii.). A brilliant aspect of Shakespeare's dramaturgy is his juxtaposition of humour and tragic events.

14

CHARACTER

'Let me play the lion too'
A Midsummer Night's Dream, I. ii. 57

Now here's a challenge! Imagine yourself in the following three situations. First, you are about to make your entrance in a tragedy in the year 499 BC in one of the great theatres of ancient Greece, in Athens or, perhaps, at Epidauros. Second, you are awaiting your cue to enter, backstage at the Globe Theatre, Southwark in London in 1599. Third, you are standing in the darkened wings of the Royal Court Theatre in Sloane Square, London in 1999.

Let's flesh out the three different circumstances. In ancient Greece, you would not have been a professional actor as we now know it, although you would probably have been paid for the performance. You might be an instructor in public speaking, a skill considered to be an important feature of a child's education. You may well have written the play you are about to perform and possibly choreographed or directed it. It would therefore be a new play and it would be written in verse. You would certainly use song and dance as part of your performance as well as the spoken word. You would be wearing a full mask and costume. It would be a day of religious festivities and the auditorium, open to the skies, would be jammed with thousands of people. It is uncertain whether or not women were present, but slaves were definitely excluded. Were you to be sitting in the audience, you would have the blue sky over your head, a glimpse of the hills and perhaps the sea in the distance. Surrounded by your fellow men, in full sunlight, you would be watching man in relation to nature.

In the Globe Theatre, you would certainly be a professional actor and would be a member of a company known as the Lord Chamberlain's Men. It is likely that rehearsals were brief by modern standards, perhaps just a few days. You would have been given your own part to rehearse along with the relevant cues but would only hear the other actors' lines as part of a rehearsal or performance. The author would certainly be present and might well be performing alongside of you. You would be performing a new play, largely written in verse. You would be wearing a costume representative of your character. Beyond the curtain separating the tiring room from the stage would be gathered between two or three thousand citizens from all classes and a sprinkling of visitors from abroad, all packed into a relatively small space beneath the London sky. Standing in the Yard, you would see the actor against the background of a sea of humanity. You would be watching man in relation to mankind.

At the Royal Court, you would also be a professional actor but not a member of a company. A director would have chosen you for the express purpose of presenting a particular text. The author may be present for much of a rehearsal process that could last up to five or even six weeks. The piece you would be performing would likely be written in prose but its form and content could be drawn from many diverse sources. You would be standing in the dark and the audience would be sitting in the dark. The stage between you would be relatively brightly lit. The audience, numbering a few hundred, would be in one room, looking through the proscenium arch at the performers in another room. You would be watching man in relation to . . . what? Modern lighting and scenic arts allow us to create whole worlds of illusion that can shift and evolve at the touch of a button.

Theatre art both shapes and is shaped by contemporary architecture and technology. The theatres in which we play are a reflection of the political, philosophical and religious concerns of the society that built them. So ancient Greek theatre reflects man's struggle with nature at a particular moment in history. Tales of past heroes and their interaction with the gods and with fate allow citizens to explore their precarious mortal existence, to debate contemporary morality and to peer into the dangerous waters of their inner lives. And, crucially, it is all done in bright sunshine. The god of light and truth, Apollo, reveals all.

Shakespeare's theatre is a Renaissance theatre. The rediscovery of ancient Greek and Latin texts in the fourteenth century sparked the explosion of the arts, sciences and philosophy, centred on Italy, that became known as the Renaissance, a rebirth. It was a revolution that effectively placed man, not God, at the centre of the universe. And man, with his own face, unmasked, is at the centre of Shakespeare's drama.

God has been pretty well banished from our contemporary theatre, which has brilliantly adapted to embrace the pluralism that characterises the contemporary world. Modern technology is perfectly suited to service an art form that can provide popular entertainment on the one hand (and remember the ancient Greeks and the Elizabethans loved this), and a theatre of ideas and debate on the other hand. Realism, naturalism, alienation, the absurd, Brecht, Strindberg, Stoppard and Churchill can all happily be accommodated in our flexible multi-purpose spaces. Pluralism and the fragmentation of our society are reflected back from the stage.

So where does the actor stand in this contemporary picture? More particularly, where does the actor playing Shakespeare stand? His author is near four hundred years dead and wrote for a theatre that was already passing before he was cold in his grave in Stratford. Plays were moving indoors and two-room theatre had arrived. Social inclusiveness was banished from the playhouses, arguably for centuries.

Let's try and understand where we are from an appreciation of where we have come from. Let's try and attempt a methodology of character building based upon an understanding of the way the craft has changed over the centuries to reflect the demands put upon it by writers and society.

Go back to our exercise in historical imagination. For the Greeks, the mask and the costume were the character. For the Elizabethans, the words are the character. In the modern world, character is an inner quality, made manifest by action and behaviour. Here we have three completely different ways of approaching character. A modern actor attempting Shakespeare must learn from all of these.

Let's start with the Greeks. We know from experience and anecdote that wearing a mask changes your behaviour. You don't need to go to drama school to find this out. Look at the way people behave at fancy dress parties. Look at Carnival in Venice or Mardi Gras in New Orleans. Something happens when you put on a mask. Somehow it possesses you. You become taken over by the mask. Powerful emotions well up inside of you. It will affect the way you move and the way you interact with others. Most important of all, the mask determines your inner life. So the Greek actor had a profoundly different attitude towards character than we do. When a character was injured or died, the mask might be changed or, more probably, the costume would be ripped or discoloured. It is also likely that they would have had a less possessive, less neurotic relationship with their character. For example, it is most likely that in the play *Oedipus* at Colonnus, more than one performer enacted the role of Theseus; they would share the mask. This was not done for artistic reasons, but to maintain the convention of only using three actors. But it certainly focuses attention on the question of function. Theseus is both a character and also a function in the story of Oedipus's final days.

So what do we learn from the Greek theatre for the building of character?

First, that the mask worked on the actor from the outside in. Second, that we should try to define the function of the role, what he or she is there for. We will return to both of these ideas shortly.

In Shakespeare, the verse line has the potential to act upon you in the same way as the mask. Throughout this book we have observed how a human being expresses himself through language, and how the form and structure of that language convey meaning. Everything that needs to be communicated by a character exists in the language. This is why I frequently say to my actors that there is no subtext in Shakespeare; it's all in the line. There is no point in adding lots of pauses for thought. Think on the line and speak as you think. And when your cue comes, be ready to speak! Shakespeare's verse, and indeed his prose, falls apart if you try and deliver it as naturalistic conversation. It isn't. It is concentrated and precise thought supported by condensed, intense emotions. The nature of the language as well as the rehearsal conditions I have alluded to mean that the Elizabethan actor would have approached his part in a radically different way to his modern counterpart. He would have read his part and deduced exactly how to perform it from the way it was written. The metaphors would have led him, instinctively, to the character's imagination. The word play would have informed him of his wit and education. The verse lines would have shown him the way in which his thought moved forward. The detail of the metre and pulse, the prosody and the appositions would have given him all the necessary instruction and ammunition to deliver the lines and command the audience. He would have used all of the techniques we have studied in this book. Did he sit down and study them? I doubt it. He would certainly have been steeped and well schooled in all of this material – he was probably a part of the company when the form was being developed – but when he was handed his lines and the relevant cues, I am sure that his process of work would have been quite different from that of most modern actors. He would have allowed the verse to teach him how to play the part. He would have allowed the verse to work on him from the outside in, just like the Greek actor standing before a mirror putting on his mask. Let's park this idea for a moment and move to the twenty-first century.

As I said in the Introduction, Stanislavski's method is the very air we breathe in the contemporary theatre. This is not just because its methodology forms the cornerstone of university and drama school courses throughout the Western world, but also because it responds to our desire to understand and value our inner lives. The ancient Greeks felt this urge no less acutely, but they did not have the scientific disciplines and discoveries to articulate their investigations. Ancient Greek investigations were conducted through works of art, drama and epic poetry. The Stanislavski method will teach you two things. It will teach you to access and familiarise yourself with your own deep, complex emotions, thereby enabling you to call on your own resources in the creation of a role or the singing of a song. It will also give you a structure whereby you can analyse the psychological profile of the character you are playing. These disciplines allow a process of identification to take place whereby you become the character. In other words, the modern method is to move from the inside out.

Now, a sharp-eyed observer will notice that we are completing a full circle here. And we are! I described the Greek actor in his full mask as being possessed by the mask, and if the mask is the character, then he is possessed by the character. Some of us have been fortunate enough to see a great actor tear up the floorboards with a sensational performance. For me, Robert Stephens *was* Falstaff. I would say that that character possessed him. Daniel Day Lewis in the film *There will be Blood* was the very embodiment of that ninetheenth-century oil prospector. Contemporary accounts of Edmund Kean describe him as being possessed by a role. They talk of being in the very presence of Shylock or Sir Giles Overreach.

This is something quite fundamental to the art of acting. It's about trans-formation, about becoming something other than yourself. It is magic and has been respected and feared throughout the centuries. You are both your-self and the character at one and the same time. Part of you has lost control and another part is monitoring and guiding that first part.

I have said on several occasions that, for me, one of the great excitements of rehearsal is to watch an actor approach a scene from both a Shakespearean and a Stanislavskian angle. This is the ideal: a marriage of the two traditions. In practice, I do not think they are that far apart as long as you have thor-oughly mastered the basic techniques, such as the ones outlined in this book. Without these you are quite limited either way!

Since our subject is Shakespeare, let us start by building our skills in the Shakespearean method. The first step I would advise is a bold one. Try and learn to sight-read Shakespeare. Take an unfamiliar passage from an early play – *The Taming of the Shrew*, one of the *Henry VI* plays or *The Comedy of Errors* – and read it out loud. At first, don't worry about the meaning at all, just try to read it clearly and incorporate all the knowledge you have accumulated through these chapters. Remember what I said earlier: speak as you think. With this exercise, we are allowing the verse to work on you just like a mask. The more you practice, the more attuned you will become to changes of rhythm, variations of colour, antithesis, etc. Try this example. It's Petruchio from the *Shrew* explaining what has brought him to Padua.

PETRUCHIO

Such wind as scatters young men through the world,
To seek their fortunes farther than at home

Where small experience grows. But in a few,
Signior Hortensio, thus it stands with me:
Antonio, my father, is deceased;
And I have thrust myself into this maze,
Haply to wive and thrive as best I may:
Crowns in my purse I have and goods at home,
And so am come abroad to see the world.
                    The Taming of the Shrew, I. ii. 49–57

Just sight-read it two or three times. (It's vital that you speak it out loud.) Allow your instincts to seek out all the information and clues that Shakespeare has given you. Allow the verse to work on you and discover whether you are getting a feel for the character. Is he confident or shy? Is he witty? Is he energetic? After you have read it at least four times, go back and ask yourself all the questions. Where are the appositions? Are there any metaphors? Are there any full stops placed in the middle of lines? Where does the rhythm vary? Is there any rhyme? Now read it aloud once more.

Don't dwell on it. Move on to another piece. Here is Clarence from *Richard III*.

CLARENCE

Methoughts that I had broken from the Tower,
And was embark'd to cross to Burgundy;
And, in my company, my brother Gloucester;
Who from my cabin tempted me to walk
Upon the hatches: thence we looked toward England,
And cited up a thousand fearful times,
During the wars of York and Lancaster
That had befall'n us. As we paced along
Upon the giddy footing of the hatches,
Methought that Gloucester stumbled; and, in falling,
Struck me, that thought to stay him, overboard,
Into the tumbling billows of the main.
Lord, Lord! methought, what pain it was to drown!
What dreadful noise of waters in mine ears!
What ugly sights of death within mine eyes!
Methought I saw a thousand fearful wrecks;
Ten thousand men that fishes gnaw'd upon;
Wedges of gold, great anchors, heaps of pearl,
Inestimable stones, unvalued jewels,
All scatter'd in the bottom of the sea:
Some lay in dead men's skulls; and, in those holes

Where eyes did once inhabit, there were crept,
As 'twere in scorn of eyes, reflecting gems,
Which woo'd the slimy bottom of the deep,
And mock'd the dead bones that lay scatter'd by.

Richard III, I. iv. 9–33

This speech is a much bigger challenge, but use the same method. Don't study it; sight-read it. You should find, after a couple of goes, that you get quite good at it. Allow the language to work on you, and you will reach a point where you start to feel that you own the speech. You will begin to get a sense of who this person is. Then, as before, go over it more slowly and try to understand as far as possible how Shakespeare has written the piece. Refer back to the chapter headings as a checklist to help with this. Now move on. Go through your *Complete Works* and find a piece from a middle play, say a Viola speech from *Twelfth Night* or something from *Henry V*.

For our next exercise in Elizabethan acting, let us return to the Greeks. Earlier I talked about function and, for our purposes, I would add the word 'relationship'. Greek tragedy was performed using just three actors and a chorus. There was at least one protagonist or principal character and an antagonist, whose job it was to oppose the protagonist. That was his function. I have always found it constructive to get my actors to attempt to define their character's function in the play, to think about what the character does rather than who he or she is.

On one level this is quite straightforward. Think back to the first mechanical scene in *A Midsummer Night's Dream*. Quince, who is organizing the play within a play, hands out the parts with very simple descriptions: Bottom is to play 'A lover, that kills himself most gallant for love'; Flute is to play 'The lady that Pyramus must love'; Starveling is to play Thisbe's mother; Quince is to play Thisbe's father; and Snug is to play the lion's part. Here Quince tells us partly what their relationship is and partly what they do. It's always important to state your relationship but then further define it in terms of their contribution to the story. Thus in the main action of the *Dream*, Egeus is Hermia's father, but perhaps his function is to oppose the marriage, to provide an insuperable obstacle to the lovers. Titania is the Fairy Queen and Oberon's wife, but what does she do? Crucially, she defies Oberon over the Indian boy and thereby incurs his revenge. I make no comment on the rights or wrongs of her behaviour; I merely state what she does. That verb 'defies' will give you a clear clue to her character. Peter Quince is a carpenter, but what he does is to organize, to direct, to lead. Hermia is Egeus's daughter and a lover, and what she does is to elope – which, of course, triggers a train of events.

At the beginning of rehearsals, I try and lay out the relationships as clearly as possible. I will do this physically, using a variation of the relationship exercise described in the previous chapter. I will ask the company to enter a given space one after the other and join the other members of the cast to whom they are related in the play. So Claudius might enter first and sit in a chair, then Gertrude might go and sit on his knee. Hamlet might stand a good way off, but still be in touch with his mother. This is often highly revealing. In *Hamlet*, for example, you soon realize that the whole action revolves around two families: Hamlet's family (the royal family) and Polonius's family. Next, I will ask all the other actors to relate to these families in some way, always trying to express their relationship in physical terms. So Horatio might stand very close to his friend Hamlet and Renaldo might get quite close to Polonius, but, subservient, might lay down on the ground at his feet. This can be fun and helpful in defining relationships. But always go further and try and get to function; what does my character contribute to the play? The above exercise is useful in any of the plays, but especially in the great family dramas like *King Lear* and *Romeo and Juliet* or in plays in which family loyalties are particularly relevant. The History plays come to mind, as does Macbeth. Status exercises will also provide you with invaluable knowledge about how your character interacts with others. These are practical – not intellectual – ways of building your identity.

Occasionally, the function of a character is 'choral', in other words they are in the play in order set up a situation or a particular atmosphere. A good example is Grandpré in *Henry V*. On the morning of the Battle of Agincourt, he appears to the nobles in the French army and says the following:

GRANDPRÉ

Why do you stay so long, my lords of France?
Yon island carrions, desperate of their bones,
Ill-favouredly become the morning field:
Their ragged curtains poorly are let loose,
And our air shakes them passing scornfully:
Big Mars seems bankrupt in their beggar'd host
And faintly through a rusty beaver peeps:
The horsemen sit like fixed candlesticks,
With torch-staves in their hand; and their poor jades
Lob down their heads, dropping the hides and hips,
The gum down-roping from their pale-dead eyes
And in their pale dull mouths the gimmal bit
Lies foul with chew'd grass, still and motionless;
And their executors, the knavish crows,
Fly o'er them, all impatient for their hour.
Description cannot suit itself in words

To demonstrate the life of such a battle
In life so lifeless as it shows itself.

Henry V, IV. ii. 38–55

This is a fabulous speech to work on, by the way. It is full of opportunities to practice all the skills we have been acquiring. Grandpré has little to do elsewhere in the play, but at this pivotal moment he delivers this astounding description. Why? To boost the confidence of the French? They hardly need his help! Its main function seems to be for the audience's benefit. It gives us a remarkable insight into the French perception of the English and at the same time provides a timely alternative view of the English to that presented by the play as it follows Henry's story. Its impact is akin to a brilliant establishing shot in a film, panning across the pitiful army and then tracking past individual details of horror or terror.

The detailed study of text in this book has provided you with the most important tools in character building in the Elizabethan tradition. Think back over what you have learnt. The character's imagination lies in his use of metaphor. His way of thinking lies in his use of antithesis, apposition and verse structure. Word play, vocabulary, length of sentence and use of colour all provide significant pointers. Allow these to talk to you about the character. Allow the verse to instruct you.

At the same time, seek out specific lines or moments in a text when you feel that you can strongly identify with the character. Look for images or situations that chime with you. As an example, I want to return to a sonnet that we examined in the chapter on metaphor. First of all, try and sight-read it:

When, in disgrace with fortune and men's eyes,
    I all alone beweep my outcast state
And trouble deaf heaven with my bootless cries
    And look upon myself and curse my fate,
    Wishing me like to one more rich in hope,
Featured like him, like him with friends possess'd,
    Desiring this man's art and that man's scope,
    With what I most enjoy contented least;
Yet in these thoughts myself almost despising,
    Haply I think on thee, and then my state,
    Like to the lark at break of day arising
From sullen earth, sings hymns at heaven's gate;
    For thy sweet love remember'd such wealth brings
That then I scorn to change my state with kings.

Sonnet 29

The whole sonnet leads up to this amazing metaphor that describes and celebrates the speaker's feelings for the loved one. It begins with a long sentence. It rhymes quite formally and has interesting and subtle shifts of rhythm. The exercise this time is to seek out points of identification between you and the character, while, at the same time, carrying on working on the language. So ask yourself: Have you ever been 'in disgrace with fortune and men's eyes'? It doesn't matter how simple the situation is, all you are looking for is a toehold, a way into the character. Have you ever felt so miserable that you 'all alone beweep my outcast state'? Remember the feeling and try to marry your private experience with your character. This procedure will support the process whereby the text teaches you. This sonnet is fertile ground for this type of investigation because it is full of situations that most of us have experienced at some time. You will find that the rhyme prevents it from becoming too maudlin and gives the story a bounce. Indeed, the more I read it, the more I think that he is deliberately exaggerating his feelings in order to make his lover smile. This brings me to a key issue: character is made manifest through action. You will learn most about the identity of a character when you expose that character to transitive action. So with the above sonnet, the question is 'What is he doing?' or 'What is he trying to achieve?' As I suggested, it might be to make her smile or to make her love him more. Again, this is a situation that most of us can identify with.

At the centre of Shakespeare's universe is man. He has a sympathetic but essentially unsentimental view of man. Capable of magnificent ideas, beautiful expression and great wisdom, mankind could also be full of folly, subject to destructive passions and prey to pettiness and gossip. The wonderful thing about Shakespearean characters is the way you can walk all around them, examining them from all angles. They are not ciphers; they have functions but are not merely functionary.

Central to his view of man is a belief in man's capacity to change – for the better or, often, for the worse. In other words, your character will be different at the end of the play from how he was at the beginning. It is useful to regard a character's progress through a play as a journey that has a beginning, a middle and an end. For your own satisfaction, and especially that of your audience, try to make that journey as long as possible. Sometimes Shakespeare will give you a very strong situation at the beginning. For example, Isabella in *Measure for Measure* is a novitiate nun in her first scene, but by the end of the play she has received a proposal of marriage from the duke. Early on in *The Taming of the Shrew*, Kate tortures her little sister, who is passionate to marry, but by the end of the play she is lecturing her on the virtues of obedience and modest behaviour. At the beginning of the play, Othello is blissfully married and called upon to save the state, but by the end of the play he is a murderer and a suicide.

Sometimes, the character is less clearly delineated at the beginning. In this circumstance you will need to make some decisions, but make them with the aim of elongating the journey. For example, in King Lear, the role of Edgar is quite lightly drawn in his early scenes. It is not until he is forced to flee and adopt a disguise that his character blossoms. He eventually becomes a man of action and a great moral force within the play. In order to elongate his journey, perhaps make him withdrawn, even bookish, at the beginning.

In previous chapters we have noted how a strong situation will cause a character to develop and change. Think of Isabella again. In the chapter on dialogue, we saw how the need to fight for her brother's life gave her a dynamism and an attack which in turn made her much more articulate. She found the words and the arguments to take on the lawyer Angelo and beat him at his own game. We have seen how Rosalind, in As You Like It, finds articulacy and freedom of expression in the Forest of Arden when she falls in love and is forced to flee. She finds her voice!

This is a central Shakespearean concept: action results in articulacy. Hand in hand with this concept goes another concept: you need to lose yourself in order to find yourself. When you find yourself, you discover your voice.

It is easy to lose yourself in strange places like forests, stormy heaths or indeed battlefields. The character is thrown off centre and has to improvise, thereby beginning to find their voice. They are outside their comfort zone, so as you draw your character's trajectory with your imagination, it is important to locate parts of yourself that are at the frontiers of your experience, parts that feel alien. You will assuredly find imagery in the text that will lead you there. For example, here is Edgar in King Lear, hunted and frightened:

EDGAR

I heard myself proclaim'd;
And by the happy hollow of a tree
Escaped the hunt. No port is free; no place,
That guard, and most unusual vigilance,
Does not attend my taking. Whiles I may 'scape,
I will preserve myself: and am bethought
To take the basest and most poorest shape
That ever penury, in contempt of man,
Brought near to beast: my face I'll grime with filth;
Blanket my loins: elf all my hair in knots;
And with presented nakedness out-face
The winds and persecutions of the sky.
The country gives me proof and precedent

Of Bedlam beggars, who, with roaring voices,
Strike in their numb'd and mortified bare arms
Pins, wooden pricks, nails, sprigs of rosemary;
And with this horrible object, from low farms,
Poor pelting villages, sheep-cotes, and mills,
Sometime with lunatic bans, sometime with prayers,
Enforce their charity. Poor Turlygod! poor Tom!
That's something yet: Edgar I nothing am.

King Lear, II. iii. 1–21

Edgar, the legitimate son of one of England's aristocratic families, has become a hunted animal. His secure world has turned upside down. There is breathlessness to the rhythm. The urgency and desperation to survive is found in the forward-driving pulse, the thoughts running on from the full stops in the middle of the lines. It is a life or death situation and it leads him directly to a brilliant means of survival and disguise, which he describes as:

the basest and most poorest shape
That ever penury, in contempt of man,
Brought near to beast.

He will, quite literally, give up everything and face the world naked. Look at the latter part of the speech. Lists dominate it. It is as if he is taking upon himself all the pain, the humiliation and the misery embedded in these images. It is a ritual of initiation that the character undergoes, and you must live through it with him. During the speech he becomes the new character. By the end, he is speaking as him:

Poor Turlygod! poor Tom!
That's something yet: Edgar I nothing am.

Disguise is a frequent visitor in Shakespeare's plays. The reasons are quite clear. Disguise is, on the one hand, a way of losing your identity; you literally become someone else. On the other hand, it is a kind of metamorphosis and the process of spiritual rebirth. Disguise gives freedom to act and freedom to speak, especially to women, and was a device particularly suited to the all male companies of actors prevalent in Shakespeare's time. The resonance of disguise, however, travels way beyond the conventions of the Elizabethan stage and strikes a chord of aspiration and recognition in modern audiences. Many people want to change but are unable to effect change in themselves. Many feel inadequate and inarticulate and uncomfortable in their own bodies. We are often unable to deal with our emotions or the situations in which we find ourselves. Disguise in art offers a challenge and a paradigm of change.

We not only witness Viola in *Twelfth Night* suffer grief and then fall in love, we live through it with her and so gain a measure of understanding.

Finally, let us focus on the trajectory of a single character. Let's take Hal in *Henry IV Part I*. The play tells the story of the education and preparation of a prince – a prince who was to become the model for monarchs, Henry V. He appears to reject all the trappings and comforts of royalty and chooses instead the vagabond life of the London underworld. Indeed he seems to revel in the company of criminals, the poor and prostitutes – the great underbelly of the metropolis. It is not hard to find parallels to his actions in the pages of any newspaper today. In a way, his life with Falstaff and his cronies is a form of disguise. This is how he describes his actions in a monologue:

Kenneth Brannagh as Henry in *Henry V* at the Royal Shakespeare Theatre, 1984. Photo: Joe Cocks Studio Collection © Shakespeare Birthplace Trust

PRINCE HENRY

I know you all, and will awhile uphold
The unyoked humour of your idleness:
Yet herein will I imitate the sun,
Who doth permit the base contagious clouds
To smother up his beauty from the world,
That, when he please again to be himself,
Being wanted, he may be more wonder'd at,
By breaking through the foul and ugly mists
Of vapours that did seem to strangle him.
If all the year were playing holidays,
To sport would be as tedious as to work;
But when they seldom come, they wish'd for come,
And nothing pleaseth but rare accidents.
So, when this loose behavior I throw off
And pay the debt I never promised,
By how much better than my word I am,
By so much shall I falsify men's hopes;
And like bright metal on a sullen ground,
My reformation, glittering o'er my fault,
Shall show more goodly and attract more eyes
Than that which hath no foil to set it off.
I'll so offend, to make offence a skill;
Redeeming time when men think least I will.

Henry IV, I. ii. 190–212

Now fast forward to the decisive confrontation with his father, Henry IV. It is a brilliantly observed scene of great humanity. The father feels angry and disappointed; the son feels humiliated and cornered. The king has berated, admonished, criticized and accused his son. Finally, Hal cracks and comes out with this speech:

PRINCE HENRY

Do not think so; you shall not find it so:
And God forgive them that so much have sway'd
Your majesty's good thoughts away from me!
I will redeem all this on Percy's head
And in the closing of some glorious day
Be bold to tell you that I am your son;
When I will wear a garment all of blood
And stain my favours in a bloody mask,
Which, wash'd away, shall scour my shame with it:

And that shall be the day, whene'er it lights,
That this same child of honour and renown,
This gallant Hotspur, this all-praised knight,
And your unthought-of Harry chance to meet.
For every honour sitting on his helm,
Would they were multitudes, and on my head
My shames redoubled! for the time will come,
That I shall make this northern youth exchange
His glorious deeds for my indignities.
Percy is but my factor, good my lord,
To engross up glorious deeds on my behalf;
And I will call him to so strict account,
That he shall render every glory up,
Yea, even the slightest worship of his time,
Or I will tear the reckoning from his heart.
This, in the name of God, I promise here:
The which if He be pleased I shall perform,
I do beseech your majesty may salve
The long-grown wounds of my intemperance:
If not, the end of life cancels all bands;
And I will die a hundred thousand deaths
Ere break the smallest parcel of this vow.

Henry IV, III. ii. 129–159

The key thing to notice here is Hal's articulacy. His use of language is astonishing. We hear, for the very first time, that clarion clear voice that was to mark his reign as Henry V. The subject of the speech is transformation and promise. That is why it always sends shivers up my spine when I hear it! Like Edgar, we are watching someone change before our very eyes.

Earlier in this chapter, I said that everything you need to know about your character lies in the text. I am convinced that this is true. To build your character, you need to develop your expertise at exploring and delivering the text. You also need to be willing and able to draw from your own personal experience to give texture and authenticity to the emotions and experiences of the play. That is the truly creative side of acting.

15

MORE JOURNEYS

'The undiscovered country'
Hamlet, III. i. 81

Early in this book I described the artistic journey that Shakespeare's company of actors undertook and the way they would have developed their craft and understanding in tandem with his progression as a writer. If you have followed these chapters, you will have by now undertaken a journey of your own. My main hope is that I have kindled a passion in you that you can pursue in whatever field you chose – as a student, as a professional or amateur actor or just as a lover of language.

The final thing I want to look at is the way Shakespeare constructed his plays. I want you to consider them not only as extraordinary stories, but also as journeys that can have political, moral and spiritual significance. Such a perspective will support the work you do on language and character. In the chapter on comedy, I described the form as a progress towards matrimony. Tragedy, I suggested, confronts us with our own mortality, but, crucially, describes a journey towards wisdom. On reflection, I believe that can serve as a useful definition for most of Shakespeare's endeavours.

Early on in his career, Shakespeare lit upon an idea for the construction of his plays that was to endure throughout his working life. It is a simple but highly productive paradigm. Allow me to describe it to you. Like all stories, it has a beginning, a middle and an end. In the beginning, a character, group of characters or even a whole society is faced with some terrible crisis. That crisis compels our character into an unfamiliar world, a world that the character struggles to control, a world of chaos – that is the middle of the journey. Finally, the character, group or society emerges in a new condition, even a new reality; they perceive themselves and each other in a new light. The wounds have been healed. The adversity of the middle section has brought them wisdom.

Let us test this idea and consider the implications for the application of all the techniques we have learnt. *A Midsummer Night's Dream* is a perfect example. There are three distinct groups of characters whose stories are interwoven in a dazzling display of inspired dramaturgy: the lovers, the mechanicals and the immortals or fairies. In the first movement of the play, each group arrives at a point of crisis that soon precipitates them into a state of chaos. The lovers, refused permission to marry, decide to elope or to pursue their loved ones; the mechanicals are so determined to produce the finest performance of their play that they choose a remote spot outside the city for rehearsal; the immortals, Titania and Oberon, quarrel over possession of an Indian boy and declare war on each other. The destination of all these characters is the wood outside Athens. In the wood at night-time, chaos ensues: human beings are turned into beasts; passions run wild and unchecked; and lovers fall in and out of love in the blink of an eye. Eventually, order is restored, but not until each character has undergone some sort of transformation from which lessons have been learnt. So the people who gather at Theseus's palace to celebrate the nuptials are wiser, more mature, deeper people.

I believe that this is a concept that we can readily relate to our everyday lives. Experience can lead to self-knowledge. Falling in and out of love is the most excruciating rite of passage for most teenagers, but, without question, it can bring maturity and self-awareness. Shakespeare's lovers go through considerable pain and moments of high exhilaration, but emerge more certain of where their true affections lie. The play is therefore like a rehearsal for life, just as the act of play for young children can teach them important social and physical skills under the protective umbrella of the game. Therefore, as an actor, it is important that you fully appreciate the shape and architecture of the play and attempt to fulfill each aspect of the journey. An audience will also emerge enriched from the wood near Athens if you have successfully included us in your journey. The aspect that requires particular attention is the middle section: the chaos. Read this passage from Act V of the *Dream*:

THESEUS

Lovers and madmen have such seething brains,
Such shaping fantasies, that apprehend
More than cool reason ever comprehends.
The lunatic, the lover and the poet

Are of imagination all compact:
One sees more devils than vast hell can hold,
That is, the madman: the lover, all as frantic,
Sees Helen's beauty in a brow of Egypt:
The poet's eye, in fine frenzy rolling,
Doth glance from heaven to earth, from earth to heaven;
And as imagination bodies forth
The forms of things unknown, the poet's pen
Turns them to shapes and gives to airy nothing
A local habitation and a name.
Such tricks hath strong imagination,
That if it would but apprehend some joy,
It comprehends some bringer of that joy;
Or in the night, imagining some fear,
How easy is a bush supposed a bear!

A Midsummer Night's Dream, V. i. 4–22

Shakespeare collects the lunatic, the lover and the poet into one group. Each is fired by this high-octane fuel of imagination, which leads them to the frontiers of experience. I would add 'the actor' to this assembly for he embodies aspects of all three! So Shakespeare is demanding that you embrace the extremities of human experience, that way the story reveals more to the audience.

The central metaphor for this paradigm is the wood or forest. As Orlando says in *As You Like It*, 'There's no clock in the forest'. You cannot walk in a straight line in a forest. A forest is full of strange noises and, like the Wild Wood in *The Wind in the Willows*, terrifying shapes and dangerous beasts. Critically, you can get lost in a forest. To put it simplistically, you get lost in order to find yourself.

Take a look at *As You Like It*. In Act I, Orlando is exiled from his family home and Rosalind, Celia and Touchstone run away to the Forest of Arden, where they meet the banished court of Duke Senior. In the forest, all sorts of unexpected encounters occur: people fall in love, are rejected and experience pain and joy. Crucially, Rosalind can rehearse her love affair with Orlando from the relative safety of her disguise. But Shakespeare knew well that acting demands no less authenticity than real life and inflicts no less pain in the execution. Therefore, Rosalind emerges from the game a much wiser creature. *As You Like It* is constructed on parallel principles to the *Dream*: a series of crises, a long movement of chaos and resolution in marriage. The forest is both benign and dangerous. It is a harsh environment in which you must hunt, even fight, for food. The winters are savage but spring is celebrated in beautiful songs. It is, moreover, a landscape of the imagination in which

Robert Stephens as Falstaff in *Henry IV part I* at the Royal Shakespeare Theatre, 1991. Photo: Reg Wilson © Royal Shakespeare Company

lions stalk their prey and rabbits run free. It is interesting that at the end of the play they are all, bar Jacques, ready to return to the city – an action of resounding moral and political significance.

In *Measure for Measure*, the duke, who has disguised himself for the course of the play, summons all parties to meet with him outside the walls of the city where he plans to set all things to right. *Measure* is not, perhaps, a play that obviously fits into the crisis/chaos/resolution model but if you look closely, you will see that indeed the play does open with the duke throwing the whole nation into a constitutional crisis by temporarily abdicating, and the draconian laws of his deputy Angelo cause widespread turmoil. The prison and its environs provide the play with a dark, dangerous crossroads in which the duke precariously juggles matters of life and death. In the final act, on the duke's instructions, everyone meets in the sunlight outside the gates and, indeed, all matters are meticulously set to right. At the close of the play, they are all ready to reenter the city; judgment has been given, lessons have been learnt and a wiser, more mature people can go back to their everyday lives. So, in a way, *Measure for Measure* offers a metaphor for change.

There comes a moment in most plays when a character has lost the compass and has no idea which way to turn. You need to be able to recognize this moment and have the courage to go there. For Isabella, it is probably the moment after her brother has rejected her plea that he should sacrifice his life for her virginity. She has argued her way through the terrible dilemma that Angelo has placed upon her, but I don't think she has a clue what to do when her brother begs for his life. She has totally lost her moral compass and only the duke enables her to survive.

Let's look at a couple more examples to see what we can glean from the structure of a play to help us with interpretation of character. King Lear is an obvious example in which a political crisis quickly becomes a personal crisis, which inevitably leads to chaos, both for the king and his kingdom. In this case, the location is the heath and the metaphor is the storm. The private agony of the king is matched step by step by a public trauma that seizes the whole state. Wars are fought, men are tortured and maimed, marriages break down and murder is committed. The storm on the heath is both a literal manifestation of nature in turmoil and a metaphor for the brainstorm that invades Lear's mind and for the conflagration that engulfs the nation. The final resolution can only be conditional; the pain has been too great. These are the final words of the play:

> The oldest hath borne most: we that are young
> Shall never see so much, nor live so long.
> *King Lear*, V. iii. 301–302

The exercise of finding the pivotal moment for your character can apply to all parts, not just to the eponymous roles. The question to ask is simple: When does my character enter completely uncharted waters? For Edgar, it might be when he decides to disguise himself as Poor Tom and become a vagrant; for Kent, when he defies banishment and returns to his master. It needs to be a moment of life or death, and it needs to relate directly to the central ideas of the play.

Henry V begins with a political crisis and a declaration of war on France.

The struggle goes well until, finally, the army faces a showdown with the French at Agincourt. Shakespeare creates a long night scene in which Henry and his army, low on morale, few in number and exhausted by the weather and a long march, must face up to failure and death. It is an unknown territory of fear, recrimination and physical hardship that eventually steels Henry and his men and fits them not only for the impending battle but also for the peace that establishes England as the premier power in Europe.

The Comedy of Errors is framed by the death sentence hanging over the head of old Egeon. Shakespeare cleverly creates a cocktail of mistaken identity, intrigue and insecurity. Characters become uncertain of whom they are, lose themselves and fall in love with strangers. The action becomes frenzied and culminates in a hectic chase scene after which, in a scene made up in equal parts of comedy and transcendent beauty, brother finds brother, husband finds wife, parents find their children and a precious life is saved. Fundamentally, the play tells a story of self-discovery.

One of the glories of the Elizabethan theatre is its ability to create changing realities. The paradigm that I have described above offers both a challenge and a fantastic opportunity to actor and audience alike. To fulfill the journey of the play, the actor must be willing and able to inhabit those strange, often hostile places. For its part, the audience must be willing to enter the play imaginatively and travel with the characters. The device that Shakespeare uses to facilitate this is the changing reality. Because reality in the Elizabethan theatre is principally created by the use of language, this allows a scene to exist on a literal and a metaphorical level at one and the same time. The storm in *King Lear* is a storm in nature, which in a film could be photographed; it's also a storm in his head. Both are real and sit side by side in creative juxtaposition. Usually the internal and the external realities are the same, as in *King Lear* or *As You Like It* or *Titus Andronicus*. Occasionally, they diverge with startling dramatic results.

Macbeth sees a vision of a dagger just before he goes to murder King Duncan: he sees the knife but we do not. We enter his nightmare world through the language and the power of the actor's imagination. Throughout this section of the drama, each protagonist repeatedly entreats the other to listen. This has the effect of creating a very special quality of silence in the theatre. Now read young Lennox's description of the same night:

LENNOX

The night has been unruly: where we lay,
Our chimneys were blown down; and, as they say,
Lamentings heard i' the air; strange screams of death,
And prophesying with accents terrible
Of dire combustion and confused events
New hatch'd to the woeful time: the obscure bird

Clamour'd the livelong night: some say, the earth
Was feverous and did shake.

Macbeth, II. iii. 53–60

Two realities juxtaposed to astonishing but disquieting effect! We have
spent the night effectively inside Macbeth's reality. We are privileged witnesses. The nightmare world inside Macbeth's head that we have been
exposed to gradually spreads throughout the nation. Here is an extract from
a conversation between an Old Man and Ross:

OLD MAN

Threescore and ten I can remember well:
Within the volume of which time I have seen
Hours dreadful and things strange; but this sore night
Hath trifled former knowings.

ROSS

Ah, good father,
Thou seest, the heavens, as troubled with man's act,
Threaten his bloody stage: by the clock, 'tis day,
And yet dark night strangles the travelling lamp:
Is't night's predominance, or the day's shame,
That darkness does the face of earth entomb,
When living light should kiss it.

Macbeth, II. iv. 1–10

Here the natural world has been infected by the evil at its centre. Soon
the political ramifications become manifest and we start to see the tell-tale
signs of tyranny that have become so common in the twentieth century: an
exiled leadership, fear and suspicion between friends, the murder of innocent
civilians and waves of refugees fleeing the country.

For me, this is what the classical theatre does par excellence: it carries the
spiritual, emotional and intellectual history of the nation. The story of *Macbeth*
never happened in England. But it could. And Shakespeare's play conveys the
Jacobean horror of tyranny and the possible consequences of absolutism. The
two History Tetralogies contain some pretty dodgy political history, but
they carry a nation's hopes for a model king and their fears of civil unrest
with perfect clarity. In many ways, the History plays provided a model for
historical analysis for centuries to come; Shakespeare's methodology of
juxtaposing the private man with his public actions was the principal means
of teaching history when I was a boy. In his Comedies he acknowledges the
pain as well as the ecstasy of love, and understands the wildness of spirit that

often accompanies our progress to adulthood and marriage. Through language we can proceed moment by moment alongside the character, sharing their shifting realities.

And through language, we, as citizens, are better equipped to grapple with politics and human relationships, our public and private lives. Without language there can be no ideas; without ideas there can be no justice; and without justice there can be no democracy.